¡Óigame! ¡Óigame!

Conflict and Social Change

Series Editors
Scott Whiteford and William Derman
Michigan State University

¡Óigame! ¡Óigame! *Struggle and Social Change in a Nicaraguan Urban Community*, Michael James Higgins and Tanya Leigh Coen

Manufacturing Against the Odds: Small-Scale Producers in an Andean City, Hans C. Buechler and Judith-Maria Buechler

The Bushman Myth: The Making of a Namibian Underclass, Robert J. Gordon

Surviving Drought and Development: Ariaal Pastoralists of Northern Kenya, Elliot Fratkin

Harvest of Want: Hunger and Food Security in Central America and Mexico, edited by Scott Whiteford and Anne E. Ferguson

Singing with Sai Baba: The Politics of Revitalization in Trinidad, Morton Klass

Struggling for Survival: Workers, Women, and Class on a Nicaraguan State Farm, Gary Ruchwarger

FORTHCOMING

Literacy and People's Power in a Mozambican Factory, Judith Marshall

Gender, Sickness, and Healing in Rural Egypt: Ethnography in Historical Context, Soheir A. Morsy

The Myth of the Male Breadwinner: Women, Industrializaton, and State Policy in the Caribbean, Helen I. Safa

Computing Myths, Class Realities: An Ethnography of Sheffield Workers in the Information Age, David Hakken with Barbara Andrews

The Culture of Protest: Religious Activism and the U.S. Sanctuary Movement, Susan Bibler Coutin

¡Óigame! ¡Óigame!

Struggle and Social Change in a Nicaraguan Urban Community

Michael James Higgins
and Tanya Leigh Coen

Westview Press
BOULDER • SAN FRANCISCO • OXFORD

Conflict and Social Change Series

All photographs taken by the authors unless otherwise attributed.

This Westview softcover edition is printed on acid-free paper and bound in library-quality, coated covers that carry the highest rating of the National Association of State Textbook Administrators, in consultation with the Association of American Publishers and the Book Manufacturers Institute.

All rights reserved. No part of this publication may be reproduced or transmitted in any form or by any means, electronic or mechanical, including photocopy, recording, or any information storage and retrieval system, without permission in writing from the publisher.

Copyright © 1992 by Westview Press, Inc.

Published in 1992 in the United States of America by Westview Press, Inc., 5500 Central Avenue, Boulder, Colorado 80301-2877, and in the United Kingdom by Westview Press, 36 Lonsdale Road, Summertown, Oxford OX2 7EW

Library of Congress Cataloging-in-Publication Data
Higgins, Michael James.
  ¡Oigame! ¡Oigame! : struggle and social change in a Nicaraguan urban community / by Michael J. Higgins and Tanya L. Coen.
    p. cm.—(Conflict and social change series)
  Includes bibliographical references.
  ISBN 0-8133-8083-9
  1. Barrio William Diaz Romero (Managua, Nicaragua)—Social conditions. 2. Political participation—Nicaragua—Barrio William Diaz Romero (Managua)   I. Coen, Tanya L. (Tanya Leigh)   II. Title.   III. Series.
HN170.B37H54 1992
303.4′097285′13—dc20   90-25258
                                                                                                 CIP

Printed and bound in the United States of America

The paper used in this publication meets the requirements of the American National Standard for Permanence of Paper for Printed Library Materials Z39.48-1984.

10   9   8   7   6   5   4   3   2   1

Contents

List of Illustrations xi
Acknowledgments xiii

1 Introduction 1

Todo a la Plaza, 1
Ethnographic Praxis, 3
Dialectics of Everyday Life, 5
Rethinking Participant Observation, 6
Applied Anthropology, 6
Ethnographic Advocacy, 6
Barrio William Diaz Romero, 8
Managua and the Barrio, 9
Demographics—The Social, Political, and Economic Composition of Barrio William Diaz Romero, 16
Land of the Lakes: The Historical Background to Modern Nicaragua, 18
Summary, 28
Notes, 29

2 The View Through the Door Frame 37

Methods of Ethnography, 37
Introduction, 38
What Is Ethnography? 39
What Are We Doing? 44
Notes, 49

3 Jodido Pero Contento 53

THE ECONOMIC AND SOCIAL CONTEXT OF THE BARRIO WILLIAM DIAZ ROMERO, 53
Introduction, 54
Structure of the Chapter, 55
Formal and Informal Economic Sectors, 56

Political Economy of the Popular Revolution, 56
The Current Economic Realities of Nicaragua, 58
Post-Election Developments in the Economy, 59
THE DICHOTOMY BETWEEN THE FORMAL AND INFORMAL
ECONOMIC SECTORS IN THE BARRIO WILLIAM DIAZ ROMERO, 60
Demographic Data, 60
Analysis of Data, 60
Economic Activity in the Barrio, 63
Shopping Patterns, 65
HOUSEHOLD STRATEGIES FOR
PROCUREMENT AND REGULATION, 67
The Curtis Household, 67
The Household of Maria Felix, 74
Socorro Blanco's Household, 79
Households of Consuelo Mendietta and Ruth Arena, 83
Ephraine Ortiz's Household, 87
SOCIAL ACTIVITIES IN THE BARRIO, 91
Housing Project, 91
The Rice Cooperative and the Barrio Store, 92
Clothing Sale, 93
Community Center, 93
Conclusion, 94
Notes, 96

4 ¡Quiero Decir Esto! 99

The Popular Politics of the Barrio, 99
Introduction, 100
Mass Organization and the History of the CDSs, 101
History of the CDS in the Barrio, 102
The "New" CDS Line, 108
The "New" Line at the Local Level, 113
Conclusion, 119
Notes, 121

5 *Afuera del Barrio* 129

External Relations of the Barrio, 129
Introduction, 130
City and Regional Relations, 130
History of Health Care, 131
Urban Renewal and Housing, 134
Education, 137
Police and Legal System, 139

Military, 140
　　　Cultural Relations, 141
　　　Belief Systems About Health and Curing, 146
　　　Calendar of Events, 147
　　　Household Fiestas, 148
　　　Popular Religion in Nicaragua, 148
　　　Political Structures, 152
　　　International Community Relations in the Barrio, 153
　　　Notes, 154

6　*Vamos a Sequir*　　　　　　　　　　　　　　　　　　　　　157

　　　Introduction, 158
　　　Everyday Life in the Barrio, 158
　　　Social Linkages, 160
　　　Ethnographic Praxis, 163
　　　So What Makes Any of This Ethnographic Praxis? 166
　　　The Struggle Continues, 167
　　　Notes, 177

Bibliography　　　　　　　　　　　　　　　　　　　　　　　　179

Illustrations

Tables

1.1	Representation of age (CDS Heroes y Martyrs)	17
1.2	Representation of age (CDS Zelada)	18
1.3	Representation of age (CDS Francisco Moreno)	19
1.4	Representation of age (authors' sample)	20
1.5	MINCOIN representation of consumers	20
1.6	Educational levels	21
3.1	Occupations (general sample)	61
3.2	Occupations (CDS Heroes y Martyrs)	62
3.3	Occupations (CDS Francisco Moreno)	63
3.4	Occupations (CDS Liberator Zelada)	64
3.5	Market prices for April 1988	66
3.6	Market prices for August 1–7, 1988	66
3.7	Supermarket prices for August 1–7, 1988	67
3.8	Prices in the barrio/local store for August 1988	68
3.9	Prices in the barrio for summer 1989	69
3.10	Market prices for July 1989	69
3.11	Supermarket prices for July 1989	70
3.12	Household budget for the Mabel Curtis family, summer 1989	71
3.13	Household consumption analysis for the Maria Felix family, summer 1989	76
3.14	Household budget for the Maria Felix family, 1989	77
3.15	Household budget for the Socorro Blanco family, summer 1989	82
3.16	Household consumption for the Ruth Arena family, summer 1989	87
3.17	Household budget for the Ruth Arena family, July 1989	88
5.1	Schools in the barrio	137

Photographs

Barrio coordinator accounting for medicine	125
Barrio residents	125
Local fruit and vegetable vendor	126
Main street in barrio	126
Final construction on barrio's new basketball court	126
Current contradictions of post-revolutionary Nicaragua	127
Children awaiting donations from sister barrio	127
Director of elementary school	128
Family outside their combined home and shop	128

Acknowledgments

"¡Óí'me! ¡Óí'me!" In the Barrio William Diaz Romero, people often shorten the formal command statement of óigame (listen to me) to the more informal phrase of óí'me (also meaning listen to me). Thus, we would like to acknowledge all the people of this barrio whom we listen to and who listen to us. With great honor and respect we dedicate this book to their hopes and struggles.

There are many other friends in Nicaragua we would also like to acknowledge. Bolivar Espinoza, an urban researcher at INIES (National Institute of Economic and Social Research), graciously gave of his time and expertise to explain the complex hegemonic terrain of Nicaragua. Araceli Garcia and the entire INIES staff were also extremely helpful. We would also like to thank Manuel Ortega for his help and advice during different stages of this research. Our thanks also go to various people in the Nicaraguan public health service and CDS offices who helped us during the investigation. Consuelo Mendietta, Hugo Medina, Mabel Curtis, Noel Curtis, Ruth Arena, Alicia Espinoza, Manuel Ruiz, Orlando Garcia, Lesbia Guerrero, and many others were constant sources of help and friendship during this project. We would also like to thank Don Pedro and Dona Gabriela for their help and support during our many stays at their world-renowned boarding house La Norma. Also, we would like to thank many of the international volunteers in Nicaragua that we met who gave us advice and support for this research and our solidarity activities.

We would like to thank the Research and Publication Board; the graduate school; the deans of the College of Arts and Sciences; and the Department of Anthropology, Black Studies, and Women's Studies at the University of Northern Colorado for their support and encouragement for this project. Our appreciation also goes to the student government and the Department of Anthropology of the University of Colorado at Denver for their support and encouragement, especially Craig Janes and Janet Moone.

Equally important were various people in the Greeley community who aided the sister-barrio project. We would like to acknowledge the People to People Peace Brigade, Al Frente del Lucha, Secundino Salazar, Father

Peter Urban, the Unitarian Church of Greeley, Elaine Schmidt, and the hundreds of community people who donated their time and materials.

There are several very important people who aided us in the production of this book. Marcia Moore-Jazayeri provided editorial assistance to us. Any remaining errors—either technical or conceptual—are the fault of the authors. Delores Belo provided much-needed help in the typing and printing of various rough-draft versions of this book, and Marcia Hackett typed the tables for us. Kellie Masterson and Nancy Rasmussen at Westview Press and Roger Lancaster were constant sources of support and encouragement during this long process. We would like to thank Dulce Camp, Ron Camp, John Payne, and Lizzet Dominguez, who worked on the video part of this overall project.

The authors would like to pay thanks to their respective families who bore with us through this long endeavor, especially Fran, Don, Cord, Shane, Waurayne, Seth, Aultia, Siobhan, and Tristan. And special recognition goes to the memory of C. R. Wilson and to all those who came before us and lacked our opportunities.

Finally, our thanks go to Reagan and Bush, who made us angry enough to go to Nicaragua and encounter a context that really does have a thousand points of light and hope.

Michael James Higgins
Tanya Leigh Coen

1

Introduction

Todo a la Plaza

At about 6:30 A.M. on the morning of July 19 (1989), we heard the booming voice of Consuelo telling us it was time to get up and get ready to go the plaza. This was the beginning of the day celebrating the tenth anniversary of the Sandinista Revolution in Nicaragua. We were living in a barrio by the name of William Diaz Romero which is located near the center of Managua. This was our fourth summer in the community, and this was to be the first time we had attended a celebration of the revolution because the previous celebrations had been held outside of Managua. The community of William Diaz Romero has a population of some 4,000 people with a mixed class composition of middle, working, and poor people. Over 140 small businesses exist in the barrio. This community has been politically active during the ten years of the revolution. We have been in this barrio for the last four years because of our research interests as anthropologists and as members of a solidarity group (from Greeley, Colorado) which had organized a sister barrio project with this community.

At 7:30 A.M., in front of the Delrado ice cream parlor, we met with Luis, Manuel, Norma, Marcelino, Hydee, Consuelo, Dennis and several other community members.[1] Manuel and Norma had brought a large banner that proclaimed the barrio's solidarity with the ten-year revolution. We all carried Sandinista and Nicaraguan flags of various sizes. Other community members had already begun walking to the plaza which was about a mile and a half from the barrio. Some were going on their own; others were with other groups—unions, fellow workers, etc. As we began to march down the main street, Ho Chi Minh Avenue, we started to encounter other groups also marching towards the plaza. The majority of the people were in white t-shirts on which were stenciled red and black hearts with the slogan of the anniversary: "Never has there been so much patriotism in one heart." Almost everyone was carrying some kind of banner or flag. As we approached the main avenue to the plaza, the number of people in the street had grown immensely, until we were now marching with several thousand people. Everyone was in a fiesta mood and joyfully shouting, "Ten Years of the Frente and More to Come." As we entered the plaza of Carlos Fonseca, we become part of the vibrant crowd which was to grow to somewhere near 300,000. The salsa music of Luis Enrique Mejia Godoy was blasting from the stage. After waiting for over an hour, the stage filled and the speeches began. The field in front of the stage was covered with bright colors, the white shirts of the tenth anniversary, and the red and black flags. There were also colorful national flags being held by persons from the many countries who were there in solidarity with the struggle of the people of Nicaragua.

The official celebration lasted only a few hours. There had been several days of parties throughout the whole city before this event. President Ortega gave a long and detailed speech on the limitations and successes of the revolution. When his speech was over, the huge crowd began leaving the plaza. We left with our friends from the barrio. They expressed satisfaction with the event and reflected on the limitations and successes of this experiment in popular change in terms of their own barrio. As we walked with them, we thought about how we were going to convey to others what these ten years have meant for the residents of this community.

What none of us thought that day was that within six months all of our perceptions would be radically altered. The election results of February 25, 1990 placed the political coalition of UNO (The United Nicaraguan Opposition) in power throughout Nicaragua. They had won the Presidency, control over the national assembly, and the majority of city councils throughout the country. People in the barrio were shocked, saddened, and surprised. The slogan of "ten years of the Frente and more to come" now was replaced with the cry of "gobierno de abajo"—government from below. This cry was proclaimed by Daniel Ortega after the loss of the election, and it meant that the revolution would continue through the struggle of the popular classes now outside the government.

Following the announcement of election results, we received numerous calls from friends in the barrio expressing their concerns about what the future now entailed for them and their community. For them "gobierno de abajo" meant continuing as they had done in the past, but now as part of the militant opposition to the new government. Now they had to rethink what the ten years of the revolution had been, why they had not been able to turn the gains of the revolution into an electoral victory, and how they were to regain the allegiance of the majority of the residents of their own community. Our friends bravely suggested that they would continue with their community plans and hopes. They also expressed new fears about attaining these goals now as the opposition.

The election results also altered how we were planning to convey to others what the revolution had meant in this community. We now also had to explore what this loss meant in terms of the community. Further, we had to find means to weave an ethnography of this community that recognized our political involvement with it while maintaining a level of critical insight to allow for a fair analysis of the social dynamics within the community. For us this involves several features. We need to provide basic ethnographic information that can illustrate the patterns of everyday life in the community. Within this narrative we also have to explore ways in which we could express our feelings of support for the aspirations of the community residents who now were divided between political affiliations to either the Frente or the new government. This requires that we critically rethink what we mean by participant observation, doing applied anthropology, and the role of advocacy for a community. More concretely it means for us, as anthropologists, explaining the emotional depth of our involvement with the people of this community in an ethnographic form of narration. These concerns have led us to explore how to develop a form of anthropology that we see as ethnographic praxis.

Ethnographic Praxis

We are seeking to present our experiences in the Barrio William Diaz Romero from the framework of what we call ethnographic praxis. What do we mean by combining the concepts of ethnography and praxis?

We suggest that an ethnographic praxis involves the combining of ethnographic analysis, the dynamics of participant observation, applied anthropology, and for us, a critical advocacy with the groups with which one is working. Let us expand this concept and suggest what other kinds of questions are generated.

Ethnography has traditionally been the attempt by social anthropologists to describe in a narrative style the traditions of other people's cultural systems. The concept refers to attempts by anthropologists to translate their field experiences into descriptions, within defined boundaries, of the everyday activities of particular groups; for instance, the relationships— social, economic, political—found in factories, or in schools between teachers and students, or in a village (Marcus and Fischer 1986). Further, it is now a method of investigation that can be adopted by those outside anthropology (Giroux 1988). Praxis has meant, in its classic sense and its modern political sense, the search for linking concepts to action, the political affirmation of one's theoretical concepts (Bauman 1987).

What actions are we attempting to derive from this ethnographic narrative of the Barrio William Diaz Romero? What are the politics we are seeking to affirm? To answer these questions, we briefly wander into the nebulous world of post-modernity and generate a set of questions which will frame the focus of this endeavor. Social anthropologists have often worked from an unstated assumption that they were the spokespersons for the unheard voices of the modern world. They, or we, were the ones who placed the "other" within the Western intellectual discourse. The concrete realities of the post-modern world have shattered such vague assumptions. The "others" have developed their own means of confronting the Western intellectual world and Western intellectuals have more or less abandoned their faith in speaking for "others." The authority of the ethnographer and her ethnography have been called into question.[2] Who speaks for whom and with what authority? The intellectual resolution of this dilemma seeks a solution by explicitly stating who the various voices are that make up an ethnography and what the textual modes of improvement are for producing ethnographies (Clifford 1988). We say "intellectual" because this movement of post-modern ethnography often seems more concerned with how to write a better ethnography than how to seek to develop what could be called the politics of ethnography or a praxis. The writing of better ethnographies is a valid goal for anthropology. However, for us, the challenge to the author of an ethnography is not just the construction of a better text, but also a recognition of the power and authority of the political systems that control the realities of the "others" which the ethnography purports to describe. In seeking an ethnographic praxis, ethnographers will have to learn to juggle the required distance for critical observation with the social space necessary for advocacy. There are no politically neutral ethnographic contexts in the post-modern world, especially in the case of anthropologists working in politically complex and changing contexts such as Nicaragua (Lancaster 1988). The difficulty is to convey the sense of the people and their political context so that it is accessible to all readers.

Does this mean, then, that as anthropologists we have to write about our subjective experiences which will support what we feel to be a politically correct position? We do not think so. We think that as anthropologists (or others) using the methods of ethnography, we ought to pay attention to the insights of feminist thinking which have proclaimed that the personal is political (Dimen 1986). We think that an ethnography which attempts to narratively describe the personal lives of the social actors within their material/symbolic context should recognize the politics of that context. In a highly charged environment like Nicaragua this is particularly important. If a revolutionary context does produce change, then that change will be in people's everyday lives. Such changes should be representable within an ethnographic narrative. Conversely, an ethnographic narrative should be able to illustrate the absence of such changes. How?

First, the narrative should address the processes of rapid change that are taking place in this popular revolution. How is this done? It involves not assuming, as in traditional ethnographies, that one is attempting to describe cultural stability but rather the dynamics of change. Further, it involves recognizing that though the ethnographic perspective focuses on the primary units of social action within the boundaries of community, such concepts as community are overdetermined realities involving the issues of class, gender, sexuality, and political economy at both macro and micro levels. In the case of Nicaragua, this involves an understanding of the dynamics of the overall popular revolution (including its critics) and how such dynamics are dialectically expressed within a context such as the Barrio William Diaz Romero.

As ethnographers, we also have to recognize that how well we can capture such complex dynamics will be determined by the collective readership of this work. In other words, we understand that the meaning of what we attempt to convey will be affirmed by the meanings constructed by the various readers of this work. That collective readership will include the people of the Barrio William Diaz Romero and others in Nicaragua. Hopefully, along with the collegiate readers of this work there will be readers interested in the issues of Nicaragua, Central America, social change, and radical political developments. To engage such collective readership we have to present a narrative that can represent the everyday life of the people of this community, within the overall social/political context of the revolution. For us, this involves a description of the dialectics of everyday life.

Dialectics of Everyday Life

The dialectics of everyday life involve representing, in the context of everyday life, the linkages between the people's existential actions, their participation within their community, and their perception of the national identity. For us, an ethnographic narrative should express how people see their existence—what they perceive as the quality of their lives. The way in which people participate in their community also has to be illustrated. This involves not just a statistical portrait, but also the texture of participation and interaction among community members. How does the struggle for one's personal existential aspirations relate to community obligation? How do such relations of individual to community engender relations of national identity?

Clearly, in the case of Nicaragua, where the discourse of the popular revolution continues to seek the construction of social processes and self evident linkages, an ethnographic representation of such developments is profoundly important. An ethnographic analysis can represent the contradictions within such struggles. This is important in order to provide suggestions where actions, political or social, can or ought to be directed.

Such a use of ethnography involves rethinking the role of participant observation and combining applied anthropology with a form of critical advocacy.

Rethinking Participant Observation

Traditionally, participant observation has been the method by which ethnographers have searched for the way to solve the tensions between their care or passion for the people they were studying with the requirements of doing objective analysis. Participant observation involves attempting to act within the social norms of a culture without being obtrusive. This has produced a tone of moral ambiguity in the writings of ethnographers. We are aware that participation affects what we observe, but we have known equally well that without participating in some fashion we cannot attain the textured types of analysis we feel express cultural knowledge. This is more complex in our situation in which we are also politically involved with the community that we are attempting to study. We have no easy answer for this problem. In the chapter on methods we more fully explore our approach to this dynamic.

Applied Anthropology

By applied anthropology we do not mean the more typical forms of consulting, but forms of active observation.[3] This entails an involvement with the community, establishing a role for oneself beyond that of an observer. If a community is planning a housing project, the ethnographic role is not just to watch how the community plans nor to plan for the community, but to eventually participate in the development of such plans. This would involve staking out a position for oneself within the community and recognizing the limits to such actions. That is, if one identifies with a minority position in a debate within the community, one could not oppose the majority (in the sense of being part of opposition groups) but only make clear what one's position is. This involves a great deal of political honesty to oneself and the community with which one is working. It implies an acceptance of a position of critical advocacy for the community which one is attempting to ethnographically capture. It means that the ethnographer walks a narrow line between a useful and effective form of advocacy and an unwanted and needless meddling.

Ethnographic Advocacy

What does ethnographic advocacy mean? For us, it means a form of critical advocacy or solidarity with the general aspirations of the community with which one is working. We are not attempting to suggest some kind of political correctness equation between the ethnographer and the community of study. We can see the importance of studying a racist community (such as a white South African community) as a means to combat racism. However, the study, in order to be a benefit to that community, should inform the members of the fallacy of their racism, not provide them a rational means to maintain their racism. Whether one could, in fact, do such a thing with a racist community we do not know. However, in the context of the struggles of Third World popular classes, we see no contradiction in identifying with their aspirations of personal self-determination and doing an ethnographic investigation of such struggles. This is, in fact, what ethnographic praxis is for us.

We feel that the Sandinista revolution has been a valid expression of a struggle of national self-determination in this confusing post-modern world. We also feel that this ethnography is an attempt to present the community of the people of William Diaz Romero and the context of this revolution in their everyday lives. This is a critical recognition that does not shy away from criticism of those actions. We feel that our criticism will be based upon our principled views of how we see anthropology and on our direct participation in our solidarity project with this community. As they say in the barrio, only those who work should criticize what's being done. We have worked as anthropologists, as participants, and as solidarity workers. This gives us a unique perspective into the processes—political, cultural, social, economic, and emotional—of this community and its involvement in this popular revolution. The criticisms that we may offer are presented in terms of commitment to the overall struggle of the people of Nicaragua and the residents of the barrio William Diaz Romero.

We see the hopes and dreams of the people of Nicaragua and the people in the Barrio William Diaz Romero as a search for a form of radical democracy. This is a dream we should be hoping for, not cynically "looking to be fooled again."[4]

Can such a book as this directly help the people of the Barrio William Diaz Romero? We think so—not so much in terms of the bold concepts declared about them, but as a means to convey the reality of this community in its own context. Ethnography can still place the unfamiliar into the familiar. That is important. The people of this community can be heard in a sense. In the chapter on methods, we explain how we think this can be done in the political context of post-modernity. We think this endeavor can concretely aid this community in two ways. In Nicaragua itself, this community's goals and strategies can have a wider audience. The people themselves can learn about others' strategies through the comparison of experiences. This work will also be published in Nicaragua. Perhaps more concretely, though realistically limited, proceeds from this work will go to the community itself. This is not a statement of nobility on our part, but a concrete agreement that we made with this community when they asked us what they would get from this project.

In the remaining part of this chapter will be a general ethnographic description of the barrio. This is followed by a brief review of the social history of Nicaragua.

Barrio William Diaz Romero

I can tell you that this place where we are talking was a trio (drying mill), called La Perla. Also, there was an ice factory here, also called La Perla. The owners were land holders of a great deal of property; they were millionaires. Here you could see the exploitation that existed between the workers and these owners. When I was a kid here, there was a mill for coffee, a mill for rice, and a wood mill. That is part of the history I remember from when I was eight or nine years old.

In the past, this barrio had two barrio committees. One was called La Perla and the other was called La Veloz. I was not participating in barrio politics at the time of the victory. I was in my union organization. Later, I was called by companero Luis Lopez Galiano to join the barrio committee. That is how the committee was organized. When I agreed to participate, I was made secretary of the organization.

At that time, the barrio was not William Diaz Romero. There were two coordinators; Luis was coordinator for La Perla, and Dona Olga was the coordinator for La Veloz. As secretary of the organization I proposed that we could function better as one barrio. Well that's the way it turned out. Luis generously accepted Dona Olga as the first general coordinator for the united barrio.

At that time, I proposed that the barrio take the name of one of the revolutionary youths of the barrio that had died in the insurrection. We called together all the block CDSs of the barrio. The coordinators of the block CDSs all wanted the barrio to be named after a martyr, like Monte Negro. All of the martyrs of the barrio were listed, and William Diaz Romero got the most votes. Since that moment, the barrio has been called William Diaz Romero.

—Orlando Garcia, Current Coordinator of the Barrio Committee

I was born and raised in this barrio. I was born near the Theater Cabrera a few blocks from here. Sr. Mercedes Barrio Boquin was the owner of all this land around here. This area used to be called barrio of barrios. It never stopped being called barrio of barrios. Now some people call this area La Perla, but that was not the name of the barrio but of a metalwork shop that is still here. Here, exactly where I am living, was the drying mill called La Veloz (Trio La Veloz). The river came through here and they dried wheat, rice, coffee, and corn. With time the trios disappeared. The whole area was destroyed by the "King" earthquake in 1972. Now we have taken this land over, we called it the Camilo Ortega housing villa (the killed brother of ex-president Daniel Ortega).

Well, here we did not fight much, but people helped the fight in many small ways. The young fighters stayed in safe houses in this barrio; we helped feed them and helped them make small weapons.

I participated in some of the activities during the early part of the insurrection. In my way, I contributed. The young muchachos would come by the metal shop and we would give them metal tubes with one end plugged up. I did not know what they did with these, but they took them. We would also make darts and pointed rods from the iron rods here in the shop. We would take three or four pointed rods, solder them together, and they would throw them in the streets to stop the trucks of the National Guard. We made a great number of these and had to hide them. We would also make metal spears so the muchachos could use them as weapons. Here people did not have many weapons, so they used these spears. They could stick them in all sorts of things. That's how I participated a little.

Here we tried to fight for the rights of the community. We surveyed the vacant land in the barrio and went to the mayor to get the land granted to us. The mayor checked to make sure the land could be given to us. They had the land surveyed for fault lines and measured the land in terms of how many lots it would be possible to give to the people. We gained a good quantity of land and there are persons who are now constructing their houses. We have given the land out because of the demand of the people in the community. However there is so little land and so many who have demands for it. We work with the people to see what can be done.

My duty on the committee is to see to the necessities of the persons that do not have houses yet, who have always rented their houses. Many of these people have been exploited very badly. They have lived in houses that cost practically nothing and have paid millions in rent. There are some people who have lived in their houses for more than 30 years and they still have to pay rent. The government now understands this and wants everyone to have houses.

—Manuel Ruiz, Long Term Resident of the Barrio and
Member of the Barrio Committee

Managua and the Barrio

This section is a general sketch of the barrio and its people. In the first part of the section we provide the reader with a general description of the city of Managua. The second part of the section is a "walking tour" of Barrio William Diaz Romero to illuminate the physical composition of the barrio and to introduce some of the people of this community. In the third part of the section, we provide a general demographic outline of the barrio.

Managua

Managua is an odd city. It has been called the "anti"-city (Envio 1989b:24). Most of the time it is popularly depicted as uncomfortably hot, dry, and dusty. It is a large sprawling city that seems to have no overall structure and no definite center to it. It has also been called a "structurally defeated city," as a result of the earthquake in 1972 which destroyed the center. One of Managua's main problems is that "it is built on ecologically and seismically fragile land," with over 100 faults being found in the city (Envio 1989b:17–33).

Managua's population is nearing one million, one third of Nicaragua's population; the population for the entire country is over three million (Nicaraguan Census 1989). The city is composed of 250 or so barrios, with the majority being spontaneous communities (squatter settlements) that arose after the triumph (Vilas 1986). Managua's growth rate of seven percent is the highest in all of Latin America and the Caribbean. Since 1979, Managua's population has almost doubled due to migration from the war and a high internal growth rate. In contrast, current Nicaragua census data indicate that the population in the rural areas has only slightly increased since 1979. The impact on Managua's population is that its infrastructure can only serve 500,000, half its population; while those using Managua's services, including Managua and its surrounding area, are at 1,500,000 (Envio 1989b:17-33).[5]

Water in Managua is shut off two days per week. This is a strategy to prevent the pollution of Managua's water supply and to preserve the health of Managua's population. When the water level in reservoir Asososca (Managua's current fresh water supply) drops below a certain level, the toxins in lake Xolotlan leach toward it (Envio 1989h:39).

Under the Somoza regime, Lake Xolotlan was a "dumping ground for Managua's sewage and dozens of industries that sprang up on its shores" (Envio 1989h:39-42). The Penwalt Corporation, operating between 1968 and 1980 and dumping an estimated 40 tons of inorganic mercury into the water, is an example of the extent of the problem. Still lacking a sewage treatment plant, the lake currently receives "130,000 cubic meters per day of raw sewage" (Envio 1989h:40). More contemporary industries, such as a recently constructed geo-thermal plant, release high amounts of inorganic arsenic into the lake (Envio 1989h:38).

Neither the necessary capital nor the technical skill to implement a sewage and industrial water treatment plant exist. These projects are estimated at multi-millions of dollars, and proposals for the use of lake Nicaragua's water are estimated at 100,000,000 dollars (Envio 1989h:39).

Another of Managua's fundamental environmental health problems is a deforested and eroded watershed (the southern watershed). It is located twenty-two kilometers south of Managua. Eroded by "making way for cotton and cattle, the population's need for firewood, the crops campasinos have chosen to produce there," and subsequent heavy rainfall, the southern watershed is a major problem for the environment which affects the city of Managua and demands major changes in land use (Envio 1989h:38).

Walking Tour: Barrio William Diaz Romero

If there is a center in this capital city, Barrio William Diaz Romero is often described as one. The composition of Barrio William Diaz Romero,

Introduction

mainly because it represents a panorama of contemporary urban life in Managua, can be used, we feel, to illustrate the context of everyday life in Managua.

The population of the barrio is around 4,000 and encompasses 30 blocks. It is a well-established barrio with some residents having family histories dating back some 100 years. The population of the barrio is quite mixed. It represents various popular sectors, middle class and professionals, mercantile and street vendors, the working class, urban poor, and marginal groups.

Barrio William Diaz Romero has water and electricity, and the majority of streets are paved. As previously mentioned, the environmental problems in Managua necessitate that the water be turned off two days a week. To compensate for the shortage, large barrels to be filled with water occupy patio areas of people's houses. At the Hospedaje Norma, you can hear the water rushing loudly very early in the morning as Pedro Mena, one of the family owners of the hospedaje, fills five barrels on Tuesday and Thursday mornings for drinking, showering, and washing clothes. It is around eight to ten in the evening when the water is turned back on.

The Hospedaje Norma is one of eight hospedajes (boarding houses) in the barrio that have sprung up at different times, mostly because of the close proximity to a bus station. The heavy influx of internationalists to this barrio after 1979 led to others of various sizes and qualities being built. Most contain a central bathroom area, small rooms with cots, and a central area with hammocks or tables for socializing. Most do not offer food. We begin this walking tour of the barrio starting from the Hospedaje Norma.[6]

As we leave the hospedaje, we make our way next door to Mirna's for lunch. Numerous restaurants dot the barrio. Mirna's is a popular place on the corner next door to the hospedaje. This comedor is actually the house of Mirna and Jose Suyani. In the last three years, a broken down truck, meaning a loss of work, and health problems encouraged Mirna and Jose to start selling sandwiches in their living room to internationalists. The demand grew and Mirna's now serves breakfast and lunch. The heavy flow of customers is tremendous work but hardly allows Mirna, Jose, and a few hired relatives to keep up with inflation.

Leaving Mirna's, we face south toward a large field which runs diagonally across the street where the new community center has recently been built and where an open field used for sports lays. On the corner of the field closest to Mirna's, nuns from the barrio convent are on their daily outing across the street to burn their trash.

While walking through the streets of the barrio, one is generally struck with the heat and the humidity. It is all the more distinctive in the disastrous structural, aesthetic, and environmental context of Managua in general. Nevertheless, many barrio residents, through their experiences, their histories, their memories, and their daily lives, have described the barrio as having a certain charm.

Walking through the streets west from Mirna's to the noisy, main street, Ho Chi Minh Avenue, we pass several neighbors who are on their way to different barrio stores, visiting, working, or running errands. We pass by several other smaller comedors, many of which are quite popular for lunch with Nicaraguans working near the barrio.

Several large restaurants also exist in the barrio. Down a few blocks north and off the main street is an outdoor restaurant somewhat in the center of the barrio. It has a large patio and bar area and is a popular place with Nicaraguans. The constant blaring of the jukebox, the attractiveness and spaciousness of the restaurant, and the generous steak meals generate a constant flow of customers, including a share of local drunks.

Sara's, another barrio restaurant further east, is a popular spot with the internationalists who pass through the barrio as well as those who live in other parts of Managua. The business Sara Castillo and her family have received has allowed them to generously expand in the last three years.

Another barrio restaurant, the Terazza, lies on the south border of the barrio. It's known for being one of the fancier restaurants in Managua. It is historically known for catering to Somoza and the upper middle class populations. With the triumph, however, the workers confiscated it and now collectively work, own, and manage it.

Leaving the restaurant and heading north down Ho Chi Minh Avenue, we approach another section of the barrio. In fact, Ho Chi Minh Avenue, recall various long-term barrio residents, was previously a drainage ditch that divided the barrio into two separate barrios. As we walk down one of several dirt streets west off of Ho Chi Minh Avenue in the barrio, we arrive at the barrio's new housing project where 42 families have been building houses during the last three years. Regardless of differing abilities to purchase materials, the basic structure of newly built houses in Nicaragua generally conforms to the earthquake style called a "mini-falda," with brick or cement on the bottom half and wooden framework on the top. Like much of Managua, this barrio has been hit rather severely by past earthquakes. The barrio is dotted with several empty lots where dense layers of earthquake rubble exist beneath the dirt. This restricts the number of lots that can be used to alleviate the general problem of overcrowding.[7]

It would be safe to say, however, that these types of houses, although representing the majority of those styles built in the barrio, still represent a minority of those in Managua in general. The majority of houses in Managua comprise the numerous squatter settlements in and around Managua. These houses, constructed of plastic, corrugated tin, bits of

Introduction

wood and whatever else is available, are usually strategies of the poorest populations who cannot afford a house or housing materials. The emergence of squatter settlements generally represents residents' self-initiated housing/economic strategies which provide services that strained government structures otherwise cannot.[8]

Apart from the more recent mini-falda style housing in the barrio, the range of housing styles and sizes is actually quite variable, generally coinciding with the diverse class composition of the barrio. As we continue west down the dirt road to the far side of the new housing project and the west border of the barrio, we pass the house of our friend Maria Felix and her family. Of the more recent urban immigrants, they may represent the poorest household in the barrio. Their housing style, for this barrio represents a squatter lean-to style. They are also exceptional in their lack of lights, water and gas. Like their housing style, their living conditions are more common to other more humble areas on the edge of Managua.

There are numerous local community stores dotting the barrio. A couple of these are on the main avenue, such as Lillian's. These local stores generally offer a diverse assortment of goods and food items such as bread, cheese, oil, cigarettes, toilet paper, sugar, rice, tortillas, ice cream, meat, and vegetables. Other smaller stores in the barrio sell various goods such as school supplies, pharmaceutical items, and assorted items such as expensively priced shampoo, lotion, and makeup.

In the barrio, men mainly find work in the formal sector of the economy while women work more in the informal sector, doing domestic work in someone's home or selling food on the street. Nicaraguan census data from 1990 indicates that since 1979, the number of employed men has greatly increased in Managua from 250,559 to 796,711. The statistics do not indicate this for women, most likely reflecting the lack of inclusion in formal census data of informal sector employment such as domestic labor. This lack of inclusion also reflects the general lack of adequate salaries and benefits accorded these women.[9]

There are 142 small businesses and enterprises in the barrio. These range from a clothing factory, "El Triunfo," to various other stores, workshops, and businesses. El Triunfo is located somewhat in the interior of this 30—square block barrio. El Triunfo is a clothing cooperative, employing and run mainly by women. They have a strong union and women's organization and are responsible for collectively advertising, distributing, and selling the items they produce. They had initiated a food-buying cooperative at subsidized prices and have been mobilizing with local community groups to find a place that can be used for day care for the majority of workers who come in from various barrios throughout Managua.

A smattering of numerous other small and medium-sized local businesses such as small metal and wood workshops, a shoe repair workshop, and several auto shops also make up the barrio's composition. Manuel Ruiz is a metal smith. Previously living down the street from El Triunfo, his new house and shop is now on the other side of the barrio, part of the 42 lots (Camilo Ortega) attained by the barrio. His new house, like his previous one is fashioned of bricks and creative metal framework. Abused as a young boy, Manuel left the house at eight years to travel Nicaragua's countryside, landing several jobs and finally taking up an offer to apprentice as a metal smith. A non-sectarian, highly-involved community member to this day, he recites stories of how he constructed sharp metal rods for others to use in clandestine activities before the triumph in 1979.

Walking south from El Triunfo we pass Francisco's. Francisco Ramirez is a long-time community resident who makes and repairs wooden chairs and tables in his tall-ceilinged house/barn where he lives alone. His house is tucked back and bordered by some trees and is in one of the more humble housing areas in the barrio. Around the corner, Carlos Martin (a shoe repair person), another long-time community resident, occupies the front room of his family house for his shop. His street is nicknamed "street of dogs" and is lined with middle-class looking, well-established houses. Carlos, along with several other men, works busily to keep up the repair work on the piles of shoes setting on the floor and shelves around them.

There is one movie theater in the barrio. It occupies a large space on the main avenue in the barrio. The theater presents mostly grade B Latin films. Just outside of the west boundary of the barrio is a large park with an elegant cultural center. It houses an art gallery, a performance area for local bands, and a dance studio where the national dance troop practices. The park is frequently used by a wide range of people from the barrio; however, the cultural center is frequented by the more cosmopolitan and middle class Nicaraguans. A large sports arena lies outside of the northern edge of the barrio, and across the street is a stadium for bull fighting. Both of these spots are heavily attended by Nicaraguans throughout Managua.

Most transportation in the barrio is by foot or by bus. Numerous bus stops dot the barrio. These bus routes lead to all parts of Managua and to larger bus stops which carry people to other cities and the countryside. Certain buses, such as the 119, are notorious for crowds and robberies. These buses are on the central routes leading to the big markets in Managua, the Mercado Oriental (with the largest black market), most commonly used by barrio residents, and Mercado Huembes, a newer and cleaner but more expensive market. Barrio William Diaz Romero also contains numerous Protestant and Catholic churches. Contrary to what is typically heard outside Nicaragua, the Catholic churches are locally defined as reactionary by barrio residents; whereas, a Baptist church in the barrio preaches liberation theology and is involved with the local CDS to cooperatively plan different sports and health-related activities.

Barrio William Diaz Romero is a barrio with an interesting political history. It is named after a young school teacher who was killed three weeks before the triumph of the revolution. As a young man, William Diaz lived with his family in a wooden house in the barrio. His house is located in the central part of the barrio and is now occupied by another family. It is quite visible. Neighbors frequently point to it when they recall the sites and sounds surrounding the story of his capture. Directly across the street from his house is a garage that has housed the local barrio government (CDS). Every June 27th, barrio people fill the area between his house and the CDS to commemorate his martyrdom through speeches, a mass, music, and dancing.[10]

Like William Diaz Romero, numerous martyrs from the barrio are commemorated with plaques on different corners throughout the barrio. Barrio William Diaz Romero is frequently described as an area of little political activity, no military actions having taken place in this barrio. There were, however, numerous safe houses operating in this barrio in the last few years before the triumph. Many people in the barrio such as Ruth Arena, Mabel Curtis, Consuelo Mendietta, Elisia Espinoza, Olga Palacio and Maritza Cortez, coordinated safe houses. Many of these women were already politicized, while many others, as is typical of many experiences heard in Nicaragua, became heavily involved through the long-term clandestine activities of their offspring. These women speak of hope, devastation, and struggle as they recall their experiences of becoming politicized. Elisia Espinoza describes herself during these times as "being born again" as she recalls hiding guns under her bed to assist her offspring.

Olga Palacio, a strong woman in her early 50's, frequently talks with pride and enthusiasm of her 30 years of being a school teacher and the history of school teaching in her family. She lives near the south border of Ho Chi Minh Avenue in the barrio. Her four offspring, most of whom still live in the barrio, were heavily involved in long-term clandestine activities. Following the triumph of the Nicaraguan people in 1979, Olga was the first to be elected as barrio coordinator.

Her daughter, Maritza Cortez, lives directly across the street from her mother and down a dirt alley. An articulate university professor and sociologist, she also works in a research institute in Managua. Like so many other Nicaraguans, her work during the insurrection, integral to Nicaragua's overall history, is reflected in her current position as current health coordinator of the barrio.

Consuelo Mendietta is an extremely articulate and energetic woman in her mid-40's. She also joined in the struggle, along with five of her young offspring. Numerous others from the barrio, such as Elisia Espinoza, Mabel Curtis, Manuel Ruiz, Ruth Arena, Orlando Garcia, Elisa Torres, Hugo Medina, Luis Lopez, and many of their family members also became actively involved in the general struggle, and today remain committed and focused members of the barrio.[11]

After the triumph, the residents were quick to form these barrio committees (CDSs). CDSs represent a form of mass organization that operate within barrios throughout the country. The CDSs generally handle local problems and concerns, and attempt to develop national programs at the local level. These range from health to adult education, price control, food distribution, and community (and housing) development. They also act as a forum for settling internal community problems. These range from planning children's parties to settling land disputes among neighbors. In the last two years CDSs, as part of a remobilization, were renamed CDCs (Community Development Centers).[12]

In William Diaz Romero, the 30 blocks have been organized into fourteen block committees, with one general committee for the entire barrio. The general committee is composed of eight elected members who serve a year without pay. This committee, as mentioned above, is quite active and has currently (April 1990) finished building a larger community center which will have room for day care, adult education, and health care. Another successful community-initiated project has been coordinating the previously mentioned housing project for 42 families in the barrio.

Finally, these community residents are continually involved in attempting to keep the barrio motivated in its support of the popular revolution. In terms of the political affiliation of the barrio, the majority have been affiliated with the Sandinistas. There had been some evidence of opposition and of growing dissatisfaction with the economic situation and the continuation of the war before the election. There was obviously a large population that swung towards UNO, the opposition party that beat the Sandinistas in February. As previously mentioned, after the initial day or two of surprise and mourning, Nicaraguans supportive of the Sandinistas have called their new strategy "Government from Below." Time will tell what effect the new government will have on the composition of Nicaragua, Managua, and Barrio William Diaz Romero. But for now, they have made new commitments to strengthen the grass-roots organization of the movement and move forward.[13]

Demographics—The Social, Political, and Economic Composition of Barrio William Diaz Romero

In this section we provide a general demographic outline of the barrio. These summaries highlight economic, social, and consumer data on the barrio and its residents.

Introduction

TABLE 1.1 Representation of Age (CDS Heroes y Martyrs, 1988/89)

AGE	MALES	FEMALES
0-4	13	7
5-9	8	12
10-14	12	7
15-19	4	10
20-24	1	5
25-29	11	7
30-34	4	9
35-39	5	6
40-44	3	2
45-49	1	3
50-54	1	3

Total number of people in CDS	134.0
Average household size	4.5
Total number of males	63.0
Total number of females	71.0
Average age of males	22.3
Average age of males 18 and under	7.1
Average age of males above 18	39.5
Average age of females	25.0
Average age of females 18 and under	9.5
Average age of females above 18	38.7

Representation of Age, Household Size, and Education

The samples we refer to throughout this section are drawn from the census data of three CDSs out of a total of fourteen CDSs in the barrio as shown in Tables 1.1, 1.2, and 1.3. However, out of these fourteen, only seven or eight operated. In addition, we present data from our own sample as shown in Table 1.4. Each CDS is approximately a block or two in size.

Mincoin 1988-89 (Ministerio de Comercio Interior)

The following is archival data based on the number of consumers in the barrio for the previously distributed (until summer, 1988) government-subsidized food packages. Table 1.5 represents the number of expendios (distribution points) in the barrio, the total number of consumers in the barrio, and four sociological categories (including three age groups, women ages 12-50, and total number of families).

Educational Levels

The range of educational levels of barrio residents are shown in Table 1.6 (A and B). These estimates are based on the occupational categories from the census materials from the three CDSs.

TABLE 1.2 Representation of Age (CDS Zelada, 1988/89)

AGE	MALES	FEMALES
0-4	9	7
5-9	10	11
10-14	11	12
15-19	7	5
20-24	4	7
25-29	3	6
30-34	8	11
35-39	8	5
40-44	3	3
45-49	1	2
50-54	1	1
55-59	2	1
60-64	0	4
65-69	3	1
70-74	3	2
75-79	0	1
80 +	0	1

Total number of people in CDS	153.0
Average household size	4.6
Total number of males	73.0
Total number of females	80.0
Average age of males 18 and under	9.1
Average age of males above 18	39.5
Average age of females	25.6
Average age of females 18 and under	8.6
Average age of females above 18	35.3

Land of the Lakes:
The Historical Background to Modern Nicaragua

The Martyrdom of William Diaz Romero

William Diaz Romero was a very fine young man. He was a school teacher. During the struggle against Somoza, like many of the youth in the barrio, he was part of the Sandinista Front. He was a messenger and provided information and news between various safe houses in the area, like the ones in our houses. He also participated in many of the clandestine activities with other Sandinista youth.

Early in the morning of June 24 (1979), the Somoza national guard stormed his house and he was taken in his underwear from the house and was never seen again. After the triumph (July 19, 1979), his mother began searching for him. In one of the Red Cross hospitals, she encountered one of William's friends. This young man was in critical condition from the torturing he had received from the national guard. He told her that William had been tortured for several days before he died. He thought that his body had been taken to the lake outside of the city, where many tortured bodies had been left by the national guard. William's friend told William's mother that he had been brave to the end and had not given the national guard any information. She searched the area around the lake, but was not able to find William's body.

Introduction

TABLE 1.3 Representation of Age (CDS Francisco Moreno, 1988/89)

AGE	MALES	FEMALES
0-4	13	7
5-9	8	6
10-14	8	8
15-19	2	7
20-24	5	7
25-29	9	11
30-34	5	9
35-39	6	4
40-44	4	5
45-49	0	1
50-54	6	3
55-59	2	2
60-64	2	4
65-69	1	1
70-74	1	1
75-79	2	1
80 +	1	1

Total number of people in CDS	164.0
Average household size	3.8
Total number of males	75.0
Total number of females	77.0
Average age of males	26.6
Average age of males 18 and under	8.0
Average age of males above 18	37.7
Average age of females	27.7
Average age of females 18 and under	8.9
Average age of females above 18	37.3

No gender given for four residents whose ages are: 24, 4, 1, 36.
No gender or age given for: 5 adults and 3 children below age 13.

> *William was a brave young man. He knew the location of the safe houses in the barrio, but he gave no information. His courage was a symbol to us of what revolutionary struggle meant. Now each year we celebrate his martyrdom here in the barrio. This celebration always begins with a mass said in his honor. We place his photo on the altar alongside that of Jesus Christ.*
>
> —*Ruth Arena and Mabel Curtis*
> *Neighbors in the Barrio William Diaz Romero*
> *Managua, Nicaragua*

Historical Background

Because the U.S. public is not familiar with history in general and is even less familiar with the specific histories of third world countries, we will provide some background information on the history of modern Nicaragua. History is understood in terms of the present; however, the present makes little sense without some sense of history.

TABLE 1.4 Representation of Age (our sample, 47 households)

AGE	MALES	FEMALES
0-4	20	15
5-9	15	16
10-14	11	22
15-19	7	17
20-24	17	12
25-29	17	15
30-34	7	13
35-39	6	9
40-44	3	5
45-49	3	6
50-54	3	6
55-59	6	4
60-64	4	1
65-69	1	3
70-74	3	3
75-79	1	2
80 +	0	1

Total number of people in sample	274.0
Average household size	5.9
Total number of males	124.0
Total number of females	150.0
Average age of males	23.7
Average age of males 18 and under	7.5
Average age of males above 18	35.3
Average age of females	25.9
Average age of females 18 and under	9.3
Average age of females above 18	37.7

TABLE 1.5 MINCOIN 1988/89 Representation of Consumers

EX-PENDIO	TOTAL # OF CONSUMERS	UP TO 3 YEARS	4-13	14+	WOMEN 12-50	TOTAL # OF FAMILIES
1	1029	110	222	697	354	231
2	802	87	150	565	283	191
3	1026	114	224	668	309	212
TOTAL	2857	311	596	1930	946	634

Ecological Parameters of Nicaragua

Nicaragua is one of the five countries that make up the land mass referred to as Central America. Nicaragua's modern neighbors are Guatemala, El Salvador, Honduras, and Costa Rica. These are all tropical areas nurtured by sun and sea winds to produce a great intercontinental bridge of great richness and diversity (Mosser 1976:20). These land masses move from the highlands of Guatemala to the shallow plains of Panama. It is land filled with volcanos, jungles, high mountain regions, lowland coastal areas and huge fresh water lakes. The quality of the land mass and its position as a bridge between the two American continents has given this

Introduction

TABLE 1.6 Educational Levels (from the sample of the three CDSs)

	PRIMARY	SECONDARY	PRE-SCHOOL
(A) Children's Educational Levels (ages 15 and below)			
Males	41	13	2
Females	32	20	2

(B) General Adult Education Levels

SECONDARY, POST-SECONDARY:	PRIMARY:	LIMITED:	MISC:
43 (41%)	54 (51.4%)	3 (.03%)	5 (.05%)

These estimates are based on the occupational categories off the census materials from the three CDSs. Sample number = 105.

land the tragedies of massive earthquakes and destructive tropical storms throughout its history (McBirney and Williams 1965). As Wolf so ably suggested many years ago, these are the lands of the shaking earth (Wolf 1959).[14]

Pre-Spanish History of Nicaragua

Since the wanderings of the peoples of the Americas began some 15,000 years ago, the different zones of Central America began to be peopled (Fagan 1989). Earliest sites (Clovis) go back some 6,000 to 7,000 years in the area, with village and ceramic technology going back to 2,000 B.P. (Stone 1972). Various populations seem to have wandered through the regions of Nicaragua, with village horticulturists occupying the Pacific side and more nomadic foragers occupying the Atlantic side. Cultural historians have come to see the Pacific side populations as part of the cultural traditions of the classic civilizations of Mexico; whereas the Atlantic coast groups are placed within the South American Indian tradition of lowland peoples. This is a tradition of lower levels of social production and complexity. The Pacific side populations developed into small city state systems corresponding on much smaller scale to the social dynamics of Mesoamerican groups to the north, where the Atlantic coastal peoples maintained only loose political structure and had no urban development (Lange and Stone 1984).[15]

For all of Nicaragua before the arrival of the Spanish, the population was estimated to be at around 1.6 million, with 75% of that population residing in the Pacific regions (Newson 1987).

The Conquest

In the early 1500s, the Spanish conquistadors in Central America were contriving various plans and plots to determine who could be the next

Cortez. They sought rich lands, precious metals, and native populations over which to gain control. In the conquest of Nicaragua, we see the first of many battles by outsiders to control the fortunes of those who reside within this territory. Cortez' control had moved from southern Mexico into Central America. He had his people in what was to become Honduras, who were planning to move south into the areas of modern Nicaragua. Conquistadors in Panama—Andes Nino and Gonzales de Alivida—were making plans to move into the region also. In 1522–23 they launched their invasion. They were able to capture gold and Indians, but could not defend themselves and were forced to retire back to Panama. The next year, Hernandez de Cordoba was more successful. He too came up from Panama, and was able to found the cities of Granada and Leon. Thus, the peoples of Nicaragua were given the honor of becoming part of the American colonies of the Spanish empire. They paid dearly for this honor. By the 1570s the population of 1.6 million was reduced to under 50,000. The vast majority of that population loss was in the Pacific region. In our present times, we have come to be unfeeling about the destruction of the peoples of the Americas. Such massive forms of genocide should still be, and are, shocking. We often like to think that these population reductions were because the Indians were not immune to the simple illnesses that the Europeans brought to the New World. This is something of a European myth, not the memories of the native population themselves (Galeano 1985). In the case of Nicaragua, it is simply false. The massive reduction of the Nicaraguan population came primarily from one source—the industry of human commerce, slavery. The Spanish used the Native American population of Nicaragua as a commodity to sell to other parts of the empire as slaves (Newson 1987).

The Colonial Period

After the establishment of Spanish rule, Nicaragua become part of the Viceroyalty of Nueva Espania. This included Mexico and Central America. As in other parts of this new empire, the Spanish came looking for riches and found that to attain such riches work was required. The various boundaries of Central America were not some kind of logical set of decisions based upon peoples and lands, but what the Spanish thought would be profitable (MacLeod 1973). To pay or reward these explorers/exploiters, the "encomienda" system was developed by the Spanish crown. This involved giving the Spanish settlers control over the labor of Indians within the boundaries of an encomienda grant. Land was not provided, but the labor of the Indians. Indians were to work on projects for the settlers and work their own land to pay tribute to those who held the control of their labor. In the later centuries this system was transformed into the classic hacienda system, where both land and labor were owned by Spanish settler descendants.[16]

As the colonial process moves into the 17th century, what is left of the native population on the Pacific region begins to stabilize. Many Indians had moved into urban centers, with Indian barrios becoming part of the urban scene. Also, the alienation of Indians from their land intensified. Indians had held lands communally and had common areas for multiple uses. The Spanish crown was, in principle, concerned with protecting Indians lands; in fact, they did nothing. Indians had too many labor demands placed upon them, with too few laborers to carry out the demands. Their improvisation continued. Their basic food stuffs were the same, but there was less of them. This is seen in the population data of the time. By the end of the 17th century, the population in the Pacific regions is 22,263 (Newson 1987). The Atlantic side had a higher population, 38,843. Remember that the pre-Spanish population was thought to be around 1.6 million (Sherman 1979).

Independence Period

With the victory of Iturbide in Mexico and his formation of the kingdom of Mexico, the peoples of Central America found themselves independent.[17] The Iturbide empire lasted no more than a year. With the fall of Iturbide, Guatemala broke from Mexico, and led the movement toward a Central American federation that was to include the regions of Honduras, El Salvador, Nicaragua, and Costa Rica (Herring 1968). Thus, in 1823, an experiment of regional governance began that is still to be resolved. The immediate and continuing conflict is over the issues of centralism versus federation, those who desire a strong central government for the whole region versus those who wish to construct a loose federation of the various regions of the area. This was both a difference between the social elites of Guatemala who favored centralism since that was to their overall advantage and the regional elites who feared economic and political loss in such a structure. The region's conservative political positions associated with centralism and liberalism were associated with the federation position. For example, those in Nicaragua who favored nationhood for themselves also separated into groups over whether, within their own nation, the government should be organized in terms of centralist principles or in terms of a regional federation (Karnes 1961).

These battles, particularly in Nicaragua, were framed in terms of the economic and political interests of the United States and England, which would favor either position so long as it supported their economic and political interests. This is the period of the Monroe doctrine which declared that Central America was the province of the United States, not Europe

(Bermann 1986). Though Nicaragua was to remain peripheral to overall social/political issues of the 1800s, it was to find itself constantly being pushed and shoved in directions dictated by the United States.[18]

As the 1800s were closing out, Nicaragua's first nationalist leader emerged. In 1893, Jose Santos Zelaya became the president of Nicaragua. What seemed to make him controversial, both inside and outside of Nicaragua, was his nationalist sentiment. He felt that the first to benefit from Nicaragua's resources should be Nicaraguans. He was no socialist or radical. He felt that the capitalist class of Nicaragua should be able to control the dynamics of its own country.[19]

Zelaya lasted until 1909, when he resigned and went into exile instead of attempting to fight the United States. In this period, the United States sent the marines who occupied Nicaragua until 1933. Because of the political contexts created by this American occupation, two historical actors and their movements have come to dominate Nicaraguan history into the 1990s. These would be Augusto Cesar Sandino and Anastasio Somoza Garcia (Arevalo 1961).

Sandino

Augusto Sandino was the bastard son of upper class Nicaraguans. There is nothing in the context of Nicaraguan social structure that makes his birthright unusual, only that many of the founders of the revolutionary movement some 50 years later would also be bastard children of upper class Nicaraguans.

Whether his birth status affected his politics is not known, but it is clear that Sandino was a nationalist who backed his beliefs with an effective strategy and organization of armed struggle against the American occupation of Nicaragua. Sandino had been active in the liberal party in Nicaragua (the same party as the Somozas), but refused to participate in civil politics until the American occupation had ended (Selser 1979).[20] Sandino was able to organize an armed resistance to American occupation. With a force of over a thousand people, Sandino carried out an effective "guerrilla war" against the American marines.[21] For over five years (1929–1934) Sandino and his forces were able to prevent the USA marines from pacifying Nicaragua.

What the USA did do was to get the warring political factions to accept a compromise among themselves and to form a national guard to be led by Anastasio Somoza Garcia. From the position of controlling the national guard, Somoza was able to build a family-run dictatorship that was to last until July 19, 1979. With the formation of the national guard under the leadership of Somoza, the USA Marines were withdrawn from Nicaragua. This met Sandino's condition that he would not stop the armed struggle as long as the country was occupied. On February 21, 1934, President Sacasa of Nicaragua, the father in-law of Somoza, invited Sandino to Managua to negotiate an end to the war. This was a tragic invitation, for it was the pretext for his murder by Somoza and his national guard. Thus ended the first phase of the Nicaraguan revolution for self-determination (Crad 1930, Frazier 1958, and MaCulay 1967).

Somoza

From the 1930s until July 19, 1979, the Somoza family ran Nicaragua as its personal business and property. During this time period Nicaragua became a symbol for the banana republic (though in fact banana production was never very significant in Nicaragua) (Karnes 1978). Anastasio ruled the country in various styles (president, leader of the liberal party, head of the national guard) until his assassination in Leon in 1956 by a young Nicaraguan poet—Rigoberto Lopez Perez. Somoza's first son, Luis, then took over the presidency. Luis' younger brother Anastasio, called Tacho by everyone, took over command of the national guard. Luis was a modernist in the sense that he felt that the Somoza family wealth and power could be maintained without the visible control of the state system. He proposed various reforms in the civil structure of the government and made some moderate changes in the economy to pursue more development of agro-exports. During this time, Tacho reorganized the national guard to pursue the emergence of a new armed struggle in the mountains that was labeled as a communist plot. In fact, those who were in the mountains were the founders of a new Sandinista struggle.[22]

Luis did allow for caretaker presidents in the early part of the 1960s, but as the political situation got more difficult, Tacho returned the reins of state power directly back to the family by allowing himself to be elected president of Nicaragua. His term ended on July 17, 1979, two days before those plotters in the hills entered Managua.[23]

Frente Sandinista de Liberacion Nacional

The National Sandinista Liberation Front (FSLN) was formed in July of 1961. Carlos Fonseca was the intellectual and political leader of this reappearance of armed revolutionary struggle for the overthrow of the Somoza dictatorship and self-determination. Many of the early organizers of the FSLN were young, university students, middle or working class, and from outside of Managua. Fonseca was the bastard son of a wealthy Matagalpan and his maid. Fonseca, Borges, the Ortegas (later members of the struggle), Daisy Zomora, Omar Cabazas, Bayardo Arce, and many other young Nicaraguans were inspired by the successes of the Cuban revolution and perceived Che Guevera and Fidel Castro as role models of action. However, it was the spirit of Sandino that anchored their struggle in the appropriate history of Nicaragua. It was Fonseca who lobbied that this revolution be based upon the thoughts, actions, and strategies of Sandino and his followers during their struggle of the 1920s and 1930s (Close 1988, Hodges 1986, and Walker 1981 & 1982).

Fonseca argued that Sandino's thoughts were part of political discourse on popular classes and culture (Ruis 1984).[24] Popular classes and culture in the simplest terms, represent all those groups outside the power structure of the elite (Black 1981). On June 19, 1979 these popular groups, organized into a revolutionary army, entered Managua. From these efforts, what was to be eleven years of popular political rule was begun.

The Sandinistas, 1979–1990

For eleven years the Sandinistas struggled to encourage the three million people of Nicaragua to build a new society that would represent the desires and needs of those composing the popular classes (Borge 1987:53–65). That attempt was focused in four general areas: (1) civil/political reform, (2) the development of a mixed economy, (3) mobilization of popular political action through mass organizations, and (4) the transformation of the conditions of peoples' daily lives.

Civil/Political Reform. This effort involved the development of a new governance structure for the country that was based upon a new constitution. For Nicaragua this involved establishing a government structured upon the separation of powers (executive, legislative, and judicial) (Diskin 1983). This also included the development of political space for opposition parties and independent media sources. This further involved the restructuring of local and regional government structures that had not existed under the Somoza era (Lanuza, Vazquez, Barahona and Chamorro 1983). In this area the Sandinistas were more successful than they might have wanted to be as evidenced by the results of the election of February 25, 1990 (Envio 1990a).

Mixed Economy. The Sandinistas had hoped to be able to construct an economy that would allow for free market growth in a non-exploitative context. This involved a model where the government controlled the centers of finance and left the majority of the productive industries in private hands. It introduced various forms of labor and land reform that were designed to develop a labor force that could participate in the overall process of planning and production. It attempted to provide tax incentives to those industries and producers that could generate jobs and materials for general development. Though the focus was to be on a mixed economy, emphasis was primarily centered on the maintenance of agro-exports. In this area there was little success. The Contra war, the United States' economic harassment in the form of the blockade, and the general world economic crisis stalled most of the attempts at economic reform (Envio 1988d:2–8, 1989a:5–16; 1989c:10–30, 1989d:33–55; 1989e:11; and 1989f:35–44).

Popular Political Action. During the period of Sandinista political control, mass organizations were developed to express the interests and needs of particular popular groups. These were primarily represented in the areas of workers (both rural and urban), ethnic groups, women's organizations, students, and community-based groups. These groups were to be autonomous from the Sandinista political structure and were supposed to be voices for their own interests. Depending upon which groups one looked at and at what time during this period, some groups were successful in representing such interests. Overall, mass organizations were not able to transform the civil political structure (Envio 1990d:23–38 and Maier 1985).

Transformation of Daily Lives. There was a genuine hope that the combined forces of this popular revolution would be a means to transform the quality of everyday life for the people of Nicaragua. They were searching for various forms of empowerment that would alter the structures of education, health, housing, and local governing that would affect peoples personal lives. Women had great hopes that there would be changes in the areas of gender roles and new opportunities for women. There were many different levels of success in this area however, the long-term effect of these kinds of changes will not be known until some time in the future.

This experiment in popular change obviously had mixed results. Even though the Sandinistas lost the elections, the various forms of new political actions and hopes generated by this revolution continue. The new government will have to deal with a political population that is more informed and organized than at any other time in Nicaraguan history. The focus of our study will be on the aspects of popular political action and the domain of the transformation of daily life.

UNO 1990–1992

The United Nicaraguan Opposition has been in power for close to a year and six months. It is much too early in the process to determine how well they are doing. The war has ended and the economic blockade has been lifted. The economy is still in a shambles. The political terrain is confused and complex. Overall living conditions for the majority have gotten worse in this short time period of formal rule. It is unclear whether the Chamorro government will be able to serve a full term. Further, it is unclear if her government can be maintained or what or who will replace it. The Sandinistas hope to be able to return to formal political power in six years through the electoral process. During the remaining time they plan to be the formal political opposition within the civil domain and to encourage the maintenance of mass organizations as a force that can govern from below.

Summary

In the remaining section of this chapter, we provide a summary of the chapters that make up this book. Each chapter will open with a short ethnographic account which hopefully can set the tone for the chapter.

"View Through the Door Frame" is the chapter on methods. Here we show how a methodology for an ethnographic praxis can be constructed from the current debate within post-modern analysis and the relationship of that analysis to ethnographic writing. We review the traditional, modern, and post-modern modes of ethnographic representation. We also review the critics of these post-modern musings and present our construction of methodology in terms of our overall concerns. The title of this chapter is a play on Evans-Pritchard's view on methods entitled "View From the Tent-Door." During one of our longest stays in the barrio, we lived in a small apartment that had an enclosed porch where we often sat in rocking chairs and watched people's activities through the door frame of that small room.

The succeeding chapters are on different components of the social structure of the barrio. *"Jodido Pero Contento"* deals with social organization. We present information on household structures in the barrio, on the politics of gender, on sexuality and age, and on patterns of social interaction. Also we address the socio-economic context of the barrio, the city of Managua, and the overall country. This includes looking at the rapid economic changes that have rocked Nicaragua most recently. We present ethnographic information on the general market and commercial structure and on the overall employment patterns in Managua. This is framed in terms of the way the informal economic sector operates and how households in the barrio are economically organized. We also present an account of the collective actions taken by barrio residents in their struggles against these economic problems.

The chapter entitled *"¡Quiero Decir Esto!"* is an account of popular politics operating within the barrio. This chapter involves looking at the relationship between the national organization of communities (CDS) and the way this structure operates within the barrio itself. We look at the way the local group is organized, its accomplishments, its limitations, and its future. The next chapter, entitled *"Afuera del Barrio,"* is a discussion of the effect of national and international forces upon the everyday lives of the people of this community. The focus is on institutional realities (schools, health, housing), political realities (solidarity movements), cultural relations, and popular religion.

In the concluding chapter, we present in a more detailed manner how our analysis can be seen as a search for an ethnographic praxis and how that search has to be constantly focused on the well-being of the members of the community of Barrio William Diaz Romero. We also provide an account of how the "gobierno de abajo" is operating in the barrio.

Notes

1. Here we are using people's first names because this is the style as expressed in Nicaragua. Even national leaders in Nicaragua are referred to by their first names.

2. Since there has been no consensus on pronoun use (he/she, etc.) in contemporary writing we are choosing to use "she." Since it is often claimed the pronoun "he" generally refers to all, we are claiming the same semantic right for "she," even though we realize that in some cases, "he" more appropriately applies. Further, we are aware that it is more often the male ethnographic voice which has been challenged on the question of representational authority.

3. For an explanation of the current field of applied anthropology see Erve Chambers, *Applied Anthropology: A Practical Guide* (Englewood Cliffs, New Jersey: Prentice Hall, 1985) and John van Willigen, *Applied Anthropology: An Introduction* (Massachusetts: Bergin and Garvey Publishers, Inc., 1986).

4. A paraphrasing from the Who's album *Who Next* from the song "Won't Get Fooled Again," Peter Townsend, 1971.

5. Compounding this already critically stressed reality has been the return of thousands of overseas Nicaraguans. Obviously many of these returning Nicaraguans were not supportive of the Sandinista revolution. Both domestic and international media have suggested that Managua alone has been flooded with at least 40,000 new automobiles. Also, there has been continued in migration to the city from the countryside and the emergence of numerous new squatter settlements.

6. Since we began our research in this barrio, we have often been asked why we are studying this community full of so many internationalists? The reason for this question is that, located in the Barrio William Diaz Romero, there are numerous boarding houses and dining places that are used by the large number of international visitors to and volunteers in Nicaragua. Many of these visitors spend a week or two in this barrio and then move out of Managua and onto the various projects that they have come to Nicaragua to work on. Therefore, they usually see only this barrio or certain parts of the barrio, those parts most frequented by internationalists. Most of these internationalists think that there is nothing in the barrio but these few businesses and the other international visitors. Therefore, how did we come to study this community?

In the summer of 1986, we were in this barrio waiting to join a construction brigade that was being organized to do some work in the San Rafael del Norte region. The project involved going to the area where the Contras had kidnapped German volunteer workers and continuing their work. However, because of visa problems, we were not able to go along and were stuck in the barrio looking for something to do. We were staying at the Hospedaje Norma, which is one of the more popular boarding houses for international visitors in the barrio. Each day we would hear tales of what people were doing all over Nicaragua, but we noticed that most people did not know anything about the community they were actually in. We knew that each barrio had a local committee structure, then referred to as the Sandinista Defense Committee (CDS). We asked where we could find some representative of the CDS so that we could find out something about the community. We were sent to the house of Hydee Rivas. She is a woman in her early 60's who was the block representative. She explained that we would need to come to the barrio's CDS meeting to meet the full CDS committee. She told us that on Sunday they were having a party to raise funds for upcoming barrio events. That Sunday we went to the party, began to meet more members of the community, and began to discuss with these members the prospects of a study of the community and the organization of a sister barrio exchange between them and our community back in Greeley. Thus, that's how we came to study this community.

7. The barrio has also been able to organize another housing project named Carlos Calero Carranza. This project has 25 lots.

8. For a fuller treatment of housing and squatter settlements in Managua see Morales, Ardaya and Espinoza's work entitled "Asentamientos Espontaneos No Son Causa de La Crisis Urbana." In Boletin Socio Economic, INIES-April, Managua, Nicaragua, 1987.

9. Current unemployment data reported by Barricada (1992) suggests a rate of over 60%. For detailed census material on Nicaragua see *Nicaragua—Diez Anos en Cifras*. Instituto Nacional de Estadisticas Y Census. Managua, 1989.

10. In 1990 the local barrio government was able to construct a new community house for all these activities.

11. Here we are identifying residents with their last names because of the biographical information in this section. Also, unless otherwise stated we are using people's real names in this study because they wanted to be identified with their real names.

12. In the new political context of UNO the CDS movement is now referred to as the national community movement (Movimiento Comunal) and the barrio committees are now referred to as barrio counsels (Consejos del Barrio). Since these are basically the same organization that we refer to as CDS in this text we will maintain the usages of CDS in order not to confuse the readers.

13. In our last visit January 1992 we noted these changes at the barrio level. As noted above the barrio committee is now referred to as the barrio council and their focus continues to be lobbying for communal concerns. They have been able to obtain materials to begin a day care center and successfully lobbied the city to build them a sports center including a full-sized basketball court and stands.

Introduction

Further, they have been successful in protecting the overall land titles (houses and community center) they gained during the revolution.

In terms of the physical appearance of the barrio everything seemed to have a fresh coat of paint. With the lifting of the blockade stores now seem to have an overabundance of goods unlike peoples pocketbooks. Several new businesses had opened; U.S.-styled video centers, pharmacies, used clothing stores and new restaurants. With the slowing down of the international visitor populations some of the older comedors and hospedajes are closing.

14. Nicaragua's land mass is 57,000 square miles. This land mass has three macro-ecological zones: The Pacific coast lowlands, the central highlands, and lowlands of the Caribbean or Atlantic side. The Pacific coast is a mixture of tropical and arid areas, the highlands are a semi-tropical area, and the Atlantic areas are tropical rain forests and plains areas. The whole region has two seasons. The dry season runs from November to April, the wet season from May to October (Ryan 1970). The land of Nicaragua ranges from the high peaks of Matagalpa to the coastal beauty of San Juan Del Sur. It moves from the plains surrounding the lakes of Managua and Nicaragua to the tropical forest that lines the Rio Coco out to the Atlantic Coast. Within the various ecological zones there is a rich diversity in flora and fauna associated with tropical areas (West and Augelli 1976).

The Pacific region is composed of numerous fault lines and volcanic developments. The coastal zone of the Pacific is composed of cretaceous and tertiary sediments, with numerous variations. The Leon/Chinandega plain is one of volcanic deposits with silty loams that have produced the best soil in Nicaragua. This Pacific area is referred to as "tierra caliente" with an annual average temperature of 25c to 35c. In pre-conquest times there were heavy forests of semi-evergreen trees, where deer and peccaries were hunted and the fresh water lakes were fished. The central region encompassed the central mountain ranges of over 2,000 meters. This is "tierra templada," with average temperatures between 20c to 25c. Forests were pine and oak, with animal populations of deer, peccaries, sloths, monkeys, and wildcats. The Atlantic region was lowland tropical—hot, wet, and humid (Newson 1987).

15. Most of the information on this historical period is from Linda A. Newson's *Indian Survival in Colonial Nicaragua* (Norman: University of Oklahoma Press, 1987). The Indian groups within Nicaragua were Oto-Maguean speakers, with three major groups present on the Pacific side: Chorotega, Maribio, and Nicarao. All seem to represent migration groups from the North. They may have displaced Indian groups that moved out towards the Atlantic side. The two major Atlantic Indian groups were the Sumus and Ramas, with the Mosquitos perhaps being a mixed group of Indians and Africans after the conquest.

These linguistic groups in the Pacific region were social formations that can be referred to as chiefdoms (Service 1962). This is a mode of production based upon intensive agriculture through irrigation. They were socially stratified systems headed by hereditary chiefs. These were small chiefdoms somewhat like city states, with high population density and minimal monumental architecture. There were no large pyramids or temples constructed. Agricultural production was the primary economic activity, with hunting and fishing playing minor roles. There were craft industries and market systems present. Land was held communally, with use rights allocated to households. Most agricultural labor was performed by males. Two and a half hectares of cultivated land were needed to provide for a household. Primary technologies were stone axes and digging sticks. The most important crops were corn, beans, manioc, sweet potatoes, cacao and cotton. This type of farming used the method of pot irrigation and some river irrigation. Orchards were developed and kept as private property. The most important fruit from the orchards were mammees, nisperos and jocotes (all still grown and eaten in Nicaragua today). Other important fruits were plums, nace, guanaba, avocado, and pineapple. Wines were made from jocates and plums and oil was made from the seeds of mammee. Important garden crops were calabashes and peppers. Important trade crops were cacao, cotton, and tobacco. Orchards and gardens were private and were used in dowries. In fact, cacao beans were used as a form of currency. Important crafts were cotton weaving, pottery, and some gold work. Trade was conducted through market systems, controlled by local cities and organized by women (Newson 1987).

The sociopolitical structure involved a separation between the hereditary nobility and a land-based commoner population. The Nicaraos had a single ruler, whereas the Chorotegas were ruled by a council of nobles. The Nicarao chiefs' authority rested on two bases: they owned the cacao groves, and they received tribute from the commoners in the form of cacao beans. The nobility were exempted from routine labor. They were responsible for maintaining the general well-being of the commoners and defending them in times of war. The rulers were not priests, but worked with the priests in religious rituals. The chiefs had their court and bureaucrats who maintained the organization of the chiefdom. Commoners did the agricultural labor, paid tribute, and composed the troops for warfare. Commoners could be sold into slavery.

In terms of kinship and marriage patterns, most information is on the nobility. They tended to be monogamous and married outside their immediate kin group. There is some evidence for polyandry in terms of saving on dowry payments. The religious system was ideologically like others within Mesoamerica, including human sacrifices and ritual cannibalism. Commoners were land-based agricultural workers, with parallel forms of ritual and religion.

On the Atlantic side, Indian groups lived in small settlement units without the development of complex political systems such as the city states of the Pacific side. There was no class division, and the division of labor was in terms of age and gender. Economic activities were slash and burn horticulture and foraging. The main crops were root crops like manioc. Craft and trade production were more limited.

16. Either out of laziness or lack of knowledge of how to use the lands acquired, the Spanish settlers used the encomienda structure to develop a slave trade with Spanish colonies to the south of them—Panama and Peru. From 1525 to 1542, slavery was the main enterprise of the Spanish settlers of Nicaragua, and more than 500,000 native Nicaraguans were shipped out of Nicaragua. In 1542 all women and children were set free; males were kept in bondage, but no new slaves could be sold. Those slaves that were not exported were used in mining and other forms of forced labor needed by the Spanish.

Introduction

To say the least, this massive depopulation of the native peoples had tremendous negative effects on this population. It created a very perverse set of feedback loops on the native population. Through this population "transfer," the remaining Indians did not physically have enough labor to carry out either their own subsistence requirements or meet the new tribute demands placed upon them by the Spanish. Decreased labor meant decreased time to work the fields, which meant having to use fields for longer periods of time instead of letting some lay fallow. This produced small yields of produce and less variety, which in turn reduced food consumption for the native population. Hunger and malnutrition in the countryside had its legacy in these first decades of Spanish rule (Newson 1987 and Sherman 1979).

Within the boundaries of the colonial rule, the Spanish left the native population alone in terms of village and work structures. Indian nobility were recognized as the "caciques" of villages, with power over commoners and slaves. The major focus outside of the encomienda was the conversion of the Indians to the Church. The Spanish began their process of urbanization and government control from these urban centers. The Atlantic side was ignored except for frequent explorations of the area while looking for wealth and slaves. Leon was the colonial capital where the governor and treasury officials resided. The emerging cities were organized in terms of Spanish civic structures. Each city had a "cabildo" (military officials), two "alcaldes" (like mayors), "algucil" (constable), secretaries, and lesser officials referred to as "riedores." Political positions could be held for two to five years. This was the civil structure which the Indians had to deal with (Newson 1987, Radell 1965, and Sherman 1979).

With the abolishing of the slave trade, the new cities of Nicaragua lost their economic base. Many began turning to agricultural production for new forms of export. As the Spanish were leaving the cities for agricultural estates, the Indians were coming to the city to find work and places to live. Two structural features of modern Nicaragua emerged from these times: an informal sector of the urban economy run by the new Indian residents and a labor shortage in the countryside to work the new estates the Spanish were so eager to begin. They never seemed to understand that those Indians that they had exported might someday be needed as workers in their own country.

The move of the Spanish settlers to the countryside to develop agricultural enterprises continued the exploitation of the native population that remained. That land which was still held by the Indians was transferred to the Spanish. Even though the encomienda was not a system of land ownership, it was being transformed into that. Because of land acquisitions and slavery, there was a labor shortage. By the end of the 17th century, wage labor for agricultural workers had been introduced into the countryside. Both the origins of agroexports and landless agricultural workers have their antecedents in this time period.

The exports that the Spanish attempted to develop were cacao, indigo plants for dye, and some sugar and tobacco. The attempt at agro-exports was limited by marginal access to external markets. The movement towards agro-exports also put strains on methods for local subsistence production. There emerged differences between those agricultural sectors linked to exports versus those that were attempting to develop goods for domestic consumption. Cattle ranching emerged to satisfy these conditions.

17. The independence period was a confused one in Central America. There were no organized movements in the region. Political concerns were between local elites in disputes over their regions, rather than with the Spanish. For example, the political tensions in Nicaragua were between the interests of Granada and Leon, not between Nicaragua and Spain. In fact many in the area preferred staying in the Spanish empire over having independence. Independence seemed more of a concern for the colossuses to the north: Mexico and Guatemala. In Central America, there existed conflicts of interest over the Spanish system of social classification and privilege. This was a complex system that gave full privilege to the Spanish, numerous privileges to those born of Spanish parents, limited rights to American-born citizens, and little or no rights to Indian and African residents (Chance 1978). Those who were involved in Central American politics were willing to forego independence and stay with the Spanish if the systems of rights and privileges were alternated to allow equal rights for those of Spanish and American birth (Rodriguez 1978).

18. Though this was the time period of conflicting political battles framed in terms of conservative and liberal issues, it was also a time for pursuing United States' support for various projects, primarily the dream of a canal linking the Caribbean with the Pacific. Nicaragua, in the middle 1800's, became a theater of absurdity with such actors as Vanderbuilt, Walker, and various Nicaraguan generals and presidents playing out a surrealist drama of revolts and counterrevolts. Though not liked by many, the movie "Walker," in its oddity of presentation, is a reasonable representation of these times. Paralleling these conflicts in Nicaragua, other parts of the Americas were involved in similar political battles between their elites. The issues were consistently about the control of national resources and potential wealth. There was no interest in or concern for the dilemmas of the peasant populations or urban poor. Their interests would have to wait for several more decades before they would become part of the national agenda. For accounts of this time period see C. W. Doubleday, *Reminiscences of the "Filibuster" War in Nicaragua* (New York: Putnam's Sons, 1886); Laurence Oliphant, *Patriots and Filibusters* (London: Blackwood and Sons, 1898); Carl Scherzer, *Travels in the Free States of Central America* (London: Longman, Brown, Green, and Roberts, 1857); and E. G. Squier, *Nicaragua: Its People, Scenery, Monuments* (New York: Harper and Brothers, 1860). These are travel logs written in the racist and colonial language of that time period.

19. This put him in conflict with many Nicaraguans who felt that should not be so, and clearly put him in conflict with the United States' political and economic interests. His biggest crime seems to have been to explore the idea of building a canal without United States involvement. One can read the press in the United States during this time and see how Zelaya was depicted as an actor who was not concerned with the interest of Nicaragua, but only his own benefit. The "revolution" that he was conducting in Nicaragua he also wished to "export" to other Central American countries (Bermann 1986). One could easily substitute Sandinista or Ortega in these articles and they would read more like recent accounts in the American media.

Introduction 35

20. Sandino spent several years in Mexico after its revolution. There he was exposed to various currents of radical political thought. In this context he was exposed to Marxism, syndicalism, anarchism, and non-traditional forms of theology, including Masonism and spiritualism. Drawing from his understanding of these discourses and his understanding of the social base of Nicaragua, he began to develop a program for national reconstruction. This included elements of land reform for peasants, secular education, nationalizing of the economy to provide for Nicaraguans (later to be called a mixed economy), anti-imperialism, and the seeking of some form of federation with other Central American countries. Sandino was strongly anti-clerical. More exactly, he was anti-Catholic as the religion was practiced in the context of the Nicaragua of the 1920's. However, he understood that the general population of Nicaragua, especially the peasants, would not accept or struggle with a movement lacking in some kind of theological focus. It may be that his attraction to esoteric forms of theology was part of his search for an alternative theology (Hodges 1986). This search for an alternative theology is still part of contemporary Sandinismo. The development of this "theology of liberation" was begun by elements of the church in the time period between Sandino and the Sandinista revolution (Lancaster 1988).

21. Sandino's forces were never captured or defeated by the American forces. In effect, he organized his struggle by fighting in the countryside with forces from that same countryside. Though guerrilla warfare had been thought of in other contexts, Sandino was the first modern guerrilla warrior in the Americas. His movement was seen by other Latin American nationalists as the struggle of a new Bolivar to free the Americas again (Frazier 1958).

22. And they had certainly been impressed by the success of Castro and the recent Cuban revolution. However, they were in fact more intent in studying the strategies of their Nicaraguan hero, Augusto Sandino, in order to copy his successes. Fidel Castro also studied the ideas of Sandino in planning the revolutionary struggle for Cuba. Donald C. Hodges, *Intellectual Foundations of the Nicaraguan Revolution* (Austin: University of Texas Press, 1986).

23. How can one evaluate 46 years of a family dictatorship? In the early 1970's the Nicaraguan economy expressed the dynamics of many Third World countries. While the overall gross national product increased, there were widening differences between the wealthy and the poor. That is, the rich were getting much richer and the poor were, in fact, getting poorer. This reality still has symbolic power in revolutionary Nicaragua, especially in Managua. If you were involved in service industries (such as activities that are referred to as part of the informal sector), these were good times. If you lived in the countryside or worked in the limited industry of Nicaragua, these were quite hard times (Close 1988).

A more general review of the context of the Somozas' Nicaragua can be gained from reviewing Jacques M. May and Donna L. McLellan's study of the ecology of malnutrition in Central America which was done in the early 70s (May and McLellan 1972). Their data was from 1969. In their study they referred to Nicaragua as an agro-export economy that produces dual systems of food production. The majority of investment went to the production of food products for export, not for domestic consumption. May and McLellan documented the seasonal employment during 1963, in the agro-export sector close to 300,000 workers. These were workers who were very poor, and basically illiterate from the lack of educational services in the countryside. Basic food crops were corn, rice, root crops (yucca), and beans. Basic export crops were coffee, sugar, cotton and cattle.

For May and McLellan, this dual economy also produced for the population a duality of diets. "Here also we have a dual type of population, an underfed majority and an adequately or overfed minority. Here also we have the awkward situation of a country with insufficient food resources allocating the best cropland to cultivation of export crops in order to earn the foreign exchange required for industrial development" (May and McLellan 1972:267). This duality also affected the general health of the population. In terms of the general health of Nicaraguans, they make the following observation: "Under the visible pathological horizon many phenomena, inimical to welfare or to the full expression of individual and collective potential and to prolonged survival, occur. Children's mental development is irreversibly arrested, productivity of the adult is curtailed; unreported disease such as debilitating diarrheas are daily occurrences; and the resistance to communicable disease is lowered. None of these phenomena show up in statistics due to malnutrition. Yet, their impact on life and development is great" (May and McLellan 1972:268). They too conclude with suggestions of policy changes in the current context. They state, "even in spite of the number of good measures taken to implement wise policies, the problem of eradicating malnutrition in Nicaragua is far from solved. It has its roots in the economic situation . . . that is, the replacement of an economy of subsistence with an economy of consumption. . . . While the basic problems confronting a developing country—especially one like Nicaragua—cannot be solved without considerable time to modify existing institutions, a significant amount of good could result from appropriate husbanding of local resources and existing knowledge" (May and McLellan 1972:270).

24. Who are the popular classes? Throughout Latin America, the popular classes or cultures have been used to describe the complex social composition of this region (Gonzalez C. 1986). The metropolitan discourses of class composition and class struggle have not been able to capture the texture or context of social action in Latin America. The reality of indigenous populations, peasants, urban poor, urban workers, informal economic actors, politically radical or reactionary middle income actors, petty producers, and elite power groups have not fit into models of social stratification or workers' revolutions (Harris and Vilas 1986). Since the early writings of Mariategui, Latin writers have been attempting to construct a discourse that could capture these various realities (Gonzalez C. 1986).

2

The View Through the Door Frame

Methods of Ethnography

In the summer of 1987, we began our formal field investigation of the Barrio William Diaz Romero. I (Michael J. Higgins) was the senior ethnographer on the project, so I suggested that we begin by doing our primary data collecting from a simple questionnaire which would seek information on household composition, work, education, and people's general views on the changes that had taken place in the context of the revolution. I further suggested that, when people asked what we were doing, we would simply reply that we were doing a census. That was how I had explained my previous ethnographic work in Oaxaca, Mexico (Higgins 1974, 1983, 1986, and 1990). However, as we were to learn on numerous occasions, Nicaragua is not Mexico.

This choice of terms led us through the various bureaucracies of Nicaragua's political and academic areas. The local barrio committee (CDS) thought the idea of our study was okay, but they were more interested in the sister barrio project we were developing with them. We were told that to do formal research in Nicaragua, one had to be affiliated with a Nicaraguan research center. Our research was perceived as formal because we were conducting a census. A census in Nicaragua tends to mean more of an opinion poll than a demographic survey. We thought that we could attain such an affiliation from INIES, the Nicaraguan Institute for Social and Economic Studies. The year before, we had met the Secretary of International Relations of this Institute and had sent him copies of our current research proposals. When we returned to the research center that summer, that secretary was no longer there. Furthermore, no one had seen our research proposal. We were able to meet several investigators who were involved in urban research, and they thought our project was quite interesting. One of them even visited the regional CDS office with us to explain our project to Roger Valles, the regional CDS officer involved with the Barrio William Diaz Romero. Roger stated that he felt that the project was a good idea, but we had to be affiliated with INIES to do the work. However, in order to be affiliated with INIES, one needed formal letters of introduction which we did not have at the time.

We stopped doing our questionnaire (census to everyone else) and just did informal interviewing and participation in barrio activities. When we returned to the United States, we began collecting formal letters of introduction from our university officials and other anthropologists we knew in the United States and Mexico. We must have sent INIES over twenty letters. When we returned to Managua in the Spring of 1988, we were confident of getting our affiliation. People in the barrio were very glad to see us and the committee members (Orlando, the coordinator, and Hugo, the political educator) seemed to feel that we had taken care of our affiliation and did not mention the status of our formal study. We went to INIES, where there was now a new international secretary, Maria Vega, who was very cooperative and was quite impressed with our letters. However, she stated that we needed one more letter from an official in the Nicaraguan government. Luckily, because of our sister barrio project, we had a friend who was the national coordinator for those projects, and he wrote us a letter. When we returned with this letter, the secretary accepted it but told us that we needed a letter from the regional CDS office, stating that they also supported our research. We shouted, "No, we do not; for it was the regional CDS that had sent us to them in the first place." She relented on this point and processed our request. Within a few weeks, we were affiliates with INIES.

Several weeks later, we proudly showed several members of the committee of the barrio (Orlando, Hugo, and Felix) our letter of introduction from INIES which stated that we were working with the committee on this project. Hugo became very upset. He shouted that they had not made such an agreement with us since we had returned this summer and that we still did not have permission to do our census until they said so, even though they had all signed such an agreement the year before. We shouted back (Nicaraguans shout about everything) that we did have permission to do our study, that we were not doing a census, and further that we had just spent several weeks getting this permission from INIES based on what they had told us to do last year. After several hours of shouting, Orlando said that he would check with the regional CDS office about who was correct. The next week he informed us that, in fact, we did have permission to do this research and that they just wanted to coordinate it with us. That had always been our plan of action. Later that month (May) we visited with the assistant national coordinator for CDS, Flor de Maria Monterrey who loved the idea of our project and strongly encouraged us to continue.

When we returned in the summer of 1989 with a video crew to shoot footage for a documentary on this community, the whole committee of the barrio, including Hugo, was at the airport to meet us. This time we were doing a movie, not a census.

—Field Notes, Managua, Nicaragua, 1988

Introduction

In his classic ethnography on the Nuer of the Sudan region, Evans-Pritchard refers to his mode of observation as the view from his tent door (Evans-Pritchard 1940). Since we spent a great deal of time sitting on our porch in rocking chairs with a view of one of the main streets in the barrio, we have chosen the title for our chapter on methods as the View Through the Door Frame. However, Evans-Pritchard was concerned with the authority of his ethnographic account, and we were concerned with how to construct an ethnographic praxis. What are the methodological strategies with which one works in such a quest? To provide an answer to that question, we will need to present a review of the methodological strategies within social anthropology, the post-modern challenge to those strategies, and how we feel we can construct strategies that can lead to an ethnographic praxis.

What Is Ethnography?

Traditional Ethnographic Research, 1900–1945

An ethnography is the account that a social/cultural anthropologist gives of her field work experience in a cultural group outside of Western society. Or that is what most anthropologists thought ethnographies were up until about 1945. Early North American (including Mexico) and Western European social anthropology saw ethnography as a primary data base upon which the science of anthropology was to be based. They all felt an urgency in their task. In North America, anthropologists guided by Boaz recorded the ethnographies of Native Americans before they disappeared. The Europeans were equally concerned with capturing the realities of non-Western life in Africa, Asia, and the Pacific before those cultures were all absorbed into the developing industrial world of Western capitalism. There was a stated political purpose to some of this work. It was felt that such research would debunk the racist assumptions held in both Spencerian evolutionist scales and German assumptions of diffusion. It was further hoped that rational knowledge about marginal groups could generate rational relations between such groups and the Western political structures.

Both schools of social anthropology approached doing ethnography in similar styles. The narrative was to be written in what was to be called the ethnographic present. This is an odd term because it did not mean that the groups were to be described in terms of how they lived now, but how they once lived. That is, based upon the way they were now living, it was hoped that their immediate past could be reconstructed so that these groups could be understood in their pre-Western context. For Europeans, this approach was not contradictory, for it was felt that these groups lacked a concept of history. For Northern American anthropology, this approach was not a problem because all cultural systems had to be seen from a relativistic ahistorical focus. The fallacy of the ethnographic present was to come back and haunt anthropology several decades later.

Each school of anthropology felt that an ethnography should provide detailed information on a group's everyday life activities. It was further believed that the only way that such information could be attained was through direct observation and participation. What was to make ethnography different from other emerging social sciences of the early 1900's was that the ethnographer was to base her analysis on actually living with the folks. This "living the experience" (Clifford and Marcus 1984) of the ethnography became the methodological dictum of participant observation. The ethnographer was to both observe and participate in the social activities of the group she was studying, but was not to encourage or propose any form of change. The logical contradictions of this position also encouraged an emotional tension in the works of social anthropology. While these early ethnographers were not concerned with the applied issues of their work, they became spokespersons for "their" groups based upon their personal experiences. This tension placed the ethnographer in a position of being an advocate for "her" group independent of her proclaimed objectivity. This early strain of advocacy represents to us the beginning threads of an ethnographic praxis.[1]

Modern Expressions

The world of social anthropology was brought into the modern world by the explosive realities of World War II and its aftermath. As the macro geo-political structures of the world were radically altered, so were its micro ethnographic structures. The ethnographic subjects who had participated in the Kula rings of the South Pacific or who patiently worked their way through the civil-religious hierarchies of their villages throughout Meso-America were now world citizens affected by and affecting the development of the modern world. What were thought to be stable societies were now seen as systems in the process of profound transformation. Foragers became horticulturists, simple agriculturalists were seeking technological means of farming, peasants were leaving the countryside for the city, and city residents were confronting the dilemmas of rapid growth in their cities. Most dramatically, the colonized subjects of the modern political world (rarely ever mentioned in the text of the traditional ethnographies) were organizing and carrying out armed struggles against their colonizers. Social anthropology was caught with its ethnographic present being rapidly dated.

Social anthropologists responded to these alterations in the ethnographic present in two related manners. First, ethnographies moved away from being naturalist narratives to being the means to test out research questions. Second, from the understanding of these research results would come strategies for the development of the practices of applied anthropology. These two related activities also produced a variety of sub-disciplinary approaches to social anthropology; thus, there began to be such anthropological activities as urban anthropology, medical anthropology, educational anthropology, etc.[2]

This was the general dynamic of social anthropology through the 50's and up through the mid-seventies. Again, it was the macro geo-political realities of the world that altered this configuration of anthropological activity. This research-applied orientation was perceived in the discipline itself as an opposition between those doing pure research as opposed to those doing messy applied activities. Applied anthropologists were seen as the ugly cousins of research anthropologists. Contained within this opposition were some political anthropologists who timidly pointed out the naive political reality of each position. There was no research that was pure. The question about applied anthropology was: Applied for whom? It was the struggle of Third World peoples (Cuba, Vietnam, Central America, and Africa) that exposed these naive positions of anthropology. It was not that work was not good or insightful or that the suggestions for change were not reasonable (most were). It was, just as in the past, that anthropology was still not focusing on how the macro world of geo-political structures was articulated within the micro world of ethnographies. Concurrent with this was the emergent feminist anthropology that stressed, along with the above realities, that there was needed the addition of the requirement of understanding the politics of gender and sexuality in these processes of social action.[3]

Post-Modernity and the Crisis of Representation

As social anthropology entered the 80's there were, and still are, two conflicting, and at times complimentary, tensions within the discipline (Said 1988). The complimentary tendency involves the recognition that the ethnographic narrative was becoming a limited form for representing what constituted the domain of everyday life in what was being called a post-modern world (Clifford 1988). Post-modernity in its various meanings seems to indicate that social realities are quite complex and cannot be represented or analyzed from singular perceptions or, more formally, from paradigms (Marcus and Fischer 1986). Thus, the means for a clearer representation of such realities requires the presentation of multiple voices or points of view. Here is where the two tendencies begin to conflict. One tendency represents a fluid alliance of feminist, Marxist, and Third World anthropologists who were, and are, looking for ways to more concretely capture the socio-political realities of emergent classes or cultures. This tendency encourages a radical break with the assumptions and styles of past ethnography. The other tendency perceived that there was a "crisis of representation" in the post-modern world that also affected how ethnographies were to be constructed and presented as texts. Though this tendency was not, and is not, insensitive to political issues, the focus was more an aesthetic critique of how ethnographies have been produced and offered a set of suggestions on how such ethnographic texts can be constructed given the realities of this post-modern world (Hooks 1990).

The New Authorities on Ethnographic Authority

James Clifford is a social historian whose domain of inquiry is the intellectual and political history of social anthropology or ethnography (Clifford 1988). Clifford is part of an emerging discourse within social anthropology over how ethnographies are written (Clifford and Marcus 1984). His numerous works have reassessed important questions about how we as anthropologists write the texts which we call ethnographies. Clifford has pointed out that we have constructed a position of authority on knowing about the "other" which we claim is based on the factual nature of our reports on the "others." In fact, the authority for Clifford lies in the sophisticated mode with which we can frame our personal experiences. That is, though we have better arguments than the casual observer, our arguments still rest on the premise that we were there. Through the use of the concepts of literary criticism, Clifford shows the different types of internal voices we use to claim our ethnographic authority. This authority often acts to mute the actual voices of the "others" that we claim to represent (Clifford 1988). Clifford wants to draw our attention to the fact that we should seek an ethnographic narrative that acts not to mute the voices of the "others" but to multiply the ways to increase the volume of such voices. The social and political realities of the post-modern world have deconstructed our old claims of authority. Clifford argues that ethnographies have to be representative of how the anthropologist and the "others" come to produce a text that will be a collaborative effort between the two (Clifford 1988).[4]

Those Other Voices

Edward Said seems to be both admired as well as feared by Clifford, Fischer, Marcus and others in this post-modern discourse.[5] Said, in his classic work entitled *Orientalism* as well as in many other critical works, has challenged the ability of the Western intellectual to produce any kind of fair representation of others outside the Western context (Said 1979). In the spirit of Foucault, he argues that such scholars are more concerned with creating the subject of their observation rather than recognizing the material subjecthood of those that they observe. The Western observer became more of the expert on the experiences of the "other" than the "other" can ever claim to be. For Said, the methods of correcting such imbalances of power are not through understanding the dynamics of what the text is, but in understanding that such imbalances of power are, in fact, representative of the general imbalance of power between the "others" (generally of the Third World) and the metropolitan centers of the West. According to Said, it is not enough just to write better ethnographies. One must also generate from such actions a means to address such concrete realities of power and authority between the metropolitan centers and the voices of others in the hinterlands of the Third World. Clearly, one step in such a direction includes perceiving the voices of the "others" as the voices of authority in understanding such struggles. For Said, this crisis of representation is not a contradiction in the construction of the text, but the reality of power and authority in the post-modern world (Said 1988).

Parallel to Said's arguments are those of feminism. Feminist scholarship has had a profound effect on anthropology (Dimen 1986). One of anthropology's liberal myths has been that it has expressed minimum sexism in its production of scholarly work and participation in the profession. The last two decades of active feminist research has deconstructed such assumptions. We have learned that there are many more sides to the ethnographic narrative than those that the heterosexual male voices can capture. Further, the presence of women in the profession had not altered such perceptions until the feminist perspective was added. Some see the post-modern crisis of representation as a reaction to feminism. Just as feminists were establishing the strength of their representations, there seemed to be a crisis of representation (Mascia-Lees, Sharp and Cohen 1989). However, there is not a contradiction here. It is true, as the post-modern group has pointed out, that there are no totalizing concepts, only overdetermined social actions. Thus, there is no such thing as women in the general sense, but women contextualized by class, ethnicity, culture, age, occupation, sexuality, etc. All that means is that all such aspects of women have to be part of what is presented as a representation of women in ethnographies (Nicholson 1990). Concurrent with such feminist perspectives have been those of gay anthropologists who correct the heterosexual bias in the narrative text of ethnographies (Lancaster 1988). The point we are attempting to make here is that the issues concerning textuality for "others" are concrete issues about their powerlessness. That reality does require new modes of representation and action.

This can also be seen in the development of popular movements in the Third World, but particularly in Latin America. In the 60's many Latin activists, writers, political thinkers, and folks began constructing new alliances of action. Such actions were focused on specific issues of housing, women's rights, jobs, economic policy, and political domination. These involved alliances between women's groups, workers, peasants, middle class, youth groups, intellectual/artists, merchants, and younger members of the military. In the actual concrete forging of such alliances there was the recognition that there were no singular voices; only multiple ones. This was not because of the logical problems presented by the realities of post-modernity, but by the material realities of various actors' social conditions. From such actions, a discourse of analysis and action emerged that was called "popular." Popular meant the odd assortments of social groups that make up the majority within these Third World societies. Popular groups became alliances of voices and actions, not dogmas of political correctness. This was the context for the growth of such movements as the Sandinistas and the current Cardenas movement in Mexico (Gonzalez C. 1986).[6]

What Are We Doing?

We are a little like the traditional bride in our approach to the question of methods: we use something old, something new, and something borrowed.[7]

In the area of traditional methods, we have done the following: We have gathered a great deal of oral history material; recorded over 25 hours of life history material; collected this material from the various sectors of the community, being sensitive to having a fair representation of gender, age, occupation, class, politics, and location within the barrio; and taped several community meetings that took place in the barrio.

We also collected twelve household genealogies from households in the barrio. These, too, were gathered with the same skewing factors as in the oral histories. This material will be used to support our analysis of household formation in contemporary Nicaragua. Along with the genealogies, we also gathered household budgets from the same households. The budgets were collected over a week's time and involved 24-hour recall interviewing. The majority of the material on the political economy of this barrio will come from these budgets. We also gathered basic "census" material. We gathered basic demographic information from 52 households and had access to census material for four of the CDS blocks within the community. We also gathered census material from various institutions (schools and government).

We have done a great deal of field work on the most traditional chores of ethnography: observation and participation. Note that we did not say "participant observation." For us, participant observation is based upon the limited assumption of ethnographic authority (Clifford 1988). We did a great deal of straightforward observation. We spent hundreds of hours attending and observing the local CDS political meetings in the barrio. We went to certain local events and national events, with the stated goal of observing what was going on and how people in other parts of Managua or Nicaragua reacted to issues and events. We were ardent observers of the media in Nicaragua. We read all the newspapers (La Prensa the least) and visited with other professional social scientists, Nicaraguan and international. We attended movies, plays, art openings, and musical concerts. We also attended folk art events (such as the procession of Santo Domingo) and international happenings such as the first international book fair held in Managua in 1987. For us, these were observational activities because our concerns were to learn as much as possible about the "honda" or style of contemporary Nicaragua.[8]

When we participated in events, it was as persons involved in the emotions, rationale, and politics of the activities. There were times when we voted on issues before the local committee. Other times we were negotiating with the committee over the structure and focus of the sister barrio project of which we were the coordinators. This was a solidarity project between the Chicano barrio in our home city and the barrio of William Diaz Romero. This project has focused on educational and medical concerns. We have given speeches to this group expressing our own solidarity as well as that of our group. We do feel that the hopes and aspirations of this popular revolution are valid and require an active solidarity.

When we visited with friends in the barrio and discussed various issues with them, it was as friends who shared and debated ideas and plans. We openly shared our feelings of concern and compassion for each other's lives. When we went to fiestas, we went as friends with emotional bonds. We felt pride and friendship as Mabel's and Noel's daughter Noelia had her mass before her "quinceanera" party (the 15th birthday). We have shared joys, sorrows, and disagreements with the people as friends and fellow actors in companion struggles.

We are not attempting to suggest that such actions do not blur or cannot be done at the same time. We are distinguishing the more traditional use of participant observation, and clearly stating that we are active supporters and participants in aspects of this struggle of the people of Nicaragua. We stress these points not to proclaim our political correctness. We do not really know what that is any more, and have felt such positions often limit rather than enhance whatever correctness there might be. We feel that concrete realities of material/symbolic inequalities of this post-modern world require all metropolitan residents to give unconditional support to aspirations of self-determination being expressed in that overall context. Secondly, as they say in Barrio William Diaz Romero, only those who participate can make the strongest criticism of what has not been done or still needs to be done. We do not feel that our expressed solidarity with this popular struggle lessens the validity of our ethnographic reporting. For us, it clarifies for readers how we have constructed our "representations." It has forced us to adhere to reporting which is as accurate as possible. It is the truth of the dignity of the people of Nicaragua and of

Barrio William Diaz Romero that attracts and holds our feelings of solidarity.

Modern Methods

The modern components in our ethnography involve our concerns with understanding social change and using that understanding in an applied fashion. Now more than ever it is necessary for anthropology to have some kind of understanding about the dynamics of the rapid social change which seems to be driving this post-modern world in which we live. A causal reading of newspapers makes this statement self evident. For us, the understanding we are seeking is not some grand theoretical model of change, but the way in which such changes are constructed by actors in their actual social and material context. If change has now become the constant, then we feel that our focus should be on the activities of such changes, not on cumbersome models of change that seem to change themselves as fast as they are produced.

What does the issue of change have to do with methods? For us, it means being able to use the comparative method in an applied sense. The comparative method involves recognizing that social action is an overdetermined reality that generates forms of acceptance and resistance at both macro and micro levels. We feel that by providing micro narrative analyses of these processes of social change, we can then focus on the how's and why's of such patterns of acceptance and resistance. This is not in order to generate theorems on such dynamics, but to provide a frame of comparison. Within the overall context of Nicaragua, such patterns of acceptance and resistance can be illustrated for the community of William Diaz Romero. This can be compared to other social dynamics in other parts of Nicaragua, Central America, or the Third World if done with ethnographic sensitivity to the means of comparison. Clearly, such an understanding of social change will be slower than the changes we attempt to understand. Such an understanding is only a guidepost for the construction of more general understandings and actions. Such a particularist approach has often been seen as a scientific weakness in the discourses of modern anthropology. We do not see this approach as being particularist, but as a conceptual and methodological struggle to fully place such endeavors within the boundaries of the social/material context for real people's actions. Further, it lends itself to a form of applied anthropology that is also more concrete.

Let us illustrate some of this with a summary of our solidarity project with the barrio of William Diaz Romero. We made our initial contact with the residents of William Diaz Romero in the summer of 1986. We visited with the committee of the barrio (CDS) and explored the possibility of a sister barrio project between this community and the Chicano barrio of Greeley, Colorado. We are members of a local political group within the Chicano barrio (referred to as the North Side) which had asked us to explore such an opportunity. We told the residents of William Diaz Romero that part of such a project would require a community study that would help their community. We explained that this study would help us explain to members of our community what were the realities of Nicaragua and the Barrio William Diaz Romero. This exchange has led to long-term commitment between the two communities. We have sent several delegations to William Diaz Romero over the three years, and have helped them in the construction of a community center, clinic, and the accumulation of sports equipment. Our hope is that in the near future we can bring people from the barrio to Greeley. We are quite aware of the fact that part of the social change that we are looking at is being somewhat generated by the activities of our solidarity project. These activities do not interfere with the content of our ethnography. In fact, they are part of the ethnography.

Post-Modern

What are we doing that is so post-modern? Well, like everyone else struggling with what all this post-modern stuff is about, we are talking about it. We are attempting to clearly and openly convey to the audience of this ethnography what we are trying to do and how we see what we are doing. Hopefully, in doing this the goals, strengths, and limitations of our approach will be apparent to readers. Readers will construct their own strategies for understanding, judging, and using the information that we will provide. We accept that the "meanings" that we are presenting will be validated in the reading and use of the information we present, not by our declarations of what is meaning or what is not meaning.

We have talked to the residents of this community about what we want to do with this ethnography and asked them what they would like this ethnography to represent. We had several meetings with the barrio's local political group to explain to them what kind of research we were doing, how we were going to write a book about this, and that this book would be an ethnography. We explained what we thought we could represent about their community and asked them what they would like represented about their community. We had to receive formal permission from this barrio's committee officials to gather basic census data. We have openly expressed to all residents what we were doing, and asked their advice and input on how we were to do this. We stressed that this research would be linked to our solidarity work in that this ethnography would provide those outside of the community with a means to know about their struggles in

William Diaz Romero. This form of interaction in the production of this text is referred to as ethnographic dialoguing (Marcus and Fischer 1986). From such dialoguing, we have constructed the following post-modern elements.

Multiple Voices

In the presentation of the material that forms this ethnography we sought out and have presented as many voices from the community as possible. That is, we have attempted to present voices that differ in terms of age, sex, occupation, residence, ethnicity, etc. This seems like basic anthropology to us. What is perhaps post-modern is that we recognize that the narrative we construct is not based upon our authority as ethnographers, but on our privilege of having these residents share their experiences and views with us. As often as we can, we present their voices directly.

Concern Over Points of View

In any work on revolutionary Nicaragua, specifically as in our case when we have expressed our open solidarity with these struggles, questions would be posed as to whether or not we presented the other side. Yes, we do. You will hear, read, or see opinions expressed by community residents that are critical of the community's political actions and of the actions of the Sandinistas. There are community residents who openly criticize the Sandinistas and who support opposition parties. Some voices are apolitical or marginal to these issues. They are a part of this community and their concerns will also be presented. Further, the different views and approaches to the meaning of this popular revolution will be presented. There is no central dogma as to what "Sandinismo" or "Popular" means at the national or local level. Among those who support the revolution and the struggle within it, there is a great deal of difference of opinion on how this is to be actualized. These voices are also presented. There are also the voices of difference based upon class, gender, and age that will be presented.

How the Material Is Written

We are concerned with writing an ethnography that is accessible to general and specific audiences. We will attempt to keep technical terms and jargon to a minimum. We will attempt to place such concerns in the footnotes. Further, we will not attempt to overwhelm the readers with excessive citations and in-house arguments with other professional experts on Nicaragua. That, too, can be left in the footnotes.

Post-Modern Criticism

We hope that the way we use these post-modern elements expresses our recognition and agreement with the post-modern critics. As stated before, we are not attempting to write a post-modern ethnography so that more anthropologists will read this work, but rather to produce a readable book that is accessible to all those interested in the issues and discussions within it, both in Nicaragua and outside of Nicaragua.

Thus, What Are We Doing?

We are attempting to present an ethnographic narrative that is linked to a praxis of personal and political concerns. The personal concerns are in terms of our comments to this community through friendships, common concerns, and the alliance of our solidarity project. The political concerns are on two levels. First, we are exploring the use of the ethnographic narrative to produce good anthropology that can be our base for action as anthropologists. Secondly, we are presenting documents that can encourage others to understand the realities of Third World political struggles and to respect and work with such struggles. Further, as stated above, we wish this project to be of direct benefit to the community of William Diaz Romero. This would involve helping them place their voices and concerns within the discourse of social change, provide a frame for the development of their own social history, and, if this project should generate funds, direct material aid to the community through the proceeds of the sale of this book.

Does all or any of this constitute an ethnographic praxis? To answer that question the ethnography needs to be presented.

Notes

1. For an in-depth coverage of this historical period in anthropology see Zigmaunt Bauman, *Culture as Praxis* (London: Routledge and K. Paul., 1973); Marvin Harris, *The Rise of Anthropological Theory* (New York: Crowell, 1968); Hortence Powdermaker, *Strangers and Friends* (New York: W.W. Norton, 1966); and F. Voget, *A History of Ethnology* (New York: Holt, Rinehart and Winston, 1975).

From this period of ethnographic research came the classic works of our forebears: Boas's work on the Northwest Coast Native Americans (1940), Malinowski's South Pacific works (1922), Kroeber's Native American Studies (1925), Mead's work on the South Pacific (1928), Gamio's work in Mexico (1922), and Levi-Strauss's ethnographic travels in the Amazon (1963). From these works, the various schools of North American, British, European, and Mexican social anthropology grew. These works are the foundation for contemporary social anthropology. It now seems that this is a foundation that requires some post-modern reinforcement.

2. Because of this, one did not study group X in its isolated context. One was concerned with seeing how various processes—modernization, development, social change, urbanism, or migration—affected the well-being of group X in terms of health, education, occupation, housing, etc. Further, in being able to establish a relation between the current well-being of group X because of its migration from its previous location into a new settlement situation, practices for aiding group X and those having to advise group X in their new context could be offered.

3. For a critical treatment of this period see Eric Wolf, *Europe and People Without History* (Berkley: University of California Press, 1982).

4. What is so profound about Clifford's observation? And what is so postmodern about such concerns? Attempts to answer such questions can be found in Marcus and Fischer's interpretations of social anthropology in the social context of post-modernity (Marcus and Fischer 1986). They feel that central to understanding the post-modern world is recognition of the developing "crisis of representation." In the post-modern world there are no singular voices or discourses which can capture the full texture of social activities, such as cultural action. This is derived from the understanding or acceptance that all such actions are overdetermined—multiple relations of social action require multiple modes of analysis using multiple representational forms (Laclau and Mouffe 1985). Thus, the crisis is over the manner in which one then attempts to represent such overdetermined processes. If one accepts the modernist assumption of the knowing subject who can dispassionately observe the actions of others, then there is no crisis. However, if one accepts that there is no such reality as a knowing subject, then one does have to address the question of representation. Further, if one is an anthropologist who claims to be able to represent the social realities of "others," such post-modern criticism cannot be avoided. Why should the anthropologist speak for "others" when they now have their own voices? Or if the anthropologist wants to present what she knows of "others," then such representations cannot rest on sophisticated arguments about being there. Such works should seek various forms of representation which would include direct collaboration with the "others" in the construction of the text. For example, if what we hope to express in this study about Nicaragua is the importance of local social action, then that social action has to be expressed in the construction of the text also. How do such concerns get translated into the text of an ethnography?

Clifford and Marcus, in an edited volume on writing culture, explore such questions with groups of other anthropologists and social historians (Clifford and Marcus 1984). In an odd expression of unity for this post-modern world, they all encourage anthropologists to construct multiple-voiced ethnographies that are open to methodological and stylistic explorations. Such ethnographic texts are to be informed by the social/political dynamics of the post-modern world. However, in addressing social/political issues, one must produce ethnographies that will not be contextually contradicted by the level of representation. Clifford and others are concerned with resolving this "crisis of representation." This concern is aesthetically motivated, not politically motivated. They do not wish to write better ethnographies so that people would enjoy reading them or so that the ethnographer may confront the social/political contradictions of such actions. They seem to desire to write the "better ethnography" as a challenge to see if such forms of representation can be constructed, given all the deconstructive limitations that Clifford and others see as the "crisis of representation" (Hooks 1990).

5. Some contemporary ethnographers find many of the issues being raised by the post-modern advocates as irrelevant or silly. For them, doing ethnography is doing ethnography, and has nothing to do with a crisis of representation. There is some truth to such objections. The crisis that these post-modernists have discovered is somewhat of a self-discovery. We think that this is an important debate, however, for it does bring to the forefront the question of what ethnographies are and what they could be. Since we are searching for an ethnographic praxis, we feel that important issues have been raised by post-modernists but in ways that often create more confusion than clarity. As ethnographers, we have been concerned with the limitations on how ethnographies are written and who has access to such texts. Our concerns, however, were directly political. We wanted our ethnographies, as accurately as possible, to represent the social/material context of groups we were attempting to present. It has been and continues to be our hope that these representations would be useful to the people themselves and to others who would be concerned about similar issues of social struggle. While this in itself is not problematic for all ethnographers, the way we pursued our endeavors may be problematic. From such concerns, we have come to the position that ethnographies have to capture the social realities of overdetermination and express the multiple voices of the complex tapestry of social action (Jackson 1989).

6. For a more detailed development of this point of view see Bell Hooks, *Yearnings* (Boston: South End Press, 1990), Michael Jackson, *Paths Toward a Clearing* (Bloomington: Indiana University Press, 1989) and Trinh T. Minh-ha, *Woman, Native, Other* (Bloomington: Indiana University Press, 1989).

7. These are the dates of our field work: (a) Summer 1986: 2 months; (b) Summer 1987: 2-1/2 months; (c) Spring/Summer 1988: 6 Months; (d) Summer 1989: 3 months; (e) Summer 1990: 2 Weeks; (f) Winter 1991/92: 3 Weeks. Total: 14.1 months.

8. During our time in Nicaragua there were three main newspapers: the Barricada which was the official newspaper of the Sandinistas, and now presents itself as the newspaper of national concern; El Nuevo Diario, which is an independent newspaper that has been pro-Sandinista; and La Prensa, which was the opposition newspaper and now is the paper supporting the new government. One of the ironies of the "free market" being pursued by the new government is that several "leftist" clubs and art gallerys are now emerging throughout Managua.

3

Jodido Pero Contento

THE ECONOMIC AND SOCIAL CONTEXT OF THE BARRIO WILLIAM DIAZ ROMERO

The economy in Nicaragua is now in a process which can be described as quite variable and which could lead into a recession. When it goes into a recession, it completely breaks the prices; and, when I said prices, this includes salaries because the salaries and the prices go together. When the economy gets to this point, it is called a recession and there will inevitably be a full crash. We are going through a crucial moment in which, if the economy fails, so will the political power of the Sandinistas because their power depends on the material base of the economy. The plan the government has right now is for a variable economics which is fundamental so that prices don't get higher. The fiscal costs of the public sector and the government also have to be reduced. Each sector (health, education, etc.) has to stay within its budget. There is a limit the Sandinista government cannot pass. If they do pass the limit, the anti-inflationary plan will make no sense.

Of course the economic problem is dangerous. We are playing with all the sectors because of the mixed economy. If the producers don't produce, the plan is not going to function. So, you see, the moment is crucial. It is really quite dangerous to play with the economy of a country.

The economy (during 1989) is being affected because of the war. National and regional projects for the development of the country are being affected by these bellicose actions. But there are other areas where there have been errors by the government in terms of the economy because of a lack of experience. That's why they are in the present situation with the economy.

—Bayardo Mendez
Economist and Resident in the
Barrio William Diaz Romero

Translated from the Spanish, the chapter title means "Things Are Fucked Up, but I'm Content."

Introduction

To understand the newly developing hegemonic terrain of Nicaragua, an analysis of how overall economic and social dynamics affect people's everyday lives is required. With the political changes of February 25, 1990, the above statement would seem self-evident. In this chapter we present what the overall political economy (which is what composes economic and social dynamics) in Nicaragua has been with the Sandinistas in power and what can be expected to develop in the immediate future. To illustrate this we will ethnographically present information on how this political economy frames the economic and social dynamics within the barrio (Higgins and Coen 1990).

Even before the outcome of the election of February 25, 1990, this was to be an important chapter, for we have always felt that the success or lack of success of this experiment in popular revolution would be determined in the last instance by the status of the political economy. It is somewhat ironic that for over a decade, neo-marxist and post-modern argumentation has been seeking to construct a discourse that could refute Engels off-hand polemic that in the "last instance" the economic base determines the overall outcome of social dynamics. As we were busy arguing the fine points of this premise and counter-premise, the peoples of the Third world were living these dynamics, not as debates about post-modernity, but as the context of their everyday lives. We are not suggesting that the outcome of the February election in Nicaragua was solely determined by the state of the economy—for the state of the economy is quite an overdetermined process generated by the hegemonic power of United States imperialism—but clearly in the last instant before entering the voting booth that was what was on the minds of the majority of the people of Nicaragua.

To try to illustrate those economic and social dynamics, we wish to look at these processes in the Barrio William Diaz Romero. The focus of this analysis is on household strategies for confronting this context. This involves looking at household formations (more traditionally referred to in ethnographic terms as social structure) and household economics. However, before proceeding, we wish to provide a set of definitions for what we mean by households.

To the people in the barrio, the term household would mean their immediate family or those that they are currently living with. Households are quite fluid social constructs here and expressions and formations change easily. There is both a fragmented and fragile nature of residential households and a long-term component of solidarity and duration expressed through family relations. This fluidity has a social history that parallels the overall history of the gender/social division of labor in Nicaragua.

However, as anthropologists, we also have a more conceptual framework for looking at households. In terms of post-modern ethnographic argumentation, we would state that households are social compositions that express strategies for "living" in the time/space context of this rapid-paced world consumer economy (Harvey 1989).[1] For our analysis, we will attempt to illustrate three types of strategies that households have composed in the context of Nicaragua. First, strategies for the procurement of monetary resources to be able to have an everyday life. Secondly, strategies for the regulation of everyday life at the household level. Third, would-be strategies of collective action among households within the same community.

A household's own particular social geography will frame how it constructs such strategies. A childless couple in their early twenties will have different strategies in these areas than a childless couple in their sixties. Or households with young children will have different strategies than households with adult offspring. In a simple sense, in households with children, these strategies can be seen as decisions about how to feed and raise one's children. However, the social geography of these strategies are composed in reference to the hegemonic dynamics of gender, sexuality, class, age, employment, and residence. In the case of Nicaragua, this involves understanding how that division of labor has been altered by ten years of revolution and the upcoming post-revolutionary period. Were new strategies of procurement, regulation, and social action composed during this ten-year period? If so, what kinds of alteration may be composed in the post-revolutionary period? In this chapter we attempt to cautiously explore these issues. Cautiously not because we do not feel able to make strong statements, but because of the humble recognition that this is obviously not a decade in which to attempt any kind of prophecy.

Structure of the Chapter

To present this ethnographic analysis of household strategies we have divided this chapter into three sections: (1) analysis of the formal and informal sectors of the economy of Nicaragua, Managua, and the barrio; (2) examples of how households construct their strategies of procurement and regulations; and (3) presentation of examples of collective and collaborative social action among households in the barrio.

Formal and Informal Economic Sectors

This discussion of urban economics in Third World cities is framed in terms of the dichotomy between formal and informal sectors. The formal sector is the area of rational relations between capital, labor, and the state—the factory, the union, and the government labor laws. The informal sector is the area of more situational relations between capital, labor, and the state—the distributor, the street vender, and the tax collector.

In the majority of Third World cities, over 50% of economic activities are located in the informal sector. For some economists, this is a drag on economic development. For others, the informal sector represents possible alternative modes of economic growth. For those who see the informal sector as a limitation on economic development, the actors within this sector are seen as unproductive. For those who see the informal sector as an alternative, these actors represent a possible neo-entrepreneurial class. Thus, the informal sector is composed of either speculators and black marketeers or petty producers and developers of new economic opportunities (Massey 1988). But who are these actors? To know who these people are within the informal sector, one needs to have ethnographic information on what Roberts calls the "substantive rationales" of these actors (Roberts 1987). Roberts states that "we need to see the urban economy as presenting those who are seeking subsistence with a set of opportunity structures. It is not jobs per se, but how jobs combine with other elements such as housing, the division of labor within a household, and the household's consumption patterns or social networks that provide different opportunity sets for people in broadly similar economic positions"(Roberts 1987:4).

The categories of formal and informal are structural concepts for understanding complex economic activities. The sectors as categories have no existential or cultural dimension. The question of productivity or nonproductivity involves the context of the material relations between capital and labor, including the process of collective consumption (Castells 1977 and Higgins 1983).

Political Economy of the Popular Revolution

What does this all mean in the context of revolutionary Nicaragua? The concept of popular classes and cultures was developed as a means for understanding the context of those who were economically active within the informal sector (Gonzales C. 1986). In Nicaragua, those in the popular informal sectors played an important role in the formation of the Sandinista Front, the struggle against Somoza, and the exploration of a new or free Nicaragua (D'Ciofalo 1988:12–17). The articulation of Nicaragua into the world capitalist system as an agro-exporter coincides with the reign of the Somoza family (Gibson 1987:15–41). The rise of cotton production in the 1950s caused a critical transformation for rural and urban populations. For the rural population, it meant the further loss of land to large growers and further dependence upon wage labor for their primary subsistence. Cotton production expelled people from the rural areas into the cities to look for work. However, since there was no significant industry in Nicaragua (Gibson 1987:20), work had to be found outside of these limited structures; that is, in the informal sector. The cities, primarily Managua, became areas where work could be found in small shops, workshops, artisan activities, and petty commercial and productive enterprises. These workers were a heterogenous group, ranging from prosperous entrepreneurs to domestic servants (Spalding 1987:1–11).

This economic position saddled Nicaragua with structural problems that affected the overall social system. The maintenance of the agro-export economy (cotton, coffee, and cattle) required the importation of basic inputs for production and exporting of raw materials. This generates a basic imbalance between the higher cost of industrial imports versus unprocessed exports. These endeavors were more capital-intensive than labor-intensive. Since people were pushed off their land and no corresponding employment emerged, there began to be a labor shortage in the countryside (Utting 1987:127–148).

This is the economic context that the Sandinistas inherited with their triumph in 1979. In an attempt to create national unity, the Sandinistas embarked upon their experiment with a mixed economy (Weeks 1987:43–60), whereas the private and public sectors could work from cooperative instead of antagonistic relations. The Sandinistas wanted to provide a context in which agro-exports would continue but would be regulated in such a fashion that it would be beneficial for the general development of Nicaragua. Further, this mixed economy was supposed to provide a set of social institutions that would adequately meet their collective consumption needs. In the first years of the revolution, there were significant achievements made in health, education, and social services (Ruccio 1987:127–148).

The Sandinistas felt that by controlling the economy (they had nationalized bank and financial systems), they would be able to direct surplus into areas of economic and social need (Weeks 1987:49–54). This optimistic plan for national unity was limited by a world-wide recession, United States economic and military imperialism, the limited participation of the private agro-export sector in this process and their open support of the counter-revolution, limited experience of the Sandinistas in economic analysis and planning, and natural disasters (droughts and hurricanes) (Vilas 1987:233–246). For the first eight years of the revolution, these conditions were dealt with through deficit spending and subsidies of basic goods. Besides the war, the main drain on the economy was, and still is, the linkage to agro-exports, which requires foreign reserves to cover the cost of imports needed for production. These factors have been a cost drain on all other plans of the revolution. Concurrent with these factors was the increase in the size and importance of the informal sector. More people were drawn into this sector because of problems in the formal sector of the economy and also because of support for collective consumption factors initiated by the revolution. Those who benefit from the new social services of education, health, and transportation are those in the informal sector (Envio 1988b:14:42).

The Current Economic Realities of Nicaragua

The Nicaraguan economy is in bad shape. To attempt to confront this situation, the government opened a second front: an attack on economic problems. In February, 1988, the government put into place a complete monetary changeover. All old currency had to be turned in for new currency at the exchange rate of 10,000 for one. This was to bring inflation under control and to force currency speculators to lose money when they converted their currency. There were also attempts at controlling prices, raising some salaries, and adjusting export/import exchanges to allow for reduction in the deficit. There was also a trimming of government costs by attempting to reduce its workforce by some 20 to 30 percent. They also began to stop subsidies on basic food goods. A key factor in these reforms was the mobilization of public participation. There were great plans to encourage people to mobilize at the local level to control prices in communities and to seek alternative solutions for the distribution and consumption of basic goods. The goal of the plan was to provide a context for exporting agro-goods at a more favorable rate of exchange. It was also an attempt to force people to consume more domestic goods instead of imports. The government did not accomplish this goal and in June, 1988, further sets of reforms were introduced (Envio 1988c:10–23). In June of 1988, the government announced a new set of economic reforms. These changes involved: (1) the devaluation of the cordoba by 515%, which generated a 170% increase in home market prices, (2) indexing the exchange rate to inflation, (3) deregulating the majority of prices and wages, (4) raising public employees salaries by 30 percent, (5) strengthening food commissaries at workplaces and closing down barrio basic food stores, and (6) eliminating subsidies to productive sectors by raising interest rates. These reforms were to accomplish the following:

- A transfer of resources from consumption to export;

- A reduction of salaries and transfer of resources to those who control capital;
- A transfer of income from popular sectors to agro-export sectors (Envio 1989d:33–55).

The rationale behind these reforms was monetarist in spirit. It was an attempt to get the books balanced, and start over again. This position was opposed by the middle productive sectors that wanted more investment in their activities (cattle and domestic farm production) and the popular sector that wanted the social programs.

What have these various sets of reforms meant in terms of the dynamics of the informal sector in Nicaragua? Certain factors in these reforms were aimed at controlling aspects of the informal sector. In fact, more people may have moved into this sector. Determining who is and who is not part of the informal sector is somewhat confusing. As stated earlier, in Nicaragua they talk about the traditional informal sector (small merchants and artisans) and a neo-informal sector (black marketeers). However, many vendors without licenses are also defined as black marketeers. Envio reports that the February reforms tended to hurt salaried workers in the informal sector (e.g., domestic workers) and that the June reforms tended to hurt the better-off vendors within the informal sector. Nevertheless, because of general problems in production and distribution, the informal sector provides access to basic consumer goods. These reforms have left all the players in the same position, however, with all of them having a great deal less currency in their pockets (Envio 1989e:11, 1989g:8 and 1989i:9).

Post-Election Developments in the Economy

One of UNO's strongest attractions for the majority of Nicaraguans was their promise to turn the economy around within 100 days. How have they done? During the last year before the election, the Sandinistas, as we described previously, had been controlling the rate of inflation. They had been keeping inflation to under 20 percent. They had eliminated the black market in currency through letting the cordoba float and had ended many of the subsidies to all sectors of the economy. And all of that was not enough. The day after the inauguration of Dona Chamorro, she had to devalue the cordoba by half. In the following month, the government had to devalue the currency four more times. There have been drastic price increases with no corresponding wage increase. This is something the workers union will not accept, as witnessed by the victory of government workers unions in issues of wages, workers rights, and social programs. UNO's one-hundred-day promised miracle was based upon the assumption that the United States government would be there with money to help. As of yet, no money has arrived. UNO found out what the Sandinistas knew all along—combined effects of the war and the USA blockade has left the national treasury empty.

UNO's problem in attempting to transform the economy is that there is not much to do that the Sandinistas had not been attempting for the last two years. UNO, however, does have the advantage of ending the blockade and opening access to markets in the United States again. They hope that overseas Nicaraguans will return to invest in the new economy, but as of yet, they have not been returning at any significant rate. Also, since it is still unclear what the Contras plan to do, UNO will not get an immediate peace dividend.

Inflation is at super high levels again. The black market in currency is back and people want higher wages. What will happen? That we do not know yet (Envio 1990c:26-23).[2]

THE DICHOTOMY BETWEEN THE FORMAL AND INFORMAL ECONOMIC SECTORS IN THE BARRIO WILLIAM DIAZ ROMERO

Demographic Data

This information has been arranged in terms of occupations, gender, and whether those occupations are included in the formal and informal sector, as shown in Tables 3.1, 3.2, 3.3, and 3.4.

Analysis of Data

We categorize "ama de la casa" (housewife) as an occupation and place it within the informal sector because running a house is clearly an occupation, and given the looseness with which the informal sector is defined, it seems logical that such work fits within the sector. Also, though it is clear that women play important roles within the informal sector, questions of gender are not often stressed in the discussion of the informal sector (Moser 1987). Placing the "ama de la casa" within the informal sector makes it the largest category of work in the barrio. However, many of those who labeled themselves as only doing housework were also involved in macroeconomic activities (selling food, doing domestic labor, or working for enterprises in the informal sector). This was not reported as work, because as residents they were responding to the formal questions of the CDS census which excluded these economic activities. Hence, people do not like to acknowledge all their sources of income, whether to avoid taxation or just to keep such information to themselves.

TABLE 3.1 Occupations (general sample, 1988)

OCCUPATIONS	MALE	FEMALE
Housewife (I-9)		********
Secretary (F-6)	*	*****
Pensioner (5)	**	***
Professor (univ.) (F-1)		*
Military (F-8)	*******	
Woodsmith (I-2)	**	
Keymaker (I-1)	*	
Seamstress/tailor (I-4)	***	*
Nurse (F-3)		***
State worker (F-9)	*******	*
Engineer (F-3)	***	
Odd jobs (I-3)	***	
Janitor (F-2)		**
Domestic (I-6)		******
Teacher (F-4)		****
Mechanic (I-1)	*	
Restauranteur (I-1)	*	
Coop. worker (F-14)	***********	***
Chauffeur (I-4)	****	
Merchant (I-11)	**	********
Carpenter (I-1)	*	
Factory (F-2)	*	*
Accountant (F-4)	****	
Private sector vendor (F-1)		*
Metal work (I-4)	****	
Doctor (F-1)	*	

Informal sector   Formal sector

Females = 25   Females = 21
Males   = 22   Males   = 37
Total   = 47   Total   = 58
                 Total = 105

Key: I = Informal sector work
      F = Formal sector work

That this barrio represents a panorama of occupations and class groups can be seen in the range of occupations in it. Further, the distribution of jobs between genders indicates a somewhat traditional allocation of work, though women are represented in many non-traditional jobs. Women are represented in the positions of teachers, university professors, doctors, lawyers, journalists, and engineers. The women in these professions are younger women who have gained access to university training because of the revolution.

It is interesting to note that there are skilled and unskilled occupations in both sectors. The only group not found in the informal sector is the professional group, though that does not mean that there are not professionals in that sector. Many say that doctors and others who have small private practices are informal.

Even with the "ama de la casa" group in the informal sector, the majority of occupations in the barrio would fall within the parameters of the formal sector. However, most residents participate in the informal

TABLE 3.2 Occupations (CDS Heroes y Martyrs, 1988)

OCCUPATIONS	MALE	FEMALE
Chauffeur (I-4)	****	
Seamstress (I-2)		**
State worker (F-5)	**	***
Secretary (F-3)		***
Engineer (F-2)	**	
Housewife (I-20)		********** **********
Accountant (F-3)	***	
Teachers (F-3)		***
Office worker (F-5)	***	**
Factory worker (F-1)		*
Merchant (I-1)	*	
Mechanic (I-4)	****	
Technician (F-3)	**	*
Laboratory worker (F-1)	*	
Carpenter (I-2)	**	
Shoemaker (I-1)	*	
Psychologist (F-1)		*
Domestic worker (I-1)		*

Informal sector   Formal Sector

Females = 23   Females = 14
Males   = 12   Males   = 13
Total   = 35   Total   = 27
                    Total = 62

Key: I = Informal sector work
     F = Formal sector work

sector in some fashion. People's incomes, resources, economic activities, and strategies of procurement are woven between both sectors.

In terms of salaries, there is a 16 to 1 difference between those with professional jobs (engineers) and those in an unskilled category (janitors) (Envio 1988b:14–42). Until the current economic reforms began, it was often claimed that one could make more selling sodas on the street than working in an office. Though this claim may be somewhat exaggerated, it is an indicator of the fluidity that exists between these two sectors. It is hard to attach monetary quantities to these occupations because of the numerous changes in wages during the economic reforms. In 1987, a school teacher received 15,000 cordobas a month, and after the changes she would have made only 1,500. However, along with these wage changes have been price fluctuations and very high inflation. When we discuss people's procurement strategies this will become clearer.

In terms of resources, besides wages or income from small enterprises, it seems that everyone in the barrio has access to dollars in some fashion. They either buy dollars on the black market or receive dollars from relatives outside the country. People live with their own dual economics. Generally for basic household goods they buy in cordobas, and for special or emergency purchases they use their dollar surplus, to buy imported goods.

TABLE 3.3 Occupations (CDS Francisco Moreno, 1988)

OCCUPATIONS	MALE	FEMALE
Doctor (F-4)	**	**
Nurse (F-1)		*
Aux. Nurse (F-2)		**
Technician (F-6)		******
Painter (I-1)	*	
Seamstress 1 (I-1)		*
Tailor (I-1)	*	
Engineer (F-2)	*	*
Accountant (F-2)	**	
Secretary (F-5)	*	****
Foreman (I-1)	*	
Sociologist (F-1)	*	
Mechanic (I-1)	*	
Musician (I-1)	*	
Economist (F-1)		*
Merchant (I-6)	****	**
Domestic worker (I-7)		*******
Housewife (I-3)	***	
Retired (2)	**	
Gardener (I-1)	*	
Military (F-9)	*********	
State worker (F-7)	******	*

Informal sector   Formal sector

Females = 10   Females = 18
Males   = 13   Males   = 22
Total   = 23   Total   = 40
            Total = 63

Key: I = Informal sector work
      F = Formal sector work

Economic Activity in the Barrio

There are over 142 commercial enterprises in the barrio. The majority of these are small businesses such as restaurants, stores, bars, and boarding houses. One also finds various kinds of workshops for auto repair, metal-working, shoe repair, tire repair, television repairs, etc. There are numerous mini-enterprises such as selling fruit drinks, tortillas, or cooked beans. There are several doctors and lawyers offices in the barrio. Also located in the barrio are a commercial radio station, a clothing factory, a large machine shop, and a movie theatre. Doing a site survey of small businesses, we were able to make the following classifications:

Work shops	34	Professional	4
Factories	2	Misc.	38
Small business	64	Total	142

What do these various enterprises mean for the barrio's economy and the dichotomy between the formal and informal sectors? First, it would be difficult to place any of these businesses strictly in one category or the

TABLE 3.4 Occupations (CDS Liberator Zelada, 1988)

OCCUPATIONS	MALE	FEMALE
Housewife (I-20)		********** **********
Domestic worker (I-9)		*********
Tailor (I-1)	*	
Military (F-5)	****	*
Accountant (F-5)	****	*
Electrician (I-1)	*	
Retired 3	**	*
TV repair (I-3)	**	*
Nurse (F-1)		*
Engineer (F-1)	*	
Reporter (F-1)		*
Doctor (F-3)	***	
Lottery agent (I-1)		*
Chauffeur (I-1)	*	
Secretary (F-2)		**
Worker (F-4)	***	*
Mechanic (I-2)	**	
Lawyer (F-2)	*	*
Administrator (F-1)	*	
Psychologist (F-1)		*
Merchant (I-2)	*	*
Technician (F-2)	**	
Architect (F-1)		*
Seamstress (I-1)		*

Informal sector   Formal sector

Females = 33   Females = 10
Males   = 8   Males   = 19
Total   = 41   Total   = 29

                    Total = 73

Key: I = Informal sector work
      F = Formal sector work

other. The clothing factory is clearly in the formal sector. The workers are unionized and wages are set by the government wage controls. There is a management structure that attempts to set production and working rates. However, the factory participates in informal sector activities in the food program that it has for workers and in its commissary programs. They contract with people in the informal sector to provide lunch for the workers. Workers form their own groups to search out means to buy goods in bulk and resell them to the general work force. Further, workers and management have a shared governance structure so that the factory is run like a cooperative. Less than 5 percent of the factory's workers live in the barrio of William Diaz Romero.

The employment provided by these various enterprises is not to the residents in the barrio per se. Most of the employment comes from people owning their own small businesses rather than from providing work for others in the barrio. For example, there is a large mechanic shop in the barrio that employs 10 mechanics, none of whom are from the barrio.

Restaurants, bars, and boarding houses are also numerous in this barrio. All fall within the formal sector because they are licensed by different government agencies. The bars tend to have a clientele from the barrio as well as from other areas of Managua. Restaurants (which mostly serve limited menus) and boarding houses are used by the "internationalists" who come into the barrio looking for inexpensive room and board. The internationalists are also typical clients for the small vendors of fruit drinks and food sold throughout the barrio.

Because of general shortages throughout Managua, some businesses will have clients from other areas of Managua. For example, there is a cheese producing store in the barrio with clients from all over the city. Bakeries, tailor shops, beauty shops, and certain repair enterprises also serve a clientele beyond the barrio.

There are several types of food vending services in the barrio, and the clientele tends to be from the barrio. There are several small stores in the barrio that sell a variety of goods, including meat, poultry, and vegetables. There were a few specialty stores that sell only meat or produce. There are street vendors who also sell such goods. There are three food dispensaries in the barrio. When the dispensaries have supplies of basic food stuffs, they are sold to the barrio residents at controlled prices.

This barrio, then, provides people with the means to meet most of their commercial and household needs.

Shopping Patterns

Like most Central American cities, Managua has a system of "mercados de abasto," general shopping markets. The market nearest the barrio is the Oriental, a large market regarded as a black market center. This means that most street vendors are unlicensed and sell scarce products at high prices, or sell large amounts of basic items, also at higher prices. This is clearly part of the informal sector. A current controversy in the markets is the presence of such vendors. Permit vendors who pay their taxes clearly oppose those who sell without taxes. However, without unlicensed vendors, there would be fewer goods in circulation. The Oriental is a large market of vendors of food products. Most of the area is unpaved and generally quite dirty from rains, garbage, and the high volume of human traffic through the area. Table 3.5 is a sample list of goods and prices at this market for one week in April. The artificial exchange rate (of 10:1) was unrealistic. The purchasing power of 666 cordobas was not equal to 66.6 US dollars. This exchange rate did not slow inflation, so that in June there was a new devaluation.

TABLE 3.5 Market Prices for April 1988
           (rate of exchange C10 to $1.00)

		PRICES
Meat	chicken	pound @ 40
	fish	pound @ 30
	pork	pound @ 45
Vegetables	tomatoes	dozen @ 80
	chayote	dozen @ 8
	onions	bunch @ 50
Fruits	melon	1 @ 13
	mango	1 @ 10
	sour oranges	1/2 dozen @ 60
	bananas	1 @ 10
Basic items	rice	pound @ 50
	sugar	pound @ 15
	pinolio	pound @ 5

TABLE 3.6 Market Prices for August 1-7, 1988
           (rate of exchange C380 to $1.00)

		PRICES
Meat	beef (tenderloin)	pound @ 150
	chicken (whole)	pound @ 150
	fish	pound @ 100
	iguana	pound @ 200
Vegetables	tomatoes	10 @ 100
	chayote	4 @ 100
	onions	bunch @ 50
Fruits	lemon	dozen @ 50
	mangos	dozen @ 100
	oranges	dozen @ 100
	pitaya	3 @ 50
Basic items	rice	pound @ 120
	sugar	pound @ 80
	pinolio	1/2 bag @ 80

Table 3.6 shows prices at this market for a week in August of 1988. Prices went up about 66%, though the exchange rate on the cordoba was 380 to the dollar. Although these goods are cheap in terms of U.S. dollars, in Managua at this time the majority of the population earned less than c2000 a month.

There are numerous government-owned supermarkets in Managua. Each store has to operate in terms of market prices. These supermarkets have more processed food products and clothing. For example, their shelves often have rows and rows of Bulgarian canned beef. The closest supermarket to the barrio is about 10 blocks away. Shown in Table 3.7 are

TABLE 3.7 Supermarket Prices for August 1-7, 1988
(rate of exchange C380 to $1.00)

		PRICES
Meat	beef (tenderloin)	pound @ 175
	chicken	pound @ 120
	pork	pound @ 150
	fish	pound @ 80
Vegetables	tomatoes	pound @ 25
	chayotes	pound @ 30
	chilotes	dozen @ 30
Fruits	sour lemons	dozen @ 50
	tamarindo	pound @ 160
	pitaya	dozen @ 110
Basic items	milk	liter @ 26
	pinolio	pound @ 75
	beans	pound @ 84
	coffee	pound @ 250
Luxury goods	English sauces	12 oz.@ 185
	mustard	8 oz.@ 115

the prices from this supermarket for a week in August 1988. Though the supermarket is cheaper than the market, it does not have a constant supply of goods.

As already stated, there are small stores and dispensaries in the barrio. Shown in Table 3.8 are the prices from these stores and dispensaries during the month of August of 1988. Prices from the summer of 1989 are shown in Tables 3.9, 3.10, and 3.11.

It can be seen that prices are not particularly higher or lower in either the formal or informal sector, but the informal sector has a more constant supply of goods for sale.

HOUSEHOLD STRATEGIES
FOR PROCUREMENT AND REGULATION

The Curtis Household

Strategies of Procurement

To begin we will focus on the dynamics of one particular nuclear household: that of Mabel and Noel Curtis. Both Mabel and Noel work in formal wage labor positions. They have both worked these jobs for numerous years. Mabel is an elementary school teacher and Noel works in a middle management position for a Pepsi corporation. They have five small children ranging from ages 7-15, and can be seen as the most classic

TABLE 3.8 Barrio/Local Store Prices for August 1988
          (rate of exchange C380 to $1.00)

		PRICES
Barrio meat store:		
Meat	beef	pound @ 160
	chicken	pound @ 120
Vegetables	chilote	dozen @ 30
	yucca	1 @ 30
	onions	bunch @ 10
	tomatoes	dozen @ 200
Mini-Market in barrio:		
Meat	beef	pound @ 160
Veg./Fruit	onions	bunch @ 10
	lemons	dozen @ 30
	bananas	1 @ 5
Cheese shop:		
	smoked cheese	pound @ 50
	mozzarella	pound @ 250
	chicken	pound @ 120
	cream	pound @ 200
	tortilla	1 @ 10
Government store:		
	sugar	pound @ 27.50
	oil	quart @ 24
	beans	pound @ 45
	soap (laundry)	bag @ 190
	powdered milk	pound @ 310

nuclear family type. So far, Noel and Mabel earn just enough to cover their monthly expenses so that none of the children need to work and can go to school. Mabel works as a teacher five days a week. However, it is common that much of her vacation and weekend time is also spent at the school or with her union in meetings and workshops. This is unpaid labor time.

Housing. The Curtis's rent a long, high-ceilinged room. It is covered with the corrugated tin seen everywhere in Nicaragua. Their house is very hot. It lacks ventilation and has only a single window facing the front. Their living spaces are partitioned by furniture, dividing a central living room area from a central bedroom that lacks even the privacy of a sheet hung between Mabel and Noel's bed and their children's. Another partition separates the cooking area.

Since 1979, Mabel and Noel have been living rent-free because of housing reform laws implemented by the Nicaraguan government. They

TABLE 3.9 Barrio Prices for Summer 1989
(rate of exchange C25,000 to $1.00)

		PRICES
Meat	beef (tenderloin)	pound @ 14,000
	chicken	pound @ 14,000
Vegetables	tomatoes (small)	dozen @ 8,000
	onions	1 @ 500 to 1,000
	chayote	1 @ 2,500
	yucca	1 @ 1,000
Fruits	lemons	dozen @ 2,000
	mangos	1 @ 500 to 1,000
	bananas	1 @ 1,000
	pitaya	1 @ 1,500
Basics	rice	pound @ 6,000
	sugar	pound @ 5,000
	pinolio	pound @ 12,000
	tortillas	1 @ 500 to 1,000
	milk	liter @ 1,500 to 4,000
	soap (laundry)	bag @ 8,000
Cheese	cream	pound @ 20,000
	smoked	pound @ 15,000
	mozzarella	pound @ 18,000

TABLE 3.10 Market Prices for July 1989
(rate of exchange C25,000 to $1.00)

		PRICES
Meat	beef (tenderloin)	pound @ 15,000 to 18,000
	chicken	pound @ 14,000 to 15,000
	fish	pound @ 12,000
	ground meat	pound @ 10,000
Vegetables	tomatoes	dozen @ 10,000
	onions	dozen @ 10,000
	avocados	1 @ 5,000
Fruits	lemons	dozen @ 1,000
	mangos	dozen @ 4,000
	bananas	dozen @ 10,000
	pitaya	1 @ 1,000
Basics	rice	pound @ 4,000 to 5,000
	sugar	pound @ 5,000

have purchased a piece of land on which to build a house as part of a barrio-initiated housing project. Like other couples with young kids, times are tough. Raising five young children leaves them with minimal savings, time, and energy. Over the past two years, they have been able to purchase many of their housing materials little by little, but they still have little time or additional people-power to begin construction of a house.

TABLE 3.11 Supermarket Prices for July 1989
(rate of exchange C25,000 to $1.00)

		PRICES
Meat	beef	pound @ 11,000 to 14,000
	chicken	pound @ 14,000
Vegetables	tomatoes	pound @ 2,500
	onions	pound @ 2,000
	chiltomes	dozen @ 1,000
Fruit	plantains	1 @ 2,500
Basics	milk	liter @ 2,500
	beans	liter @ 7,000
	coffee	pound @ 20,000
	cheese (dry)	pound @ 3,600
Luxury goods	English sauces	12 oz.@ 7,500

Shopping/Finances. Shopping on Sundays is a specifically joint activity. Sunday mornings Mabel and Noel leave the kids at home and head to the market. Shopping on Sundays at the market is for gathering the bulk of the fruit and vegetable items for the week. Mabel and Noel purchase meat on another day at a shop outside of their barrio. That shop is chosen for the quality of its meat and its low prices.

Their arrival at the market by bus seems to put into motion a well-oiled routine that combines a very social, enjoyable weekly public outing with a functional task. Mabel and Noel, carting their separate durable shopping bags, divide up and hunt for the best buys. In the intensely crowded and bustling market, they seem to know where the other is and return simultaneously to discuss prices, the quality of goods, and other sections of the market that contain the cheaper, sought-after Masaya fruit. Mabel and Noel are enthusiastic in their tasks. This is a weekly outing without the children that they seem to enjoy doing cooperatively. The Curtis family also engages in spot shopping on a daily basis at the numerous little stores close to their home.

Household Budget, 1988 and 1989. Here we summarize the household budget information, gathered from Mabel's and Noel's reported purchases during one week in 1988. Their food purchases make up 83% of their total expenditures for that week. Additional purchases included a much-needed but very expensive pair of shoes for one of the children, and a small amount of money sent with the kids to school for the purchase of a snack. For one week the Curtis family divided these food items between them: 13 pounds of meat (chicken, pork, beef), a small portion of beans (possibly enough for 1 meal), 2-1/2 dozen eggs, 24 liters of milk, 18 loaves of bread, tamales (enough for 1 meal), 30 tortillas, morongo (rice, blood, herb patty fried in oil) enough for 1 meal, and 9 lbs. of rice.

TABLE 3.12 Household Budget for the Mabel Curtis Family, Summer 1989 (rate of exchange C25,000 to $1.00)

ITEM	AMOUNT	PRICE	WHERE
Fish	7 lbs.	70,000	mar.
Meat	10 lbs.	110,000	supermar.
Eggs	1 cart.	25,000	bar.
Milk	19 lit.	29,500	bar.
Tortillas	30	30,000	bar.
Cheese	4 lbs.	14,500	supermar.
Carrots	4 lbs.	10,000	supermar.
Tomatoes	4 lbs.	10,000	supermar.
Aguacate	1 doz.	20,000	mar.
Mangos	50	5,000	mar.
Lemons	100	5,000	mar.
Pina	6	6,000	mar.
Onions	4 lbs.	12,000	mar.
Chiltoma	25	3,000	mar.
Vinegar	1 lit.	8,500	mar.
Gueneo	25	35,000	mar.
Ice	14 bags	7,000	bar.

Daily Purchases
Jul. 3   12,500
Jul. 4   12,000
Jul. 5   6,000
Jul. 6   14,000
Jul. 7   6,500
Jul. 8   293,500
Jul. 9   70,000
     TOTAL = c414,500 or $16.58

Household Income
Mabel   c600,000 a month
Noel   c2,000,000
Total =   c2,600,000 or $104

Average percent of monthly income for household expenses = 63 percent.

Key: Mar. = Oriental market
      Supermar. = Supermarket
      Bar. = Local barrio stores

Not included in the budget allocation was the purchase of fruits and vegetables. A healthy portion of vegetables and especially fruits are traditionally purchased and eaten on weekends, especially Sundays. This is important for assessing their diet for its nutritional quality.

In the summer of 1989, we again gathered budget information from this household; the data are shown in Table 3.12.

Strategies for Regulation

Kin, Friendship Networks, and Visitation. Like many families in Nicaragua, Noel and Mabel's kin are quite divided politically. Noel's father was an officer in Somoza's military and Mabel's father received a decent wage working in customs on the Atlantic coast. With the ouster of the Somoza regime in 1979, the majority of their kin on both sides of Mabel's and Noel's families fled to Miami. Generally, for people in Nicaragua, this means that these relatives in the U.S. will become a source of dollars. The "rules" surrounding the speculation about who in Nicaragua receives dollars and who does not is a more favorite topic of "gossip" than a public admission of one's own dollars. Therefore, Mabel and Noel have not mentioned receiving dollars, except a small amount sent occasionally from her father for his grandchildren. But we suspect that they, like most people, have some hidden dollars that they can count on.

In terms of visiting patterns, the Curtis family seems to be friendly with several brothers, sisters, aunts, and uncles from both sides of the family in and around Managua. Apart from drinking buddies from their work places, kin members (rather than neighbors) seem to be the more frequent guests at the Curtis household, even though many have already left the country.

August 5 is a big holiday for the "popular classes" in Nicaragua. It is the commencement of 2 weeks of celebrations for the patron saint of Managua, Santo Domingo. (For a more detailed account of this celebration see Chapter 7.) This week of celebrations has grown into two entirely separate celebrations held in two locations. The "lower" parade is for the popular classes, and the "upper" caters more to the better-off Nicaraguans and expatriates returning on vacations.

It is customary on this day for the Curtis family to take a bus to the opposite side of Managua to watch the "lower" parade. While waiting for the parade, the adults drink rum as the kids drink water, and eat fruit and candy brought from home or sometimes bought from a vender. This event culminates several hours later with rivers of people clothed in traditional Indian garb, bodies greased with burnt oil or dressed in animal costumes. After the parade, the Curtises typically gather at the nearby house of Noel's sister and family for a traditional meal of soup or nacotamales (tamales filled with meat and vegetables).

Other time spent with kin is the customary swarm to the Nicaraguan beaches on Easter. Noel, Mabel, and their children look forward to this and make the trips as frequently as possible when they have the time, money, and transportation. Noel's uncle lives in a beach house in Masachapa (southern Nicaragua on the Pacific coast). On these occasions, it usually happens that Noel gets access to a Pepsi truck on short notice and the family packs and leaves very quickly to spend a few days at the beach with kin.

Reflections of Daily Life: Gender and Sexuality. Mabel and Noel have stated that they are jointly committed to "pulling the same cart." Domestic chores seem to be fairly equally divided between them. We have frequently witnessed Noel sweeping and mopping the house. He seems to quite enjoy the task, as do the children. Besides rocking in rocking chairs, sweeping is the second most popular national pastime in Nicaragua in general. Noel is quite proud of his egalitarian attitude toward domestic work. We have never witnessed him demanding or expecting Mabel to serve him food or even coffee.

Though generally quite jovial, Mabel sometimes laments the frustrations of the day-to-day grind of daily survival. Like all Nicaraguans, she wonders when the hardship will end and when they will ever get ahead and be rewarded for all of their sacrificing. Mabel is a militant Sandinista and has participated intensely in barrio and national activities. But she dreams of life in the U.S., earning dollars and living a better life, even though she strongly criticizes and feels deeply the atrocities committed by the U.S. government in Nicaragua.

Mabel is ordinarily enthusiastic and hopeful. At times, though, she is also somewhat reflective of her past life, one that holds heavy memories. Mabel mentions the somewhat luxurious material life she was provided by her father in her childhood as compared with her life now. However, she sadly laments that her mother was the poor maid of Mabel's father. Her mother, Mabel states, experienced a very oppressive life. Even though Mabel's father claimed responsibility for Mabel and her brother, he never married her mother or cared about her. Mabel's mother's life of limited options was reflected in the strong stress she put on Mabel to have children. Mabel never thought otherwise. Mabel now declares, however, that she never would have had so many children. She expresses half jokingly and half seriously that they have ruined her life. When she talks about going to the U.S., she talks of going alone. However, she hasn't left and, up till now at least, she views her and Noel's work and constant struggle as necessary in being able to maintain their family at a minimal level.

Mabel's strong leadership abilities are seen in her intensive involvement in local and national activities supporting the Sandinistas, both before and after the ouster of Somoza in 1979. Her comments reflect her hopes and desires, like those of so many women in Nicaragua, for the changing position of women. Many women feel that this "hope" is not being addressed as quickly and with as much insight, and commitment by men in their everyday relations with the women they live with. Many men continue to see it as their right to have other women and children, even though responsibility for them remains in question. This position, in turn, unjustly assumes that women are not granted the same right. Mabel's formal education, respected community involvement, and secure job no doubt have given her considerable leverage that other women do not have yet. But, even Noel's seeming gentleness, enthusiastic involvement with the children, and sharing of domestic chores may not be enough. The impact of these complex gender realities, however, no longer needs to be accepted by women like Mabel in Nicaragua. As is periodically seen in Barrio William Diaz Romero, some women are throwing out their husbands to form more economically stable, women-centered households. In these households, domestic work can be divided equitably between the women of the household, providing more free time for everyone. Further, these new and creative housing arrangements and their accompanying economic realities are welcomed and provide women with an opportunity of more control over the extent and pace of the individual freedoms in their lives and in their homes.[3]

The Household of Maria Felix

Strategies of Procurement

The next household that we will describe is that of Maria Felix. She was the main informant from this household for gathering our data. This household is comprised of Maria Felix (age 41), her husband Modesto Rodriquez (age 43), and their two daughters, Moestra 13, and Milagro Pilar 7. Occasionally a daughter, Plurda (age 22) from Maria Felix's first husband and her children Alvero, age 3, and Luciella Carmen, age 2, will reside in the household. Plurda does not have a spouse. Raphael Venturas (age 25), also a son from Maria Felix's first husband, is also a fluctuating household resident like his half sister Plurda. On any given day, there may be one or two other related people around the residence, although there does not seem to be much permanency to their stay. On the same lot but in a separate lean-to structure, resides Modesto's mother. They did not mention to what extent they may have cooperative activities with her, however.

Maria Felix was born in the rural area outside of the Pacific coast city of Leon. Her husband is from Chontales, which is also a rural area. Her two eldest offspring were also born outside of Leon. Her two youngest were born in Managua.

This family could be described as economically very marginal, one of the poorest families in the barrio. By marginal, here, we are referring to their class position in terms of their living conditions and their household expenditures. They have lived for 15 years in the barrio. Both her and her husband's families were in agriculture, and migrating to the city was seen as an improvement in their standard of living. They live on the edge of a colonia (vecindad) behind a big lot where a housing project will go. They live in an extremely humble, one-room structure which is divided between a partitioned kitchen area and another room where they sleep. They have a dirt-covered patio in front where they keep some plants and a few chickens as a form of savings for consumption and/or profit.

Neither Maria Felix nor her husband read or write. Both have only one year of primary school. Their two adult offspring have attended some adult education classes that have been offered in the barrio.

Finance, Domestic Chores. Maria Felix is the only steady source of income in the household and, most of the time, she is the only source of income. As a rural resident, Maria Felix made and sold hammocks. Upon arrival in Managua as a very poor woman, her options were limited by her class position and the lack of unskilled or accessible jobs in the formal economy. Jobs in the informal sector, such as domestic workers and vendors, are the most common jobs taken by rural residents migrating to the city. Since hammocks cannot be eaten and tortillas can, she began to make and sell tortillas out of her house because less surplus money is needed for investment in materials, the economic return is faster, she sells some tortillas every day, and a large portion of their household diet consists of the surplus tortillas that she did not sell that day. Additionally, tortilla scraps are used to feed their chickens.

Her husband works very erratically. He does odd jobs both inside the barrio and outside the barrio when he can find work. More frequently, he may work as a security guard or help vendors sell fruit at the market; therefore, he has no job security and his pay is marginal. The neighbors gossip throughout the immediate vicinity that Modesto is an alcoholic and does his share to drink much of the household income. Some feel sorry for Maria Felix and lament that she will never get ahead with him around.

The two youngest children only seem to attend school about 50% of the time, if that. This occurs mainly because their unpaid labor is needed at home to help their mother make, sell, and deliver tortillas or help with the other daily domestic duties, such as watching the house while the family is out working.

Her household food purchases amount to 84% of the household budget, virtually all of their total allocation. Broken down into food groups, they spend 68% on high proteins. This consists mostly of beans bought at subsidized prices. Fourteen percent goes for cereals, reflecting a low allocation because she produces tortillas; 11% goes for fruits and vegetables, and 27% for sugar. Their left-over income all goes towards production costs. Adding her weekly production costs to her food costs, this still amounts to 292.5 cordobas over her reported earnings for 1 week selling tortillas. Therefore, they seem to be operating at a deficit. This all indicates that, like most barrio residents, they probably have some credit links, there is some gift-giving going on, other household members are not reporting part-time income, and Maria Felix most likely does not report all of her income either.

TABLE 3.13 Household Consumption Analysis for the Maria Felix Family, Summer 1989 (rate of exchange C25,000 to $1.00)

FOODS EATEN		AMOUNT
Soup (eaten with bones, pipian, yuka, onion)	24 bones 1 onion 1 pipian 3 pcs. yuka	3 lbs.
Rice		2 lbs.
Cheese		1/2 lb.
*Tortillas (Sometimes they eat the tortillas she doesn't sell.)		
Bread		2 loaves
Milk		4 liters
Frijoles (beans)		3 lbs.
Sugar		1-2 lbs. per person every 15 days
*Pinolio (corn drink made with water and/or sugar.)		
*Coffee		

*No sufficient data on amounts for these items.

Their diet consists, however, mainly of rice and beans (which they consume every day) and tortillas, with a general absence of meat, eggs, milk, chicken, vegetables, fruit or pasta. It is mainly, then, more carbohydrates than meat. This information is shown in Table 3.13.

Maria Felix also has "reproduction costs." This money is not spent on food. It is used to get provisions for the reproduction of living and working conditions (Bennholdt-Thomsen 1984:41–44). The work of the housewife is unpaid. Apart from reproductive costs, Maria Felix's earnings are also spent on buying food for the family's daily consumption. This, then, involves both "domestic production" and "subsistence production." "Domestic production includes household maintenance and is a subset of subsistence production." Bennholdt-Thomsen describes subsistence production as "work related to pregnancy, childbirth, nursing and education of children, as well as that required in the production and transformation of food, clothing, housing, and the physical and psychological demands associated with sexuality" (Bennholdt-Thomsen 1984:42).

Summer 1989. The household was a little better during 1989, for Modesto had stopped drinking and was working as a stevador in the

TABLE 3.14 Household Budget for the Maria Felix Family, 1989 (rate of exchange C25,000 to $1.00)

ITEM	AMOUNT	PRICE	WHERE
Beans	4.5 lbs.	30,000	bar.
Rice	4.5 lbs.	27,000	bar.
Tomatoes	1	3,000	bar.
Onions	3	2,000	bar.
Sugar	1.2 lbs.	2,500	bar.
Cooking oil	1.5 lit.	6,000	bar.
Mangos	4	2,000	bar.
Brown sugar	1 lb.	7,000	bar.
Ice	1 bag	3,000	bar.
Soap	4 bars	16,000	bar.
Corn	10.51 lbs.	273,000	mar.
Molino	7	28,000	bar.

Daily Purchases
Jul. 3   156,000
Jul. 4   63,000
Jul. 5   19,500
Jul. 6   34,000
Jul. 7   32,000
Jul. 8   76,000
Jul. 9   18,000
 TOTAL = c399,500 or $15.98

Household Income
Husband's salary   c160,000 a month
Maria   c100,000
            Total = c260,000 or $10.40

Based on their reported income, this household still runs on a deficit.

Key: Mar. = Oriental market
      Supermar. = Supermarket
      Bar. = Local barrio stores

market. Below are the figures for their household expenses during the first week of July. This information is shown in Table 3.14.

Strategies of Regulation

Community Involvement, Kin, Friendship Networks, Visitation. Outside of the immediate household, Maria Felix participates at a very minimal level in the more formal neighborhood activities and meetings. About 2 years ago she became the third member asked by the committee of the barrio to become a part of a newly-formed tortilla cooperative for the barrio. The purpose of forming the tortilla cooperative was to ensure the three women involved in the endeavor a supply of flour on a consistent basis. However, this was proven to be less simple than thought in the beginning. When extreme shortages in flour and basic food items became scarce in Managua, the CDS found itself in no better position to secure flour than anyone else. A shortage is a shortage. Another reason for starting a tortilla cooperative was to regulate prices to guarantee affordable prices to people in the barrio or to influence other competition to lower its prices. Related to this are the realities of the war and general Third World shortages. This mandates that, whether in plentiful times or in times of shortages, the priority is given to the countryside over the cities, especially Managua.

Many of her neighbors, who would ordinarily like to support these types of barrio-initiated endeavors, have avoided buying tortillas from Maria Felix because they do not like the "unsanitary" conditions of her house. Other neighbors, however, mentioned purchasing elsewhere because of other reasons, such as having a preference for the taste of someone else's tortillas and/or previous patronage of a particular person or friend. Maria Felix does, however, have several steady customers nearby that she counts on on a daily basis, without the customers generated by participation in the sporadically operating tortilla cooperative.

Reflections of Daily Lives. Maria Felix expresses little concrete understanding of her class position. There are just some who live better and some who don't. There are those with money and those without. That's just the way things are, she says. She articulates very little concerning revolutionary activities before and after the time of the triumph. She does not express what it was for, and therefore seems unsure of how she may have benefited or how to take advantage of what opportunities may be open to her and her household members now.

Because she is a member of the poorest class and a woman, the immediate opportunities (literacy, legal reform, political and economic participation, and equal rights in families) (Stevens 1987) were made especially available to her in one sense. However, her access as stated above has been slowed by a lack of knowledge about how to begin participating.

The incorporation of some of the poorest women into the revolutionary process involves understanding of their complex and difficult situation, the economic alternatives open to them, and educational campaigns directed towards these poorest and most alienated individuals and households. The effort to incorporate these folks, like everything else in Nicaragua, requires surplus money, time, and people power.

Gender and Sexual Contradictions. Another constraint inhibiting Maria Felix from realizing her possible benefits and taking advantage of them are the complex gender realities of an imperfect and constrained revolution. Studies of women of every class and every social sector overwhelmingly point to a major unresolved obstacle to increased women's participation: the tremendous burden of family and household responsibilities (Stevens 1987:9–10). In Steven's article on women in Nicaragua, she states that women (mothers, daughters, and sisters) put in 17 hours a day in domestic work. Men (fathers, sons, brothers) in comparison contribute and average of a mere 50 minutes a day (Stevens 1987). Maria Felix's class position, rural origins, and gender situate her in a burdensome domestic context. The lack of participation by her husband in domestic affairs has been compensated by the help her two daughters provide. This situation however, in turn, limits her daughters' ability to get ahead. Maria Felix's class position, gender and lack of time make it difficult for her to access the various institutions such as health and education, which further limit her chances to improve her life. As long as women continue to bear their "double burden," equal participation in education, employment, and politics is virtually foreclosed (Stevens 1987:1–18). Even though there have been significant social advances which have made women's participation more feasible, the "shell shocked" (Stevens 1987) economy has severely limited the opportunities for everyone. On top of all of this, the priority to the countryside has meant that changes in the urban areas such as Managua have come more slowly.[4]

Socorro Blanco's Household

Strategies of Procurement

Socorro is a single woman and the head of her household. She is engaged in various types of unskilled labor activities. She has two teenage daughters aged 16 and 17 from different fathers, whom she has raised alone. Her work efforts have enabled them to attend school instead of having to work.

Internal Dynamics: Domestic Activities, Work. Socorro and her daughters live in the last section of a colonia. Their household structure consists of a small (10' x 20') three-room wood and cement structure.

Socorro pays a small amount for light and water but receives free housing, like the majority of other Nicaraguans, because her rent has been frozen for five years under the new housing reform law. She has relatively few material possessions, but about average for a three-person household in the barrio. Of the three connected rooms in the colonia, Socorro and her two daughters occupy two of them. Both rooms have cement floors and doors opening to the dirt path in front. To the side of their household structure is a sizeable outside dirt patio area. Numerous potted plants dot the patio area. A wire pen in one corner holds some chickens that are being raised for family consumption or to sell. Underneath a small patio roof is a worn hammock and a carbon stove. Construction materials are piled in one corner. She has managed to purchase them in increments, along with other barrio residents, as part of the barrio's housing project.

Finances, Shopping. Socorro appears to be quite skilled at acquiring a sufficient amount of money, food, and help when she needs or desires it. She is very assertive, independent, and resourceful. She receives little in terms of monthly allotments from either of her daughters' fathers. At times, though, they provide gifts of food such as chickens and vegetables. Besides the minimal compensation in food received from the fathers of her daughters, Socorro appears to be quite involved in other exchange networks with friends and neighbors. On a more visible level, Socorro works in her home, washing and ironing clothes. Socorro reports that this is her primary form of income. Her daughters share this work with her in their spare time.

Since we have known her, Socorro has worked briefly at a restaurant where she quit after two weeks. She states she quit because of the poor pay, boredom, and dislike of working for a boss. She subsequently quit that job and went back to her washing and ironing because it offered her more freedom and flexibility.

Whatever her flexible and diverse sources of income may be, her income has been enough to allow her daughters to go to school instead of needing to work to bring in added income or to help Socorro around the house.

Socorro has received minimal formal education. In that typical loud and animated Nicaraguan vocal style, she explains that as a result of the revolution (1979), she was able to attend adult basic education classes in the barrio. But raising her daughters alone has still affected her ability to take full advantage of the benefits offered in her barrio since the revolution. In discussing her participation in the adult education classes in her barrio at night, she mentions having been hesitant to leave her daughters alone unattended. Nevertheless, in her strong determination, she did complete the three years.

So far, Socorro's daughters have completed the second and fourth years of secondary education. The oldest daughter, the more reserved of the two, was just married, but for general lack of space, her husband still resides most of the time with his family of procreation. Socorro's youngest daughter is outgoing and seems to enjoy the cosmopolitan opportunities which are open to her. This is evidenced by her active long-term involvement in the barrio as a volunteer health brigadista for the past four years. This position involves attending educational training sessions in the barrio and at the hospital, and participating in the various vaccination and general health campaigns in the barrio.

Household Budget Data. Compared to the majority in our sample, Socorro's household eats rather well for a three-person family. The man who lives alone in the household unit next door throws in some money each week for food as he is generally included in their household meal plans. Their budget reveals a diet quite high in calories, protein and nutrients. In their case, this high consumption parallels their total weekly allocations for food–92%. This is also quite high and would seemingly leave them only a scarce surplus.

Between the household members these high protein foods are shared for 1 week: meat, 6 lbs. (including chicken, pork, beef, and liver); cheese, 1 lb.; cream, 21 lbs.; and beans, 10 lbs.

They also eat adequate amounts of rice, bread, tortillas, milk. They eat some fruits and vegetables and eggs. Out of their total weekly food allocations for 1 week, 35% went towards proteins, 21% went towards cereals, 13% for fruits and vegetables, 5% for sugar, and 26% went for miscellaneous items like beer, ice, refrescos (fruit drinks).

Their non-food costs go for sending a small amount of spending money with her daughters to school three times a week. Socorro also purchases a newspaper three days out of the week.

Summer Budgets, 1989. Shown in Table 3.15 is the presentation of her household expenses during the first week of July in the summer of 1989 (rate of exchange c25,000 to $1.00).

Strategies of Regulation

Exchange, Visitation, Community Involvement. Socorro's interactions are quite involved and broad, extending to diverse groups, at least at the barrio level. These interactions seem to indicate an exchange of confidences, information, and goods. Some of her closest ties in the colonia involve friendships with her nearby neighbors. This includes a group of men who seem to do nothing but drink and sit under a tree across the street. This group of men either doesn't work or works an occasional odd job. Socorro has hired several of them at different times to help pick up loads of bricks, roofing, and other building materials and deliver them to her new lot. They occasionally have helped with the actual construction of her house as well. In the initial stages, these strategies seemed to aid her ability to move along quite rapidly with the construction of her house.

Socorro is very involved with the barrio committee (CDS). Her strong political commitment seems to extend to having strong friendships with many other active committee participants. Socorro's vibrant involvement in the barrio's CDS structure is a great asset to the barrio's continued functioning. She is not timid about confronting men, leaders, or those of higher class backgrounds. Her strong character, resourcefulness, and positive outlook seem to be acknowledged and respected by many people in the barrio.

Socorro was part of the original organization of CDSs in her barrio immediately following the revolution in 1979. Instead of an elected position, she now holds an ad hoc position revolving around the local housing

TABLE 3.15 Household Budget for the Socorro Blanco Family, Summer 1989 (rate of exchange C25,000 to $1.00)

ITEM	AMOUNT	PRICE	WHERE
Meat	8 lbs.	320,000	supermar.
Eggs	3 doz.	30,000	bar.
Cheese	9 lbs.	85,000	bar.
Beans	10 lbs.	70,000	bar.
Tortillas	10	10,000	bar.
Coffee	1 lb.	20,000	mar.
Sugar	4 lbs.	20,000	mar.
Cooking oil	1 lit.	20,000	mar.
Tomatoes	4 lbs.	12,000	bar.
Chiltoma	3 doz.	3,000	supermar.
Lemons	1 doz.	2,000	bar.
Aguacate	3	5,000	bar.
Platano	2	5,000	supermar.

Daily Purchases
Jul. 3   211,000
Jul. 4   42,500
Jul. 5   74,000
Jul. 6   38,000
Jul. 7   27,000
Jul. 8   151,000
 TOTAL = c544,000 or $21.76

Household Income
In cordobas c1,500,000
In dollars $60.00

All of this income goes for household expenses if these weekly figures are averaged for a month.

Key: Mar. = Oriental market
      Supermar. = Supermarket
      Bar. = Local barrio stores

project in the barrio. Her position involves coordinating people, transportation, and materials for the attainment of roofing materials.

Socorro's desire to be involved in mass organizations extends beyond her immediate involvement in the local CDS. There is no woman's organization (AMNLAE) in her immediate barrio, and to be involved would take up too much time, she reveals. Her active community participation is all done in volunteer time and can be quite consuming in time and energy. In spite of this, she seems to enjoy her involvement and feels that it is worth the effort.

Gender, Sexuality, and Reflections on Everyday Life. Socorro appears to very much enjoy the company and friendship she has with several men. They seem to admire her as well. Socorro is very intelligent and her comments reflect the realization that freedom can accompany not being attached. Like other Nicaraguan residents, she has been generally affected by the Nicaraguan economic crisis. But despite being a single parent, her financial security seems quite adequate, relatively speaking, for her household size and needs. Unlike others who received lots, Socorro's earnings have provided her with enough to hire out the help of her male neighbors. She has somehow been able to afford it and it saves her time and energy.

In terms of her relationships with her daughters, Socorro embraces the government-supported increased access that modernity offers them in their everyday lives. She has always maintained an open dialogue with them on sexual education. Socorro stresses that this is very important to her. This behavior was influenced by the more closed relationship she had with her own mother, Socorro reflects. Sexuality was an area during her own young adulthood in which she did not receive much instruction. Thus, Socorro desires that her daughters be well informed, and she is committed to making sure that these issues are not shrouded in mystery.

Both of Socorro's offspring are of wage-earning ages and help Socorro with her work. This, in addition to Socorro's humble background which marginalizes her to the area of domestic work, her single-parent status, and school-attending instead of working offspring have been realities in limiting her immediate choices.

However, Socorro's creativity, determination, and involvement in the local committee organization, in addition to the adult basic education she received, have allowed her to maintain an adequate subsistence level. It is also a lifestyle that is relatively free from the constraints imposed by the male domination Socorro views as accompanying marriage.[5]

Households of Consuelo Mendietta and Ruth Arena

Strategies of Procurement

In this section, we are providing an analysis of two households headed by females. The first household is that of Consuelo Mendietta which we do not have specific budgetary data on. The second household, that of Ruth Arena's, is presented with budgetary data. They are grouped together because they provide similar examples of multi-generational female-headed households.

Consuelo Mendietta, age 44, rents part of her sister's house. She has seven offspring in all. She lives with her two adult daughters, Patricia (21) who is single, and Betty (27) and her 2 young children, Eselia (8) and Nelson (5). Betty's husband sleeps at his mother's house because of lack of adequate space, however, most of his mid-day meals are eaten in Consuelo's household, where the majority of his evening hours are spent. Consuelo's youngest son Dennis (17), an active member of the Sandinista youth, goes to school and does not contribute to the household income at the moment. Consuelo's older son, Manuel Ruiz (19) has only recently returned from a six-year stay in Cuba where he was studying military science, a career and commitment he made when he was quite young following the revolution in 1979. Upon his return to Nicaragua, he was immediately assigned a prominent leadership post in a southern war zone for several months. The scholarship he received to go to Cuba, the stipend, and training have greatly assisted his family's economic status. With the money he sent home while in Cuba, his mother, Consuelo, was able to purchase materials and complete most of the construction of her new house. Like others from our sample, Consuelo also received a lot from the barrio committee. Her unfinished household structure is very spacious and made from cement blocks. This house will eventually accommodate her offspring, their children and her mother. Her male companion, who is also the carpenter of her house, may also reside with her, at least temporarily.

Consuelo's other daughter, Sylvia, Sylvia's husband Enrique, and their baby Cynthia, live in a small house in another part of Managua. Juana Ruiz (25), yet another daughter, is in Bulgaria on an academic scholarship. She has completed three years and will complete another three. Also in the house is Consuelo's mother, Marina Espinoza (69). All these folks share the house with Consuelo's sister Marian (39), her husband Oscar (40), and their son Oscar (11).

Household Inventory. Consuelo's sister and her husband are the actual owners of the house. The cement house they now live in is fairly new and quite large. The house has glass windows with bars, tin roofing, and a cement floor. It has three large bedrooms. In them six beds accommodate ten individuals. There is a central patio area, a large kitchen area, a dining room, a large living room, and a front porch. The house contains many items such as pillows, bedclothes, a gas stove, various pots and pans, dishes, cups and spoons. There is a dining room table with six chairs, several large wooden closets, a vinyl couch set for the living room, seven or more rocking chairs, and coffee tables. The enclosed toilet has a standard ceramic sanitary bowl. All family members have an adequate supply of nice clothing. There are electrical outlets, a water faucet in the kitchen, and a courtyard. Their appliances include a food blender, a radio, a record player (with numerous tapes and around 50 records), an electric iron, an electric sewing machine, a wash basin, and a television set. There are framed pictures, numerous books, toys, plants and a recently purchased cardboard box containing several young chickens. When needed, they can usually get access to a car owned by Sylvia and Nelson, who live across the city but spend most of their time with this household.

Finances. Consuelo's household is definitely one of the better-off in the barrio. They have an adequate surplus to purchase school items, clothing, food, and basic essential items. Consuelo has also been able to purchase the majority of materials for the construction of her new house when prices were extremely expensive and out of the range of the average person in the barrio.

They have received numerous benefits as direct results of the revolution. Consuelo completed only primary school; however, her household's income has been greatly upgraded by the fact that all of her elder offspring have so far received university educations. Two of them, as previously mentioned, were granted full scholarships to study abroad. Consuelo's offspring's committed involvement to the Nicaraguan Revolution, both before and after the 1979 triumph, inspired the same consciousness and hope in her to participate to the fullest extent possible in the reconstruction of the country. All of these factors, then, contribute to this household's economic and functional stability.

In sum, Consuelo's family is quite large, her children are all grown, and most are working and contributing income. As far as we know, none of the children worked when they were young. All those who are old enough have attended the university. The income generated from this family is an obvious benefit, even in Managua's urban context of low wages and incredible inflation. This household is divided into two-expense and domestic-chore-sharing units. The units are divided as follows:

Unit 1 consists of Consuelo, a pensioner; Patty, who is with the National Dance Troop; Betty, who works in the research division of the College of Education at the university; and Nelson, an economist (a government job). These jobs are all in the formal sector, and are usually not accessible to the country's most marginal population. The sharing of their somewhat adequate wages, in the current context, is of utmost importance to the household's general maintenance and survival. Consuelo receives additional income from her other offspring, the son who studied in Cuba and the daughter still in Bulgaria. In addition, like most Nicaraguans, Consuelo relies on additional dollars sent monthly from relatives residing in the U.S. Consuelo admits to receiving some dollars, but the amount, since it can be a cause for public scandal and embarrassment or just plain envy, is not revealed.

Unit 2 consists of Marian, a travel agent worker; Oscar, a government worker who was recently laid off in government reductions; and Marina who receives money from relatives outside of the country. This unit contains three adults with incomes and one child. Oscar was recently laid off, reducing their available income. However, because they are the actual owners of the house and share all the facilities jointly, we assume there must be some reciprocity between the two units, especially when households change due to persons losing jobs. It can be seen, in the case of reductions in income, that large households with many workers can provide a supportive backup in crisis situations that smaller households or households with more non-working children than adults would have.

Domestic Chores, Shopping. Both of the units in this household maintain their own separate household budgets. The first unit contains Consuelo, her two youngest offspring, and her older daughter's family (husband and two children). Consuelo does not work, but is pensioned. The working members of this unit turn their income over to Consuelo in sharing household and cooking expenses. During the day, she takes primary responsibility for the weekly food buying at the market and the cooking for her unit. The other unit, containing Consuelo's mother and Consuelo's sister and her family, do most of their own shopping and cooking. The mother seems to take care of the primary domestic chores for her unit.

Summary of Expense Sharing: Ruth Arena's Household. The extended female-headed household containing Ruth Arena is also shared by four other adults and five children. Like Consuelo's household, Ruth and her mother are now "spouse-less" and quite content with this present arrangement. In contrast to Consuelo's household, which is divided in terms of expense sharing, the individuals in Ruth's household share expenses. Ruth and her mother receive pensions. The other three adults work and contribute adequate salaries to the household. All receive wages and are employed in the formal sector. All of these factors contribute to the economic security and stability of this household.

Relative to the majority of households in our sample, the members of this household consume an adequate diet, nutritionally and in terms of quantity. The diet consists of rice and beans but also includes portions of meat (beef and chicken), eggs, milk, vegetables, and fruit. Their food purchases for one week (1988) are shown in Table 3.16.

Overall, in terms of their food expenditures for one week, this household spent 40% on high proteins, 24% on cereals, 20% on fruits and vegetables, and 1% on fats. The rest was spent for miscellaneous items such as ice cream, crackers, and condiments. The budget for Ruth's household for July, 1989, is shown in Table 3.17 (rate of exchange c25,000 to $1.00).

Strategies of Regulation

One of the most interesting aspects of the domestic sharing takes place in both Consuelo's and Ruth's households. This occurs when Ruth and Consuelo take on the primary child care responsibilities for their grandchildren, even when the children's parents are around. The time and everyday commitment to this task may be atypical for the barrio because of the fact that neither Consuelo nor Ruth work for wages during the day. It remains to be seen whether this is typical of households like these in Nicaragua, and whether these child maintenance strategies will change

TABLE 3.16 Household Consumption for the Ruth Arena Family, Summer 1989

FOODS EATEN	AMOUNT
High Proteins	
Meat	5.5 lbs. + 1 chicken
Cheese	1 lb. + 4 balls
Cream	2 liters
Eggs	2 dozen
Milk	44 liters
Beans	2 lbs. + 12 spoonfuls
Cereals	
Bread	11 loaves
Tortillas	30
Rice	4 lbs.
Pinol (ground corn)	1 lb.
Fruits and Vegetables	
Tomatoes	6
Carrots	1
Onions	3
Green peppers	3
Corn	several
Squash	several
Cucumbers	1
Pitaya	3
Lemons	2 dozen +
Bananas	2 dozen
Cooking bananas	9

when the households change and move due to increased housing opportunities. Nevertheless, Consuelo and Ruth seem to quite enjoy this role the second time around. Whatever the reason, the benefit this provides for the children's working mothers is obviously a tremendous help to them. We wonder how this situation might be addressed differently, however, if a non-working male was present instead of women like Ruth and Consuelo?

Like numerous contexts around the globe, Nicaragua, too, is a case where reality still lags somewhat behind public policy. Nevertheless, having been informed by public debates that confront gender issues on many levels, and general experiences with men, they have certainly given Ruth and Consuelo the strength, courage and ability to find ways out of the unjust circumstances they had experienced previously.[6]

Ephraine Ortiz's Household

Strategies of Procurement

Internal Dynamics: Household Inventory, Composition. This household type is not typical for those found in the barrio as a whole. It is

TABLE 3.17 Household budget for the Ruth Arena Family, July 1989
(rate of exchange C25,000 to $1.00)

ITEM	AMOUNT	PRICE	WHERE
Meat	13 lbs.	194,000	bar.
Eggs	6	6,000	bar.
Milk	42 lit.	105,000	bar.
Cheese	10 lbs.	79,000	bar.
Cream	3 lbs.	40,000	bar.
Butter	1 lb.	36,000	bar.
Vegetables	assorted	55,000	bar.
Fruits	assorted	45,200	bar.
Bread	15 loaves	51,500	bar.
Cakes	8 pieces	20,000	bakery
Crackers	1 pak.	3,000	bar.
S. bananas	4	29,000	street vendor
Coffee	1 lb.	20,000	mer.
Paste	1 lb.	9,000	bar.
Pozal	3 oz.	9,000	bar.
Beans (cooked)	7 spoons	7,000	bar.
Sweets	assorted	71,500	bar.
Cooking oil	1/2 gal.	35,000	bar.
Soap	2 bars	11,000	bar.
Newspapers	12	24,000	bar.
Cigarettes		24,500	bar.
Medical expenses		38,000	
Clothing (assorted)		410,000	mar.
Wages to houseworkers		110,000	
Dance lessons for children		69,000	
Telephone calls		2,000	
Miscellaneous		20,000	

Daily Purchases
Jul. 8   182,000
Jul. 9   85,000
Jul. 10   221,500
Jul. 11   246,000
Jul. 12   565,000
Jul. 13   155,000
Jul. 14   169,000
 TOTAL = c1,624,000 or $64.96

Household Income
In cordobas c1,650,000
In dollars $66.00

Average percent of monthly income for household expenses = 68 percent.

Key: Mar. = Oriental market
      Supermar. = Supermarket
      Bar. = Local barrio stores

Jodido Pero Contento

comprised of Ephraine Ortiz (age 69), his son Alejandro (23), and Alejandro's son Alejandro (4). The mother of the baby Nuvia Sosa Veneva (27) also lives in the neighborhood (barrio), but the baby resides most of the time with his father.

They live in a small, windowless, wood 3-room house with cement floors. The living area is the largest, with one corner separating off and leading into the humble kitchen area. A small bedroom is off in another corner, and a closet or large storage area is in another corner of the living room. The bathroom is separate from the house in the patio area. They have a wooden crib that the boy uses to sleep in, even though he has outgrown it by a few inches. Also in the house are two single beds, two plain wooden chairs, a long drafting table, an enormously large snake skin on the wall plus several of Alejandro's architectural drawings of places in the barrio, a T.V., a radio, two stoves (gas and kerosine), a big wheel toy, two very nice large hammocks, and two cheap wooden rocking chairs. They have mops and brooms, essential items to every Nicaraguan household. They have lights, water, and a kerosine lamp. They have a desk and three small tables. Their house, upon first appearance, appears tidy and clean but relatively humble and sparse in furnishings. In square footage, it looks like approximately twenty feet by twenty feet.

Their household unit is built onto the back of a large two-story house. The house has doors on two sides, leading out to a fairly spacious dirt patio area. They moved to the same general area of Managua one month after the earthquake in 1972 which completely destroyed downtown Managua and many other parts as well. The household then moved to this residential unit a year after the revolution, in 1980. Ephraine and his son pay no rent. This is typical for most people in Nicaragua as part of a government policy of frozen rents. Ephraine thinks it might actually be a benefit to pay rent though. This, he feels, could give him more control against eviction by his unfriendly neighbors in front.

Work, Finances, Domestic Activities. Ephraine is a retired carpenter. He now draws a pension of 670 cordobas monthly. He is a composed, stoic-looking, very articulate elder senor. He has a third grade education and has had fourteen offspring with five different women. Eleven of his children are still living. Ephraine says he has been "unlucky in love." He traveled around Nicaragua when he was very young, looking for work. After being fired a couple of times, he was eventually able to apprentice with a "maestro de obra" to become a carpenter. This, in turn, became his life-long profession. His son, Alejandro (22), is in his second year of architecture school. He works as a supervisor of construction and receives 1,000 cordobas monthly.

Ephraine says that he has had to learn how to cook now that he doesn't live with a woman. He and his son share expenses. Because his son works during the day, he takes over primary child care of his grandson during the day while Alejandro works. He has a quick mind and is very organized with his budgets and keeping track of his expenditures. He says he learned to cook by experimentation, which led to several burnt and awful-tasting meals. He also describes how he slowly acquired some skill after some of the neighbor women showed him how to make certain things. He now claims that he likes to cook, but also admits to its drudgery. The realization that domestic work is real work translated into quite a humbling experience for him, admits Ephraine.

In terms of the Ortiz' household diet, 43% of their total expenditures for 1 week went for food items. This reflects quite a large surplus available for the purchase of non-food items as compared with the majority of households in the sample. This household's relative economic stability is aided by Ephraine's fastidious budget organization. In addition, it is facilitated by the reality of a small family consisting of two adults bringing in monthly income and only one small child to provide for. The mother who lives nearby also contributes money for her child and takes care of him certain days out of the week. This week's budget is actually somewhat untypical for Ephraine and his family because of the purchase of some expensive non-food items. These consisted of two tanks of gas, a regular expense for cooking, a razor, blades, some clothes, some laundry soap, a new mop handle, some costly bike repair expenses needed for Alejandro's job selling candy on the streets. The purchase of the non-food items was derived from additional income for which the figures were not reported to us.

However, out of their food purchases for the one week (1988), 41% of it went into purchasing proteins (including meat, beans, cheese, eggs, and milk). Thirty-two percent went towards buying breads and cereals, 16% went towards the purchase of fruits and vegetables, and 9% went towards fats and sugars. It must be noted for all of the households in the sample that the amount spent on sugar does not necessarily reflect the consumption patterns. Because sugar, bought at a subsidized price at this time is fairly cheap and takes on the qualities of a food substitute for many poor families. A typical consumption of sugar is approximately 1–2 lbs. of sugar per person every 15 days.

Strategies of Regulation

Ephraine is very gentle, affectionate, and teasing with his young grandson. It is obvious that he enjoys him. Ephraine doesn't seem to leave the house much to visit. He usually goes out for a walk while his grandson rides his big wheel around the barrio in the evenings. He seems to be involved in very limited exchange networks with kin and neighbors. He has mentioned the especially tense relations he has with his neighbors in front. He notes their continual attempts to evict him, and behavior of the kids who frequently harass and throw rocks at him. In dealing with this situation, he occasionally calls on the police to manage the disputes. Ephraine is minimally involved in barrio activities to the extent that he bought rice at low prices when the barrio organized a rice cooperative to supply the barrio, and he annually attends the barrio's celebration of their martyr.

As we mentioned above, the individuals in this household live modestly, but within the norm of other barrio residents. Ephraine's sharp memory and his insightfulness in budget organizing help them to manage adequately in terms of diet and meeting basic needs. A lifetime of experiences, the fact that their household is small, that they only have one child, plus dual incomes (architect and pensioner) aid their subsistence maintenance.

Rather than ending up bitter and bruised from his numerous failed relationships and dealing with the rather "independent-minded women" in his life, he is quite reflective on his life. Ephraine appears comfortable with admitting failures and acknowledging personal inadequacies. At 68 years of age, he has traveled through numerous household arrangements. Ephraine is able to admit humbly that he is still learning.[7]

SOCIAL ACTIVITIES IN THE BARRIO

In this section we wish to briefly present examples of social projects in the barrio that were materially helpful to households in the barrio. Though these were projects organized by the barrio committee they provide households with a means to collectively confront many of the current economic problems. Though many of these projects were developed in 1988 and 1989, this community is currently attempting to keep this going as their expression of "government from below." We look at the barrio's housing project, the rice buying collective, planning for a barrio store, and the building of a community center.

Housing Project

There is a general housing shortage in Managua. The economic crisis has caused shortages of building materials. In 1986 the barrio lobbied the city housing authority for access to vacant lots in the barrio so people could build houses. They were given a large lot in the center of the barrio that was subdivided into forty-two lots. These lots were given out based upon need and involvement in the barrio's political and social activities. If two people had the same need, but one had been more active in the barrio's affairs, the lot was generally awarded to the person who had been more active.

The coordinator of the barrio (a housing contractor), provided families with a basic household plan with which to build their houses. Each family was given a lot and had to clear the lot to ready it for construction. Because of cost and shortages, the families have attempted to organize various buying cooperatives to get materials. Those in the cooperative were able to get bricks, steel reinforcing rods, cement, and roofing at wholesale rates. However, only about half of the 42 households had the funds to join the cooperative, and only about half of those have been able to purchase enough materials to finish their houses (Vance 1987:139–165).

In 1989 there were seventeen families close to finishing their houses. The next problem is to get water. When they began their project, it was assumed that water was available since the lots were in the barrio. They learned that they had to dig their own water trenches, provide the pipes, and pay a hook-up charge. They again collected funds and began to search for a collective solution to this new problem.

The Rice Cooperative and the Barrio Store

In 1989 the barrio's CDS committee organized a rice-buying cooperative, buying directly from producers or large wholesale warehouses, repacking the rice, and selling it directly to residents. A commission was formed to collect money from residents in the barrio (c2,000 per household) to buy the rice in bulk. The residents who had paid into the fund were given the first allocation of rice. The remaining rice would then be sold to residents in general. People had to show their food ration cards to be able to buy the rice. They were able to sell the rice at about 20 to 30 cordobas below market prices. They were then able to sell five pounds of rice to each household that wanted it. The proceeds from the sale were used as seed money for the next round of buying and selling. They would buy the rice in bulk, store it in the meeting room of the CDS, and announce the days that they would be selling rice. The selling was organized as follows: they put a scale up, weighed out the amount of rice people wanted to purchase (up to five pounds), and then poured the rice into containers or bags that the people brought with them. The sale and distribution would take about two or three days. People would come to the CDS meeting hall, wait in line, present their food cards and money, and receive their rice. In general this was a very successful project. However, there were external factors which limited the project.

First was the general inflationary trend. That is, between the time they collected money and sold the rice, the bulk price went up. Residents were told that they could get five pounds of rice for c2,000, but the price increase meant that they could only get three pounds for c2,000. The collective could have gotten cheaper rice if they had gone out to the countryside and purchased directly from producers; however, they had no means of transportation out to these areas. A second problem was that although prices went up for all goods, people's wages did not go up, and fewer people had money to allocate as seed money. One of their rice-selling ventures had been covered by a loan from a local merchant in the barrio, but this was a one-time deal.

As a result of this experience, however, the residents became interested in exploring the development of a general barrio store which would buy at wholesale and sell cheap. Though this project would have to confront all the same constraints as the rice project, people think that it is a plan worth developing.

Clothing Sale

Similar in intent was a plan originating from the clothing factory in the barrio to sell at wholesale directly to the residents. The factory commission brought several hundred shirts, pants, and skirts on the weekend and sold them directly to residents at minimum mark-up. The barrio provided the space, the volunteer labor, and the publicity for the event. The sale was held on the weekend and was quite successful. The prices were low, the quality of clothing was good, and there was a wide variety of items. The barrio charged a buying fee of c20 which went to a fund for the children's day fiesta. The success of this sale gave more encouragement to the idea of a barrio store.

Community Center

During the last five years, the barrio has been planning a community center. Plans have run from an official day care center to the current plan of a simple building for community-based activities, including job training classes for residents. The commission that has been responsible for the developing and building of this center is commissioned by members of the barrio CDS committee and local merchants. People feel that if the community was to build a center, then the commercial sector of the barrio had to be involved as barrio residents. This created further blurring of the boundaries between the formal and informal sectors of the economy.

The community center was finished during the month of March, 1990. The center contains a pre-natal clinic and they are still planning to initiate night school classes into the center. The center will be used for community meetings and other activities. They have also paved the patio area in front of the center, and plan to hold dances on the weekends to raise money for community events.

Conclusion

Political Economy

As stated earlier in this chapter, UNO is finding, like the Sandinistas before them, that to run the country based upon agro-export is quite difficult. As we point out, such an economy can be profitable if there are limited social or collective consumption costs. Ten years of a popular revolution have empowered the population to except and defend their social gains. This was demonstrated in the strike by the government workers when they won their demands on job protection and social benefits several months after the election of UNO. Further, UNO is learning that attempting to manage such an agro-export economy in the current world economic context is not a matter of ideology but of the international pecking order. Though they were the darlings of democracy in the election, that victory has not turned into hard cash coming from the United States or other countries. In fact, UNO is in the position of hoping that the Soviet Union continues its economic aid especially in the area of oil imports.

In the area of inflation, there seems to be a return to super inflation patterns. In fact, the government is now minting a one million cordoba bill. As they learned in the strike of the government workers union, the unions were willing to tighten their belts when they felt the government was on their side, as in the case of the Sandinistas. Without such a feeling of support they have and will demand better wages and working conditions (Envio 1990c:3–18).

Strategies of Procurement and Regulation

Were there new strategies of procurement and regulation at the level of household organization that were generated by the dynamics of the popular revolution? There were, but some were generated by the difficulties of the war and its effect on the economy. All of the households that we knew in the barrio had developed various strategies for dealing with the fluctuating rates of exchange and prices. There were general patterns of bulk buying and looking for the cheaper prices for goods. Also, since there was not a great deal of price fluctuation between stores in the barrio and the markets, shopping patterns were more in terms of availability over price. As also stated in this chapter, everyone had some kind of access to dollars; thus, particular households constructed their own dual economies of cordobas and dollars.

In terms of the aspirations of the popular revolution for new or free Nicaragua, there were new strategies of procurement and regulation. In terms of procurement new strategies would be those that were reflected in collective attempts to solve economic problems like the rice-buying or clothes-buying programs they attempted. They were never able to successfully get the store project going, though it is still a goal they want to work on. In the area of regulation, there were two areas that would represent new directions: gender roles and education. As illustrated by Mabel and Noel, some household men were rethinking their roles in terms of domestic labor by accepting the responsibility of doing some of the domestic labor. The question of gender roles, obligations, and need changes in those areas was a constant topic of discussion in most of the households in the barrio. If the issues were not being transformed, the reality that they could be transformed was now part of this community's social world.

During the ten years of the revolution, access to education and improvement in household living conditions were apparent. All of Consuelo's adult children had gained access to higher education through the revolution. Further, pursuit of higher education was not gender biased. Both males and females were taking advantage of these opportunities. It will be harder for the new government to stop these demands for education that are now part of how people organize their household strategies.

In the next decade we will have to watch how households in this community are able to deal with the new hegemonic terrain and to what degree they will construct new strategies of household maintenance.

Social Action

At this point, the community activists in the barrio are actively involved in a struggle for a "Government from Below." As previously stated, they have finished their community center and still envision developing projects that will be of economic aid to the barrio. The persistence of these actions remains to be seen.

Current Conditions: 1990–1992

Todo es duro (everything is hard). This is how people in the barrio perceive the current economic conditions. They state that now the stores are full but their pockets are empty. UNOs economic policies have stabilized prices, however wages remain very low. Local media sources estimate that the basic food basket costs around c900. ($180.). Whereas the average salaries are around c400–500 monthly. Clearly, for us as anthropologists and as members of a solidarity group with this community, how well the residents of this barrio can confront and alter this economic terrain is of utmost importance. The praxis that we are searching for and that this community has gained through its own struggles will be part of the final determination of this hegemonic battle over the shape and direction of Nicaragua's political economy (Envio 1990d:23-38).[8]

Notes

1. Harvey (1989) argues that in the current context of capital accumulation, the requirements for rapid turn-over and profit-making compresses the material conditions of peoples time and space. The feeling that one does not have enough time or space to do things that one wants to do, is what Harvey is referring to. Thus we are suggesting that households are involved with constructing strategies for living with such time and space compressions.

2. For the most current information on the economy in Nicaragua see Envio's issues years 1989, 1990, and 1991. We have placed in the bibliography citations on the most current essays on the economy. Currently the gold cordoba has an exchange rate of c5 to one USA dollar. There has been a relative price stability over the last six months. However wages have been very low in relation to prices. Barricada (Jan. 1992) contends that the basic food basket cost about c900 a month, with the majority of people only making around c600 a month.

3. The Curtis household in the summer of 1990 was facing several changes. Both Mabel and Noel were facing problems with their jobs because of their Sandinista affiliations. Mabel has lost her job as the director of an elementary school. Noel thought that his job was currently secure, but that he might have some problems in the future. His lack of formal education is also a problem. Their youngest son—Noel—had been through major surgery for bone cancer, and Amy, their second daughter, had lost the sight in one eye from a construction accident. Mabel's father was planning to return to Managua from Miami, and Mabel expressed a strong desire to go the United States on her own. Their overall material and living conditions were about the same.

In January of 1992 the Curtis household is holding their own. They have finished their new home and have moved in. Mabel has a part time teaching position in a barrio school and Noel has not lost his job at the Pepsi factory, though his wages are lower. The children are all still in school and their health is good. Mabel holds onto her desire to work in the states to attain more money for the household.

4. The household of Maria Felix and Modesto had been radically altered. When we went to visit with them in the summer of 1990, we learned that Maria Felix and her two daughters were now living back in the region of Leon. Maria Felix had left with another man. Modesto and his mother's family were still living in the humble housing compound in the barrio. Their overall material—conditions with the exception of Maria Felix's absence—was about the same. Conditions for this household in January of 1992 were about the same.

5. Socorro Blanco and her household had completed their house in the new housing project by the summer of 1990. The house is on its own lot, and is larger

than the apartment that they had been living in. The house has lights and water. Socorro and her daughters were very upset over the election loss and the state of the economy. Though there seemed to be no major alterations in the material conditions (in fact there had been an improvement in terms of finishing their house), she felt quite depressed by the current conditions in Nicaragua. She was thinking about moving with her daughters to San Salvador to join in the revolutionary struggle taking place in El Salvador.

In January of 1992 Socorro and her household are about the same. She did not move to El Salvador. They have made some improvements in the house and have purchased a new stereo system. Her oldest daughter has a two year old child, and the younger daughter has just gotten married and is expecting a child.

6. During the summer of 1990, Consuelo's household was about the same. All her adult children were still working at their various jobs, she was still living with her mother and sister, and struggling to finish her house. Part of the problem with the construction of her house was it size. Her house was to be much larger than many others in the project and she had not been able to attain all the funds needed for its construction. Ruth Arena and her household were also doing about the same. They were fearful of the future, because many of the adult children's jobs were with the state, and they were not sure how secure these jobs were going to be. Ruth was still getting dollars from her brothers in the United States and her mother was still receiving her pension. They were also facing problems with the owners of their house, who now want to collect back rent and start charging a much higher rent in cordoba de oro.

The households of both Consuelo and Ruth are about the same in January of 1992. Consuelo has finished most of her house, and her daughter Betty lives in the house with her children. Consuelo's oldest son has left the army and now works in the private sector. Due to drastic reductions in the army he is now working in an area for which he was not trained. Consuelo is still very active in barrio affairs. Ruth's household is somewhat the same. Her oldest daughter has moved to the United States and her oldest son has returned from his studies in the former Soviet Union.

7. Ephraine Ortiz's household was about the same. The previous year his son had left for Miami. Ephraine and his five year old grandson had many new material items provided by the son. There was a new t.v., a new bed, many new toys, some new appliances and Ephraine had new glasses. He felt that his son had not forgotten them. Though he was not sure how the economy was going to do, he felt that the new government might be about to make some things better. Ephraine and his grandson no longer live in the barrio.

8. At the January 1992 rate of exchange of c5 = U.S. $1.00, current barrio prices for various foods were as follows: (1) meats—beef 9.50/lb., chicken 6.00/lb., pork 9.50/lb.; (2) vegetables—tomatoes 2.00/lb., green peppers 3.00/doz, cabbage 4.00/head; (3) bananas 1.00/each; and (4) basic items—rice 12.00/5 lbs., beans 1.50/lb., coffee 7.50/lb., milk 2.70/litre, cooking oil 5.00/litre, eggs 4.50/doz., and bread 3.00/loaf.

4

¡Quiero Decir Esto!

The Popular Politics of the Barrio

*Where there is ill health
Make a healthy community
Where there is diarrhea,
Boil water for children
Where there are flies, burn the garbage
Where the school has been destroyed
The community needs to repair it
Where there are robberies, we need vigilantes
Where a combatant has fallen because of the
War of aggression, help and give attention to
His/Her family
Where there is a mother of a cub (soldier)
Mobilize to see and help her
Because we are the masses
Because we are the community*

—*Poem from the National CDS 1989*

The structure of the committee of this barrio was formed by the necessity for organizing the population to determine its needs. In the barrio people started to get integrated into the revolution. How were we to unify? We had to talk about the general problems as well as the problems of this barrio. After these kinds of talks, the barrio committee was formed.

They are not now barrio committees, they are now called committees for community development. We do not have leaders, but coordinators. This is part of the new communal concept. That's where these committees come from. Dona Olga was the first coordinator (some ten years ago) then Luis Lopez, then Ausmundo, then Hydee, and most recently Don Orlando.

This new communal concept started in 1985, even though we were going through the heaviest times of USA aggression against us. We always saw the communal

---

Translated from the Spanish, the chapter title means "I want to say this!"

concept as the way to develop our needs. But as a result of the 1985 aggression of the USA, which was equal to an invasion, all of our projects were slowed down. They were slowed down because we had to give priority to national defense. Now we are ready to start this new communal concept. What we care about is to be able to unify for the good of the whole community. That's the new conception.

For example I can say that I'm a Sandinista and you are from the Social Christian party, but if there is a diarrhea outbreak among the children in the barrio, it is not important which political party you are from. So that's our goal—to involve the whole community. It doesn't matter what side you are from or what your ideology is. That's the way to improve the community.

This new line doesn't come from Commandante Cabezas, it comes from the people. The necessities of the people that we talked about. Each community has its own necessities. For example, if the clogged drains of our streets need to be cleaned out, we have to do it, not Commandante Cabezas. We do not care if Commandante Cabezas has a house, we care if we do! This new concept of community action is not that of Commandante Cabezas or Commandante Herria; these are changes that come from the people.

In the future we have to have more education centers and more health centers for this community. It has to grow. The education centers are not enough and there are not enough places for health care. It has to grow. We have to give answers to our children and the young. The changes we are making are to make a better life for our children. Our children are the future of this revolution, so that's why we have to take care of the our children.

—Consuelo Mendietta-Barrio,
resident and active participant in barrio politics

Introduction

Politics in the barrio revolve around the dynamics of the CDS in the community. The CDSs are the local governmental and lobbying structures for the residents in the barrio. The local committees are part of the national mass organization for community development.[1] Each barrio or small community is supposed to organize and maintain such committees. Over the last ten years, these groups have been more urban than rural, for the rural populations have different organizations that address their needs. To illustrate how these dynamics operate in the barrio, we present: (1) a review of the history of the CDS organization; (2) the history of the CDS in the barrio; (3) a review of the new directions being developed nationally for CDSs; (4) how these processes have been and are operating in the barrio; and (5) what are the directions that local organizations such as the CDSs will now take in terms of the election results of February 25, 1990.

Mass Organization and the History of the CDSs

In the latter part of 1978, as the Sandinistas began attaining military victories in such cities as Esteli, Leon, and Matagalpa, it was in those urban zones where liberated committees for civil defense emerged. These were groups organized to help those fighting or to provide what social services were possible in war conditions. After the triumph, these groups were transformed into Committees for the Defense of Sandinismo. These groups were reorganized to expand the activities they had carried out during the insurrection and to mobilize their communities to support and participate in the popular revolution. The new activities involved organizing militias for local protection, organizing health brigades, developing adult education classes, maintaining revolutionary vigilance, organizing community stores, and planning the housing needs of their communities.

A structure was created that was supposed to feed information and plans up and down the structure. The most elementary unit was to be the block CDS committee. Each block in the barrio was to have its own committee, generally composed of three people to be elected by those on the block. Their duties would be to organize the block in terms of these various activities and to represent the block's interest to a general barrio committee. The general barrio committee would have representatives from each block and commissioners who would be responsible for the various activities of health, housing, etc. This committee would also have the formal office of coordinator, barrio secretary, treasurer, and the offices of the commissioners. Coordinators were elected through open elections throughout the barrios, and commissioners would be elected at general assemblies. Each barrio committee would send representatives to a zonal council, which in turn would send representatives to a regional council, which could likewise send representatives to a national council of the CDS.

At the barrio level, up to 1986, the Committees for the Barrio were composed like local governmental structures. They had authority to authorize food ration cards, control over sale of land within their communities, power to control prices in local stores, and the power to certify the residency of persons seeking forms of social assistance. That is, to qualify for certain government services, one had to have proof of where one resided, which required a formal letter from one's "comité del barrio." Where people were organized, this worked very well; however, in some areas, this could and did lead to abuse in the use of local power. In 1987, there began a new direction in the CDS, designed to energize these groups again. From their inception, the CDSs were to be non-sectarian and membership was to be based upon community involvement, not party affiliation with the Sandinistas. This was always a problem. Only militant party members would give the kinds of work and time required to participate in these CDSs.[2]

History of the CDS in the Barrio

Before the triumph, the barrio had been divided by the main avenue that runs through the community. One side of the road was La Perla and the other La Veloz. During 1979 and 1980, each barrio was organizing its respective CDSs when they began discussing joining the two into one barrio. This would be important because both barrios were surrounded by two of the more wealthy communities in Managua (Carmen and Bolonia), they felt that they would be better able to draw upon more resources if they were a bigger community. Out of this merger, fourteen square blocks joined into one barrio with a population of over 4,000. The first coordinator was Olga Palacio, who was followed by Luis Lopez, who was followed by Hydee Rivas, Ausmundo Sandoval, and then the current coordinator, Orlando Garcia. The name of the barrio was chosen in a general assembly, where names of those from the barrio who had "fallen" during the revolution were proposed. William Diaz Romero, a young school teacher killed only weeks before the triumph, was chosen for the martyrdom and because he was a symbol for the barrio and its struggle.

This barrio had problems somewhat different from others. The poor barrios of Managua had been the most militant in supporting the Sandinistas, and had formed very active and politically militant CDSs. They were also the communities that needed the most, especially in the areas of basic services—water, electricity, roads, and housing. These were things that the Barrio William Diaz Romero for the most part already had, but it still had its particular needs or plans. The barrio needed to be politically organized in order to participate in new programs of education, health, and food allocation. It needed to have input in plans by the local, regional, and state government agencies organizing around the above issues. The barrio's most basic needs were to get a day care and community center built and to attain land titles to vacant lands in the barrio so that families could get lots to build houses. They were also desirous of building a sports area for the youth in the barrio.

They wanted a day care/community center because many of the women in the barrio worked and needed this service. The community center would be where they could have their meetings, hold nightly classes in adult education and conduct workshops in sewing and typing, etc. Housing was a major priority because this barrio had been severely hit during the earthquake of 1972, with only limited reconstruction taking place. Within the barrio some households had four to five families living together in the same house. Though no one was homeless, they were cramped into very limited space. The creation of a sports center was to provide the youth of the barrio with something to do.

Let us explain how this all operates on a day-to-day basis. In Barrio William Diaz Romero there were fourteen block CDSs, each composed of three members. These committees were to hold open meetings twice a month, to solicit the concerns of residents and take them to the general committee. The block CDSs were responsible for maintaining a census for each block. The censuses were used to provide food ration cards, to keep track of health records of children in the block for vaccination campaigns, and to organize blocks when there were general barrio activities such as vaccination campaigns or clean-up campaigns. During our time in the barrio only about one-half of the block CDSs were active and well organized. All blocks had coordinators, but some blocks did more than others. Part of the reason for limited activity at the block level was the smallness of the barrio as well as the effective organization of the general barrio committee.

El Comité del Barrio did act as local government for the barrio. Its structure was as follows: a coordinator, vice coordinator, and five commissioners. In the language of the revolution, when there were problems in the community, commissions not committees were formed to solve these problems. Some commissions were ad-hoc, whereas others became permanent. In Barrio William Diaz Romero, the following commissions were permanent ones:

1. Political Education: This commission was to keep the community at large informed and knowledgeable about local, national, and international political issues and encourage people's participation in different political actions.
2. Community Relations: This commission was in charge of solving the various kinds of conflicts that could emerge in the community, whether they were over land, high prices in the stores, or misdeeds of the committee itself.
3. Housing: This commission was concerned with organizing and developing a housing project for the community.
4. Health: This commission was in charge of providing health education to the barrio, organizing vaccinations campaigns during the year, organizing health alert campaigns (against dengue or diarrhea), and planning a health clinic for the community.
5. Food distribution: This commission was in charge of policing the food dispensaries in the barrio (now gone), checking on prices in the stores (now also defunct because there are no price controls), and organizing food buying cooperatives.

6. Finance: This commission was charged with keeping track of barrio finances and expenses.[3]

Each commissioner was elected or appointed at an open assembly, and he or she would then organize a support group from the community that would help with the work. Since these commissions do most of the work for the general community, they tend to take over the functions of the block CDS; in fact, many of the commissioners were also the block CDS coordinators from their part of the barrio.

Those who made up the general barrio committee and commission worked very hard for this community. The general committee would meet on Monday nights to set the agenda for the barrio assembly on Friday and to address issues brought up at the previous assembly. On Tuesday nights the housing and community relations commission would have an open meeting (these two commissions have become one over the last two years.) On Wednesday nights the health commission would meet, on Thursday nights the food distribution commission would meet, and on Friday nights they would have a general barrio assembly which was generally attended by 75 plus persons.

The Friday night assembly was supposed to start at 7:00 P.M., but always began at 8:00 P.M. because everyone would watch the current Brazilian soap opera on television before coming to the meeting. Around 8:00 P.M. people began wandering into the CDS meeting room. This was a long, narrow garage that the local handicapped sewing cooperative had made available to the CDS. There were long benches along the side of the garage and in the middle was a small table where the coordinator would sit and run the meeting. On the wall was a large black and white photo of Daniel Ortega and Sergio Ramirez—president and vice-president of the country at that time. The walls also held various posters and slogans of the FSLN and educational posters from health campaigns. As the benches filled up, people took folding chairs and sat out in the driveway. As people came in they chatted and gossiped with everyone. It was noisy and looked like anything but a general assembly. Around 8:20, Orlando would quietly begin to tap his pencil on the desk in an attempt to bring the meeting to order. After several minutes, this would work. The meeting was opened by a report from the political educator, Hugo. He would provide a news summary for the week and interpret those events in terms of their political importance. For example, once we were at an assembly that fell on the 4th of July. That night Hugo spoke about the United States War of Independence, how it had been and continues to be an example for all the Americas, and how sad it is that the United States is currently against social revolutions instead of supporting them. Hugo's presentation was followed by reports from each of the commission representatives. That was followed by particular issues that the committee had put on the agenda such as planning for health campaigns. This was followed by an open session, where people could bring up problems, complaints, and news items that they wanted to discuss. This was where block coordinators or residents themselves would bring up issues. Those who had conflicts that the committee felt it could resolve were placed on their Monday night agenda to be discussed and then reported on in the assembly the next week. These meetings are quite noisy, with many points of view being expressed. Robert's rules of order did not apply. It is at these meetings where, when people want to be heard they shout out "¡Óigame, ¡Óigame! (listen to me, listen to me)." To better illustrate how these meetings work, we present three cases: the battery shop, the cheese shop, and the pre-fab house scandal.[4]

The Battery Workshop Problem

In June of 1987, at one of the Friday night assemblies in the barrio, a group of residents from a colonia in the barrio came with a complaint about a battery workshop in their colonia. A colonia in Managua is several houses or apartments linked together, like a vecindad in Mexico. One of the residents in this colonia operated a battery shop, selling and repairing car batteries. The problem was that the acids from the batteries were being flushed into the water system of the colonia and people were fearful that it was going to pollute their water and cause them health problems. They explained this to those at the assembly. Various questions were asked, possible suggestions for solutions were discussed, and the committee of the barrio said they would report back to the assembly the next week as to what could be done. This represents the types of community dilemmas that the CDS confronts. How do people maintain their livelihood? Can or should such pursuits be monitored in terms of the general interests of the community? The next Monday night, when the general committee was holding its executive meeting, it was decided that Consuelo, who was the health commissioner, should visit with the public health center for the barrio. She would get someone from the public health department to come out to inspect the battery shop to see if it should be shut down because it was a health hazard. This is, in fact, what happened. At the next Friday assembly, these activities were explained to those attending and to those who lived in the colonia. It should be noted that this was only a temporary solution, because the next year the colonia residents returned, to complain that the battery shop had started up again, causing the same problems with the water and health. They went through the whole process again.

The Cheese Shop and High Prices

Up through 1988, barrio committees had the jural authority to attempt to keep local merchants within the official price ranges established by the government. This was a difficult problem, for the only way they could fully enforce this power was by shutting down the businesses of merchants who were charging too much. This was practically all the merchants. In Barrio William Diaz Romero, there is a cheese shop that produces and markets its own fresh cheese. Because of the war and the general economic crisis, inflation was high and prices seemed to go up every day. Cheese is a popular food item in the barrio. It is nutritious, easy to serve or cook with, and—most importantly—easily attainable because the shop was located in the barrio. People from other parts of Managua would come to the barrio to purchase cheese at this shop. The problem was that the shop often raised its prices above what they were supposed to in terms of the official prices. The owners claimed that there was just no way they could produce and sell the cheese within this price structure. This conflict was a constant issue brought up at the assemblies in the barrio: How to get the owners of the shop to stay within the official price structure. They would send delegations to talk to the owners; they would write letters of official protest; they would threaten to take them to the office of small businesses and request that the shop's operating license be revoked for price violations. However, this was a threat that was never actualized. At this time (1987/1988), the economic crisis was intense. Inflation was high and the supply of goods and services was getting more and more limited. One service that was severely limited was transportation. The city bus system was slow and crowded. So even though as the CDS they had the power to shut down this shop, to do so would mean the loss of the shop in the barrio and the resulting problem of having to travel to other parts of the town to get their cheese. Thus, the conflict was between having the convenience of a cheese shop in the barrio versus having the CDS enforce the price policy. They never took the option of shutting the shop down, but kept up a constant lobbying of the owners to keep their prices as low as possible. Now, however, the point is moot, for the national price policy has not been continued.

The Prefab House Scandal

In 1986, the barrio committee was able to obtain from the national housing authority title to a large tract of land in the middle of the barrio.[5] The barrio committee put into effect a program for families in the barrio to attain lots on this land on which to build houses. The committee allocated 42 lots. Through the committee, groups were formed to purchase building materials in bulk in order to save on cost and to get access to building materials when they were available. At this time (1987), building materials were expensive and scarce. This was because of the war and because rural areas, not cities, were given priority for building materials. Thus, the process of saving money, finding materials, attaining transportation to get the materials, and then organizing the groups to go after materials was long, frustrating, and conflict-generating. At this time, a former CDS block coordinator offered a deal to several families that had received lots to provide them with pre-fab materials to build their homes. The cost of the pre-fab material was much cheaper than the blocks and cement that people were attempting to buy. She further promised them that they could get quick delivery. Some eight households gave her their funds for the pre-fab material. When the pre-fab materials did not show up the woman stated she was not able or willing to return people's money. There were numerous meetings with the committee over this and it was a very hot topic of debate at the assemblies during the summer of 1987. Basically, the committee could do little directly because this was a deal that these families had cut with her, outside the structure of the buying committees organized through the CDS. They attempted, however, to pressure the women to respond and defend her position. At one very tense meeting, she attempted to defend herself on the basis that this was a good deal and that the materials would, in fact, show up. This still has not happened. However, she was quite angry at the barrio committee, and spoke loudly and often throughout the barrio about what jerks the committee members were. She, not they, was telling people the truth in terms of all these problems. One night at a meeting on building materials, this problem was being discussed. Orlando, the coordinator, was quite upset by this woman's attacks on the committee. According to Orlando, "to attack the committee was like attacking the revolution, and to attack the revolution was to attack the Sandinista party and its programs," and they—the committee and community—should not allow this to happen. There was much discussion about this, and the mood was that Orlando's attack was too strong. This was a local community problem, not a threat to the revolution or the Sandinistas. Alicia, a strong community member and supporter of the revolution who had not bought into the pre-fab option, pointed out that such criticisms went too far, for no matter what all the complexities of this problem were, the basic reality was that they were all still neighbors with this woman. The solution to the problem had to be based on the community's concerns, not developed into issues of support or non-support for the revolution.

This example also illustrates a concern felt by many people about the operation of the CDS. The concern was that the CDSs were more than community-based action groups; they were, in fact, the local representatives of the Sandinista party. It was felt that in many communities CDSs made their decisions in terms of perceived political correctness over community needs when or if these were different. It was also felt that one had to publicly express adherence to the party line in order to get the committees to help in terms of getting food cards or resident status. Though we did not see the committee in Barrio William Diaz Romero operating this way, many residents expressed such views. It clearly seemed that in other communities in Managua there were more serious problems. Again, in 1986 and 1987, this became a national debate among all CDSs. How should they democratize their structures and move away from being perceived as a sectarian front for the Frente?

The "New" CDS Line

In July of 1988, Omar Cabezas, as the new national director of the CDS, published the following comments in El Nuevo Diario:

> Then, we want to make a call to all the people of Nicaragua to organize on whatever they want and for the good and the development of the community so that you don't have to ask permission from anybody in this country.
>
> We can organize regardless of political positions, whether to make a well, or to repair the roads or to make a center of culture where children can dance folkloric dances, or to plant an orchard. If Mrs. and Mr. of the barrios that live well want to organize because they want to receive a lesson in gardening, or if they want to get together to form a club of whatever, they can do it. And if the people want to organize to see if they can receive potable water, or to pave the streets, or if they want a baseball league, or to organize to make a society of witches, or a society of "wijas," or of spiritual players, they can do it.
>
> To organize all the world for what they want and to organize the way they want to. The one that wants to organize a block, that's his problem. The one that wants to make a committee, he can do it. The one that wants to do other things, he can do it. They can organize and accommodate how they want. They can organize in the form that is more convenient, or most enriching, or the most enjoyable.
>
> If they think they can solve their problems, that's the way they have to organize it—without formulas or without rules.
>
> The only way to learn to organize is to organize. This is the only way. There's no other way. In that way they can encounter and enhance their structure (Cabezas 1988a).

Why were the CDSs going back to their roots? There were numerous reasons, but most important was the remobilization of the general population to seek collective solutions for their most current and pressing problems. In Managua, there are officially 250 barrios that compose the city. In 1989, less than 50% of those barrios had active and effective CDSs. Of those that were active, many had problems of factions or small elite groups that have used these structures for their own limited benefit. There have also been many active CDSs (primarily in the spontaneous/squatter communities throughout the city) in the city and in the smaller urban centers of Leon, Esteli, Matagalpa, and Jinotega.

The remobilization of the general population was warranted by the over nine years of war and the resulting economic crisis brought on by that war. The early joy of organizing communities had been replaced by frustration and fear. The frustration came from the complexity of rebuilding the nation; the fear from the war that had cost so much in life and destruction. Fear and frustration were combined in the attempt to deal with the chaotic terrain of the economy. Over the last few years, it has often been only the most politically motivated who have stayed active in CDS activities. CDS activities take a lot of time, effort, and commitment. Also, to constantly work within such activities, while others do not, encourages a certain amount of cynicism toward the masses that one was supposed to be representing. In addition, because those who have stayed involved were also the most politically active, they also then were committed Sandinistas. This did give the CDSs a sectarian style that was not supposed to be part of the organization. A local elite emerges that feels itself to be politically correct in expressing the interests of the local residents, who at the time are, in fact, quite distanced from those local concerns (Cabezas 1988b).

A similar problem, though not one associated with sectarianism or affiliation with the Frente Sandinista, was the concern that local leaders can and have used their positions of authority within the CDS for personal gain or for granting personal favors to their followers. During the decade of CDS activities, this has been the most common complaint made against the local structures. People felt that if they wanted to get their food cards or get access to programs of urban renewal, they had to get along with their local committee and express their support for the revolution in order to attain these benefits. This was against the concept of how CDSs were supposed to operate. Some of these types of charges have been true in certain communities; whereas in others (like Barrio William Diaz Romero), these charges were half truths and reflected the dynamics of small group interaction. There have been CDSs in which favoritism has been the mode of operation; however, in others it has more to do with those who participated in the affairs of the barrio, knew what was going on, and were in the right position to take advantage of programs being developed. Many problems that were perceived as favoritism came from the fact that some people were better at reading their context than others. Some people knew how to use structures better than others and can, in turn, help those they interact with the most to also learn to use such structures. In the case of direct favoritism, the removal of leaders was needed; in the case of interpersonal dynamics, it would involve the CDSs pushing harder to incorporate more people to participate in all levels of community planning and action.[6]

Another factor involves the history of how communities have been organized. Those communities that lack basic services—water, electricity, roads, etc.—are more active and motivated than communities that have such services. However, as communities begin to attain such basic services, their levels of activity begin to decline (Higgins 1974). This pattern is visible in the dynamics of spontaneous communities in Managua (squatter settlements). Through their CDSs, these communities have attained or are in the process of attaining such municipal services. When they do attain their basic services, participation in the CDSs begins to decline. This is a pattern that has been noted in many urban communities throughout Latin America. The problem with this is that, with or without basic services, there are a series of other issues and problems that communities have to constantly address: health, education, community housing, and access to affordable food stuffs. These require a motivated, mobilized community.

What were the "new ideas" that Omar Cabezas proposed for the CDSs? He felt that the organization of barrio committees throughout the country had been uneven. Some barrios were well organized throughout the country; others were not. For Cabezas, the lack of organization was not from a lack of political consciousness or because of counterrevolutionary sentiment. Cabezas believed the primary problem was that local committees were not addressing concrete local issues. This came from too much bureaucracy at the top of the national structure and too much sectarianism expressed at the local level. Cabezas stressed that sectarianism should be battled to death through community persuasion and discipline. No Nicaraguan should be marginalized from community involvement for political reasons. All the people are needed to build a popular revolution. Cabezas' dream is a united country, working through and with their difference to build unity. Like an ant colony, where all work for a common goal, Cabezas wishes to see in all the barrios of Nicaragua—Moors, Christians, Tinos y Troyanos—people organizing themselves "al gusto del cliente" (at the pleasure of the client). Actions have to be grounded in the context of the community itself. If a barrio has a problem with its school or health clinic, it should organize to solve that problem (Cabezas 1988a).

What do these sentiments mean in terms of new policies and structures for the CDS's activities in barrios? Cabezas asks,

> What do the CDSs wish to do? Because Nicaragua is a poor and developing country suffering through a war of aggression, the people can assume that

¡Quiero Decir Esto!

the government is not like a father who can or will solve their problems. The way to solve problems is for people in their repartos, barrios, communities, etc. to work to resolve their problems. CDSs need women and men of good faith, who wish to work for the development of their communities. We want an immense movement of solidarity of all Nicaraguans working like cooperative ants to attain their popular goals. People do not need permission to work on the development of their barrio projects; they need to be doing it (Cabezas 1988a).

Cabezas ponders, how in the name of God can all the needs of Nicaragua be dealt with through community-based organizing? Because he answers, that is where our (Nicaraguan) strength is. Thus he calls out to all Nicaraguans to begin this process.

To engender these new attitudes, Cabezas proposes that barrio organizations entertain the following structures. There should be a general committee for the development of the barrio. This committee would act as a coordinating structure over activities taking place in the communities. All activities and projects have to be democratically run. There is no need for any kind of centralized leadership, but there is a need for a constant construction of sets of community alliances to get things done as defined by the community residents themselves. All these activities are to be as open and democratic as possible. Coordinators are there to coordinate, not to play political games because of their positions. Cabezas stresses that without a community base to actions, such actions have no base at all.

In terms of these new directions, the national CDS was also to be restructured. Instead of zonal or regional offices sending programs down to the local groups, it will now be the responsibility of the local groups to develop their own plans and projects, with zonal or regional CDS staff persons acting as promoters to help community groups with their hopes and plans.

Cabezas states,

We have a dream. We dream that Christians, atheists, Mormons, communists, people who do not belong to political parties, will put their differences aside and begin to solve their problems. We also dream that the old, the young, the children will work daily like ants for the improvement of their own communities. We dream that after the worker gets home, after the student is finished with her studies, after the merchants close the shop, when the taxi driver has finished his route, and all others, they will meet to work vigorously like ants for the welfare and improvement of their communities (Cabezas 1988a).

To further promote this new line of action, the national CDS office developed various materials and handouts to promote these ideas. Below are some examples that we collected.

One handout is a pamphlet with the following statements and simple poems.

> There is a place
> Where you can give
> And you receive
> The same
> The best
> There is a place
> That you can make shine
> And attain
> Wellbeing for all
> There is a place
> With the force of love
> And faith, participation
> And work for all
> Integrate into your barrio
> And participate for one time
> And feel that you have given Your best[7]

Another handout is a comic strip in which numerous ants give the various bits of advice:

> To begin with, if you lack food, plant a garden in your patio or in your neighbor's. If possible, plant tomatoes, chiltomas, yerbabuena, cilantro, rabanos—in pots, in barrels, in old tires—plant as far as the sidewalk—plant, plant!!!
> So as not to leave a vacuum without planting, you also need to go to the cooperatives all over the countryside. Buy in bulk and get better prices.[8]

The final song contained in these handouts is entitled:
Hay que sonar (We have to ring out, to cry out, to strike out):

> One must ring out—strike out
> One must continue to strike out
> One must construct
> One must continue to work
> El barrio is the ideal
> It is the better place
> To help others
> To be fraternal
> To be in solidarity

¡Quiero Decir Esto!

To be loving
To be honorable
To be good neighbors
To be agreeable
To be honest
To be responsible
To be good people
To be involved
To be wild/passionate
To be revolutionaries
To be strong
To be united
To be a good player
To be a good parent
To be a good child
To be clean
To be healthy
One must strike/cry out
The sound of overcoming and building CDSs

The "New" Line at the Local Level

How did local communities respond to this call for remobilization? To work like cooperative ants? To work for the betterment of their communities? To examine these questions, we look at how the people of the Barrio William Diaz Romero have dealt with these requests.

Local Democratization and the Realities of Gender and Class

The response in the barrio to these new lines was one of acceptance and support. In fact, many felt that they were already moving in these directions. What this involved for the barrio committee was some restructuring of the committee positions and getting new block coordinators elected or re-elected. This involved recruiting new members to the general committee and getting some of the block CDSs reactivated. On the general committee several members left their commission and new ones were elected. In terms of reactivating the block, this involved the general committee going out to each block CDS and getting the people on the block to reelect their coordinators or choose new ones. The area where these new directions confronted constraints were in the areas of gender and class.[9] To explain these dynamics, we need to compare some past actions in comparison to new activities.

When we first met the members of the barrio committee, it was almost evenly balanced between women and men.[10] Orlando was the coordinator;

Hugo, Jose, Luis and Felix were the male members of the committee; and the females were Consuelo, Mabel, and Lesbia. Of the seven active block CDS coordinators at this time, five were women. When we returned the next year, Consuelo, Mabel and Lesbia were no longer on the committee. Lesbia had been in charge of community relations. This involved organizing the people who had received lots in the housing project to work together to buy materials for house construction. Lesbia was from a middle class family, one of the more affluent in the barrio. They own a lot of property and run several small businesses. Her involvement in barrio politics was one of a commitment to the struggle over immediate necessity. These three women were active, assertive, and articulate. They would often challenge the males in the committee if their behavior was sexist. Also, because of either their own class background or because of changes in household fortunes because of the revolution, they were quite cosmopolitan. They were well informed about national and international issues and could speak for other women in the barrio on issues that were affecting the status of or opportunities for women. This gave the committee depth and strength. These women had left the committee structure because of various conflicts over how materials for the housing project were purchased and distributed. When we returned in the spring of 1988, there was only one woman on the general committee—Ruth, who had taken Consuelo's place as the commissioner of health. Again, most of the block coordinators were still women. In the summer of 1989, the committee had been restructured again. This time there were again three women on the committee. Dona Olga (the first coordinator of the barrio) was a retired school teacher with a prestigious history of revolutionary activity. Her daughter Maritza was also on the committee. She was a university professor of sociology who was quite assertive and cosmopolitan. The third woman was Norma. She was the wife of Manuel who was now the commissioner of community problems. Norma was the commissioner for keeping track of the monies collected for various community projects. She was a hair stylist from the Atlantic coast who was assertive in her own particular style.

The importance of describing these women's styles and background is given in terms of the gender and class dynamics that are expressed in politics at the barrio level and how this affects efforts at democratization of those politics. The majority of the people who attend barrio meetings and functions were women. The majority of recipients of lots in the barrio housing project were women who were single heads of households. Many who volunteered to work on local activities and events were also single female heads of households. They also tended to be the poorer members of the community and were not always comfortable with being assertive. Let us give some examples.

¡Quiero Decir Esto!

Socorro is a women in her late thirties. She has two teenaged daughters and one grandson. She lives in a small two-room apartment in the barrio. She is quite active in barrio affairs although she has not held a commission on the committee. She works at odd jobs and is quite skilled at knowing how to obtain the necessities required to maintain her household. She is quite verbal and will confront the committee publicly on issues in which she thinks they have been in error or in which the situation requires more information. Though poor, she is in no way voiceless.

Rosario is also a woman in her late thirties. She is a domestic worker with five children ranging in ages from one-and-a-half to sixteen years. She lives in a one room house located in one of the areas of lots that have been allocated to barrio residents requiring housing. There are numerous fathers to her children. She had previously been renting a house from which she had been evicted. The barrio committee got her the lot, loaned her some funds for the construction of her house, and helped with the building of it. She attends most of the barrio assemblies and functions. However she rarely speaks out and has never publicly opposed the barrio committee on any issues. In private, however, she will express many doubts and opinions about the actions of the committee, but she at times lacks a sophisticated understanding of the politics involved with the revolution. Her teenaged daughter has expressed support for the Contras, though she cannot articulate a reason for her support.

Rosario's neighbor is Julia. Julia is in her late twenties, has three young children, and is married to a construction worker. Julia is from Rivas (in southern Nicaragua) and has a very rural presentation of behavior. She and her family also live on lots allocated by the barrio committee. She attends most barrio assemblies and events. She never publicly speaks or offers an opinion on issues and activities. She is not very articulate nor does she seem to be well informed on political issues. Her husband has been a member of an opposition union that had taken a very negative position against the government over a strike of construction workers.

Rosa Esmeralda is a women in her late forties. She is a janitor at the office of the city transportation center. Her husband—Pedro—is a night watchperson. Their children are grown and they have one grandson. They finished their house in 1989. She is active in barrio affairs and attends most of the assemblies. On occasion she will enter into debates and take strong positions. At times she is not well informed on certain issues, but expresses what she feels to be her position based upon her legitimate feelings. She is not always sure of all the issues between the government and the contras, but she knows the war is wrong because it hurts too many people. She feels that if people knew of the suffering this war has caused mothers, they would not support such actions. What she understands about the revolution, she supports.

What is important in terms of these women (and males in similar class positions) is that they represent the type of persons who have to remobilize to keep community activities going. For many of them, however, their class and gender backgrounds encourage them to be silent instead of expressive. Single female households are very prominent in the barrio. Issues of child care, birth control, physical mobility, autonomy, and abuse are very real to these women. However, they did not often know how to articulate these issues and are willing to let the committee (male or female) speak for them. The committee, because of its class and gender background, often does not understand how to break through that silence. The presence of females on the committee does not automatically provide a means to bring out the voices of these women because of difference in class backgrounds and the opportunities of such backgrounds. The absence of such women on the committee will guarantee the continued silence of these poorer women.

One of the problems is for the barrio to recognize its own internal class and gender structure. The rhetoric of the popular struggle proclaims a unity of action that has to be constructed, not proclaimed. The passivity of Julia and Rosario is not often understood by the more militant members of the barrio committee (male or female) because it is felt these women have received benefits (lots) and should be more supportive of barrio programs. More micro level dialogue and interaction would be one strategy for confronting these realities. Luis, in addressing how to mobilize the poor members of the community, insightfully suggested that they work like the Christian-based communities and go out and work slowly and intimately in a less threatening context with such household members to learn their perceptions and concerns. This is one area where we are able to help. We attempt to convey such impressions back and forth within the community. This is a slow process with no quick and easy answers. Without recognizing such problems, however, the process of democratization can been limited.

Housing Project

Over the last four years, the barrio committee has been organizing to obtain lots for residents on which to build their homes.[11] Since the earthquake of 1972, there has been a severe housing shortage in Managua. The aftermath of the revolution, the contra war, and economic crisis have further intensified this shortage. The barrio committee has been very successful in getting the titles to vacant lots in the barrio. The land is given to people at a very low cost with very long-term payments and little or no interest charges. To get allocated a lot, households have to present a petition stating their needs to the committee. This is not much of a problem. There are numerous households in the barrio that contain four to five families sharing very limited space. We have demographic data on three households in the barrio that have over thirty members living in a very limited space. The barrio committee would evaluate the level of need and other criteria exhibited by the requesting household. This criteria ranges from having children within the household who have done their military services to members of the household who participate in barrio activities. These criteria are liberally applied, and as the barrio gets access to more lots, they are able to honor the requests that they get. There is more social than political pressure going on. Those who participate know what is going on and who is involved with these projects and are better able to position themselves to do their personal lobbying. This is more a question of small group dynamics than political correctness. However, there are questions of class and gender.

The barrio originally obtained forty-two lots in the center of the barrio for reallocation. Only two members of the committee obtained lots. Numerous people who were active in barrio events did get lots, but so did some households that did not particularly meet the general criteria or were not too active. However, once one got a lot, one generally became quite active in barrio affairs. The barrio committee organized various "commissions" to purchase basic building materials. Because of the war and the economy, it was very hard to find building materials (cement, cement blocks, metal roofing material, etc.) and even harder to accumulate the funds to be able to pay for them. The idea behind the commission was that, through collective buying, they could be bought in bulk and thus get a cheaper price. However this is where micro class differences immediately emerged. Consuelo, with adult children working, found it easier to put her money into these collective buying projects than Socorro with her non-working children. Also, working women who were single heads of households had harder times obtaining the funds to buy materials and pay for a work crew to do the construction. This is an important factor, for in order to keep a lot, some level of construction must be completed each year or the lots could be lost. Another problem emerged when materials actually arrived. When a shipment was obtained, it was often not the full amount. For example, the commission for building blocks may have collected 100,000 cordobas to purchase 50,000 blocks. However, the plant could only provide half of that amount. This is a problem because by the time they could fill the order for the other 25,000 blocks, the prices would be higher. This was a constant conflict because it meant delays in construction and problems in distribution. For example, one household may have put in 10,000 cordobas for its blocks, whereas another family may have only put in 2,000—because they had less money or because they were building a smaller house. However, the household that had put in 10,000 would want only its blocks now and felt that those who put in less should wait for the next shipment. This would have meant, however, that for their 2,000 they would get fewer blocks because the price would have gone up. This was and is a constant problem in the plans to obtain building materials and has generated a series of conflicts among the residents over the way materials got distributed. It did come down to the fact that those who had funds got their houses built, those who did not have surplus funds are still working on how to build their houses. However over half the households were able to finish their houses. Nevertheless, they encountered one more surprise. It was thought that since they were building in a developed urban area, water and electricity would be no problem. That was true; however, it could only be obtained by paying for the wiring and putting in water pipes. They would also have to pay for the connecting fees for both. To meet this crisis, they again had to form a new commission, collect more money, buy materials, and organize work groups to put the water pipes in. This time, in the spirit of new democratization, rules and procedures for this project have been openly debated. They will only buy when they have enough funds for everyone. They have encouraged people to do it on their own if they have the means. They have also organized meetings with city officials to seek alternate plans for water and electricity that will not be expensive. This is still in process.

There are other projects that demonstrate these dynamics. However, since they also involve the operation of the economy in the barrio, these examples are dealt with in the chapter on the economy. The best example of how these new politics can operate can be illustrated by describing the "encuentro" or encounter between the committee of the barrio and Baptist church in the barrio.

El Encuentro

In the later part of July, 1989, the local Baptist church and the barrio committee had a joint meeting. The meeting was to explain to the congregation of this church why it should work directly with the committee on joint projects for the betterment of the barrio itself. This event was quite a show. There were around fifty church members attending. They were from the Barrio William Diaz Romero and the neighboring barrio of Martha Quezada. They were people who were not particularly in favor of either the Sandinistas or the local committees, such as that from Barrio William Diaz Romero. The encounter involved several different presentations by the church leaders, the most intensive being a long lecture given by a theology professor visiting from the Baptist seminary in Managua.

He presented a very sophisticated argument as to why church members should become active in barrio affairs. His first premise was that humans were not just biological organisms, but social beings. The social world included politics, economics, and social relations. He stressed that such realities had been organized either in terms of equality or stratification. For him, what Christians stood for was a means to construct a social world that was based on dignity, equality, and unity for all at the community level. This included the domains of gender and personal relations. He stressed that there were two types of politics—macro forms that referred to state power and micro that referred to the responsibility of being a member of one's own community. This was the message that this church was attempting to convey to the members and those from the barrio committee. They wanted to be a part of this community's endeavors to improve the community. This was not an endorsement or a critique of the government or its revolutionary politics, but a commitment of faith in the process of community action at the local level. It was what Christians were required to do by their own theological beliefs. They wanted to help the barrio with its clinic, community house, and sports teams. It wanted to be part of the development of a dialogue within the community in terms of its direction and priorities.

Reaction from committee members and barrio residents was mixed. The more politically militant members attempted to express their interest in this opening dialogue, but stressed it was equally important to acknowledge the macro political process that made it possible for all groups of Nicaragua to get together to begin such exchanges. The more pragmatic voices of both groups stressed the importance of the dialogue, not what brought them together.

The meeting ended with the pledge of both groups committing themselves to work cooperatively for the betterment of the community. Their first joint action was the sponsoring of two local baseball teams for the barrio.

Conclusion

If local politics were in the process of changing, as encouraged by the new CDS line we have summarized here, why did that not lead to more voters approving of the overall Sandinista positions?

Though the committee in the barrio was always active and had been quite successful in attaining programs for the barrio, they were always limited in terms of how many people they could mobilize within the barrio. General assemblies never were attended by more than fifty to sixty people. However, since they had assemblies every Friday night, this is not a bad turn out. For their barrio celebrations, especially the annual one for the martyrdom of William Diaz Romero, somewhere around 250 to 300 people would attend. However, out of a population of 4,000 that is a small percentage.

There are several factors here. One is that participation in the committee's affairs meant work. Those who attended would find themselves involved in activities that did require time and resources. This was a limiting factor. Another, was that many of the people who did attend and participate on a regular basis, were also people directly involved in projects of the barrio—such as the housing project—or who were militant Sandinista party members whose participation was also part of the party involvement. When people obtained what they needed from the committee, sometimes they would participate less. Ironically, since there was an active attempt to make committee activities less sectarian, many of the more militant party members limited their involvement so that others would take their place. That did not happen.

There was also a problem with factionalism and envy. At the personal level, at times people did not or could not get along with the members of the leadership of the committee. This produced different levels of resentment and would encourage others not to participate in barrio politics. Also, some people felt that those on the "in" of the committee were able to receive material benefits over others in the community. When the barrio received donations from solidarity groups, it was felt at times that the committee members got most of the "things" that were to go to the barrio. Here is an example of where participation in affairs had an effect. Sometimes the barrio committee would decide to give their "gifts" away to those present at a particular meeting. Thus, if you were a regular attender of meetings, you stood a chance of getting something which others who did not attend would not have a chance at. More often than not, the committee was fanatic about controlling all the donations and going through the most elaborate structures for distributing, sometimes taking months before "things" were distributed.

In the various cooperative buying groups, there were always the problems of collecting funds and distributing the materials. Many people felt forms of favoritism were emerging.

On the whole, we strongly feel that this expression of local politics and the empowerment was quite real at the level of barrio affairs and activities. Given all the problems that we have discussed throughout the chapter, in this barrio local political power was working.

Then why did the Sandinistas lose? Again, they lost the election, not the revolution. Clearly, what could not be affected at this level was the reality of the United States-backed war of aggression against the people of Nicaragua and how that war and the attempts by the government to deal with that war ruined the economy of the country. That did affect the barrio. They were being pressured also in this severe economic context.

The quality of their lives was being reduced. The streets of the barrio were in bad shape, the street lights did not work on all the streets, their schools were underfunded, their earnings were being restricted and reduced. People felt fearful—there was more crime, prices were high, and everything was hard or a hassle to get done. People were frustrated and tired. Since they were just as poor or poorer after ten years of revolution, some people began to wonder why they needed a revolution. These feelings and frustrations were often expressed within the area of these local political structures. Community leaders attempted over and over again to explain how the war and the economic crisis were generated by United States aggression. Perhaps they were too successful in their explanation. People in the barrio and around Nicaragua seemed to understand that reality and seemed to be willing to allow for macro political change to see if that could, in fact, make things better. We will all find out soon.

Notes

1. A profound component in the development of the popular revolution in Nicaragua is the development of social movements within the dynamics of mass organizations. Here we need to present a conceptual statement on what is meant by social movements and mass organizations. There is an emerging discourse on social action that reads social movements as collective actions attempting to alter the symbolic/social order of authority and power in post-modern society. Struggles for rights of women, ethnic self-determination, and concern for the ecology are movements which seek to radically alter the pre-suppositions of modernity. They are not always concerned with the control over production in the Marxist sense of class conflict, but in terms of redefining how the system operates in terms of social and personal liberties. For many, this includes material freedoms, but only as one of many liberties that have to be attained. For new social movements, actors are involved in dynamics that address collective dilemmas but incorporate personal domains as sources for having to resolve such dilemmas. That is, the women's movement does not exist simply to gain equal pay for equal work, but also to redefine what we mean by both work and equality. Such social movements do not neatly fit into the bi-polarity of left and right, but in fact also generate the redefining of political confrontation (Melucci 1989).

In the historical sense of mass organizations, especially within European leftist practices, mass organizations represent attempts by political parties to seek ways to control mass concerns by framing them as always an expression of some kind of class or economic contradiction. However, in Latin America over the last two decades, there has emerged a social/political discourse that has been defined as "popular." This discourse has emerged out of the fragmented social division of labor found throughout Latin America. The European model of class action has never fit in Latin America. Indians, Afro-Latinos, Europeans, Asians, Arabs, Jews, rural and urban poor Mestizos, highly diverse mercantile classes that are structured formally and informally, and social oligarchies of wealth are not reducible to workers versus owners of production. From the struggles of Bolivar to the triumph of the Sandinistas, struggles in the Americas have been a panorama of social actors with a concurrent variety of desires and aspirations attached to struggles of independence or nationhood. These struggles have always been dramas of multiple voices. Third World peoples are not immune from the libertarian hopes being declared for social movements. This panorama of actors within the popular struggle expresses the concerns of women, workers, ethnic and cultural groups, merchants, middle class, peasants and the urban poor. They have struggled to attain a new society, not through homogenous sectarian commands but through creative confrontation in rebuilding their society through the diversity of their unity. So that in the case of Nicaragua, mass organizations do not act as fronts for the Sandinista party. Instead they provide ordinary people—the masses—with a means for concrete political access based upon their maintenance of organizational structures designed to articulate their particular concerns—including their questions of autonomy and individualization (Envio 1990e:44). At this junction of Nicaragua's social history, these mass organizations seem to reflect what this new discourse on social movements is suggesting about the dynamics of social action in the postmodern world (Higgins 1990).

2. For more information on mass organizations and popular movements in Latin America see: Bartolome and Barabas, *La Dinamica Etnica en Oaxaca* (Mexico, D.F.: INAH, 1986), Coraggio, *Nicaragua: Revolution and Democracy* (London: Allen and Unwin, Inc. 1985) and "Social Movements and Revolution: The Case of Nicaragua" in *New Social Movements and the State in Latin American* (Holland: CEDLA Publications, 1985), Evers "Identity: The Hidden Side of Latin America" in *New Social Movements and the State in Latin American* (Holland: CEDLA Publications, 1985), Gonzales C., *El Poder al Pueblo* (Mexico,D.F., 1986), Harris and Vilas, *La Revolucion en Nicaragua* (Mexico,D.F: Ediciones Era, 1986), Henry, "Urban Social Movements in Latin America" in *New Social Movements and the State in Latin America* (Holland: CEDLA Publication, 1985,pp. 155–176), Hodges, *Intellectual Foundations of the Nicaraguan Revolution* (Austin: University of Texas Press, 1986), Melucci, *Nomads of the Present* (Phil.: Temple Univ. Press, 1989), and Slater, "Social Movements and a Recasting of the Political" in *New Social Movements and the State in Latin America* (Holland: CEDLA 1985, pp. 57–84).

3. Current commissions in the Comité del Barrio are health, social problems, housing, and cultural programs.

4. For the best analysis of CDS and other mass organizations in Nicaragua, see Gary Ruchwarger's book *People in Power* (South Hadley: Bergin and Garvey, 1987). Ruchwarger also has a new book out on a worker's farm cooperative in Nicaragua, *Struggling for Survival* (Boulder: Westview Press, 1989). Because of his long-term experiences in Nicaragua Ruchwarger is quite an insightful author on developing trends in Nicaragua.

5. For a good general review of problems with women, housing and development see Moser and Peaker, *Women, Human Settlements and Housing* (London: Tavistock Press, 1987). Also see Morales, Ardaya and Espinoza's work on squatter settlements in Managua ("Asentamientos Espontaneos No Son de la Crisis Urbana," in *Buletin Socio Economic,* INIES-April, Managua, Nicaragua, 1987).

¡Quiero Decir Esto!

6. For a more detailed analysis of problems of factionalism and favoritism in CDSs, see Ruchwarger's, *People in Power* (South Hadley: Bergin and Garvey, 1987).

7. This song is followed by a statement of El Secreto: "Various international organizations affirm that no government can by itself solve all problems. Even less so us, a poor developing country trying to fight a war. The secret is all of the people. The solution is to become like the ants. Unity is the force; unity can make peace.

"Now, more so than ever, there has to be an organization for the development of the community and, for this, you do not have to ask for the permission of anyone. Do not wait for someone else to arrive to organize. Meet in the streets yourselves.

"Do not be afraid to make mistakes; the only mistake is not to try. Organize as you wish, for what you wish. Work for the betterment of your community. The message is clear—unite the moros y cristianos (Moors and Christians).

"Do you all know how to shake? In the CDS we are shakers. The sum of all our efforts is to organize for results in our communities. The nails for these efforts are the committees for community development."

8. This was followed by another song entitled "Por Eso":

Young, old, and children of the barrio
Because we are many
Because we like our flock
The barrio is our place
For this, too, is also your place
We are all assembled together
A carnival of crazies
To make a fiesta, to give a little more
To burn the garbage
To play jambol with a rag ball
To vaccinate To run bag races
To reconstruct the school
So as not to loose classes
To organize groups of dancers
To make "maratones"
To make sports fields
To plant
To make poetry, as we can do
For happiness in these hard times

9. For a more detailed look at questions of gender and class with particular reference to Nicaragua, see Maier, Nicaragua, *La Mujer en la Revolucion* (Mexico, D.F.: Ediciones de Cultura, 1985); Molyneax, "Mobilization without Emancipation? Women's Interests, State and Revolution in Nicaragua," in *New Social Movements and the State in Latin America* (Holland: CEDLA Publications, 1985, pp. 123–154); Nicholson, *Feminism and Postmodernism* (New York: Routledge 1990), Stevens, "Women in Nicaragua," in *Monthly Review Press* Vol. 39-1-18 1987; and Vance "More Than Bricks and Mortar: Women's Participation in Self Help Housing in

Managua, Nicaragua," in *Women Human Settlements and Housing*, Moser and Peader, eds. (London: Tavistock Press, 1987).

10. See Massey, *Nicaragua* (Phil.: Open Univ. Press, 1988) and Moser and Peaker, *Women, Human Settlements and Housing*, eds. (London: Tavistock Press, 1987).

11. The barrio CDS now represents not only William Diaz Romero, but the members of barrios Martha A. Quezada, La Reforma, and El Carmen.

Orlando Garcia, the barrio coordinator for the "communal movement," accounts for medicine received from their Greeley, Colorado, sister-barrio organization.

Barrio residents known for participating in the insurrection against Somoza in 1979.

A local fruit and vegetable vendor.

Main street in barrio.

Final construction on the barrio's new basketball court.

Current contradictions of post-revolutionary Nicaragua: William Diaz Romero, a pro-Sandinista barrio, receives funding from the conservative city government for a basketball court. This sign shows the cost of the project.

Children awaiting packages of clothing, school materials, and toys brought down by sister-barrio delegates from Greeley, Colorado.

Director of Casa Nasaret, barrio elementary school, reviews plans made with barrio members and sister-barrio delegates about school's future needs.

A barrio woman and her grandchildren sit outside their house that also serves as a small store.

5

Afuera del Barrio

External Relations of the Barrio

In the summer of 1988 there was a health alert in the barrio concerning "dengue." Dengue is spread by mosquitos. The effects of dengue can be several days in bed for adults or, in the case of small children, death. The barrio residents organized themselves through their the CDS to deal with this health concern. The campaign was carried out over a weekend and the barrio was, for the time being, free from this health problem.

An organizational meeting was called at the local barrio level to deal with its own immediate and specific health concerns. The meeting was attended by all representatives of the pertinent health services, including the regional health center (centro de salud) director and some of her cohorts, as well as barrio-elected CDS members, including the locally elected coordinator of the CDS of Barrio William Diaz Romero, the local health coordinator of the CDS, volunteer health participants including trained youth "brigadistas" (youth who participate in work brigades), nurses who live and work in the barrio, and local community members.

In terms of the actual eradication procedure, it was important for all volunteers to know that dengue only infects clean water supplies. In order to participate in this eradication campaign, we joined a friend of ours, Francisco Perez, who was his local block coordinator.

We met Francisco on Saturday morning at the CDS building in the barrio. After filling two plastic containers with pesticide, we proceeded to the block of which he was coordinator. We went house to house introducing ourselves and explaining that there was a dengue alert. We explained that this was in response to high levels of mosquito larvae in the water systems of this barrio and that this information was derived from the monitoring that was done by the zonal health center (centro de salud) on a monthly basis and would be done in coordination with them. The majority of people we encountered were interested in what we were doing, allowed us in, and were for the most part amazingly cooperative. In only two cases were individuals hostile, wanting to have nothing to do with the whole process. Their attitude did not surprise or alarm Francisco. He explained to us that this type of reaction was

---

Translated from the Spanish, the chapter title means "Outside of the Barrio."

typical of these particular individuals. We were quite lavish as we dropped several spoonfuls of pesticide in all clean water storage areas such as the tanks of uncovered toilets, buckets of drinking water, showers, cement sinks used for doing laundry, and plant areas.

After we disinfected each house, we would record the amount of disinfectant used and in what places. These records were then turned back in at the end of each day to the zonal health worker. Most of the participants then gathered after finishing for the day to socialize and discuss how their days went. Copies of the results of each individual block were left with the barrio committee and a copy was taken by the zonal health workers back to the "Centro de Salud." The results were reported to the general barrio members at the following CDS meeting. Barrio coordinators then relayed the information back to their local blocks to individuals who may not have attended the barrio meeting.

—Field Notes, Managua, Nicaragua, 1988.

Introduction

In this chapter we wish to present the context of the external social, economic, political and cultural relations that affect the realities of everyday life in the barrio. The types of external relations we will present will involve patterns of interaction between the residents of the barrio, the city and region of Managua, national patterns, and international factors. This context of external relations is analyzed in terms of the goals of the popular revolution and what changes might be developing in the current post-revolutionary conditions.

At the city and regional level, we look at health and urban programs in relation to the barrio. At the national level we look at education, the legal system, the military, religion, cultural activities and politics. At the international level we look at commercial and economic factors that affect the barrio and how the international volunteer programs have affected this barrio.

City and Regional Relations

The structure and functions of city governments in Nicaragua are still in the process of development. The current municipal law (1988) establishes requirements for city councils, the mayor's office, and town meetings. In the case of Managua, the city council has twenty seats. Seats are attained by winning the majority in the national election. Thus, UNO currently has sixteen seats in the Managua city council. The city council, through information attained in town meetings, is to be the legislative body for the cities. The mayor's office is to be the executive or management office for the cities. Like most Latin American cities, city government revenues are limited to taxes attained at the municipal level (mainly taxes on market vendors) and what they get allocated by the federal government.

The mayor's office (before the elections) was in charge of health services and urban issues. Though the lines of authority were not clear because these agencies where also federal programs, it was the mayor's office where the barrio residents would go to lobby issues of health and housing. For example, it was to the city government that the barrio committee lobbied to get water pipes into their housing project. The barrio committee, more often than not, would lobby a particular agency in relation to a particular problem or attempt to use the zonal or regional offices of the CDS to solve problems. This was because there was no clear understanding of what city governments were supposed to do. During the Somoza era, all forms of political authority were centralized through the federal state. Up until the municipal law of 1988, the Sandinistas had attempted to use the mass organization and mayor's office as the base to city government. What the structure and function of city governments will be with UNO is not known.[1]

History of Health Care

Health Conditions and Programs: Somoza Era

The Somoza government, in power since 1934, was never very concerned about going beyond minimal public health care. Public health care was neglected, as was any other social service that might have benefitted the masses of peasants and urban workers (Eitel 1986:30). Providing services for the poor majority became mainly the task of charity organizations and various foundations which would provide minimal services funded with scarce resources from the state.[2]

Overall, the health system under Somoza was characterized by disorganization. "More than 24 institutions were involved in the management of health services" (Envio 1988a:24). Each of the organizations were autonomous in their financing and budgeting. This contributed to their fragmented, hence unintegrated approach. The system of vertical control "benefited from institutional fragmentation and made for ineffective hospital delivery" (Donahue 1986:13). "The lack of broad-based community participation in the health sector resulted in little accountability of the health professionals to the community" (Donahue 1986:13). Evidence of this is cited in a 1974 health sector assessment, stating "that the average health center was operating at about 40% capacity in terms of patient visits per medical hour" (Donahue 1986:14).

The countryside was a stark reality. The rural areas had no health facilities of any kind. People had to drive 50–80 miles to the nearest facilities in the city. In Somoza's time the gap in health care between rural and urban folks only widened (Envio 1988a:24).

Health Care After the Revolution

After the victory of the Sandinistas, the overall health care system was restructured in terms of the following set of assumptions:

1. Health is the right of all and the responsibility of the state.
2. Health services should be accessible to the whole population, with priority given to the mother/child relationship and to workers.
3. Medical services have an integral character: both individuals and the environment are to be treated.
4. Health work should be carried out by interdisciplinary teams.
5. Health care activity should be planned.
6. The community should participate in all of the health system's activities (Donahue 1986:14 and Envio 1988a:24).

Health care has been free or at very low cost and women have played a large part in this area. Women make up the majority of volunteers in the neighborhood level health campaigns and training programs. This is still seen primarily as a women's issue. Reproductive rights and child care have been issues that have been especially asserted by women since 1979 and recently debated in the open forums discussing the new constitution. The majority of Nicaraguan women still expressed a wish for bearing children. Their concerns primarily involve a desire for more control over the timing and number of their pregnancies. Many of these constraints are war-induced, such as a shortage of contraceptives along with other medical supplies and lack of sufficient numbers of child care centers (Perez 1988).

As mentioned above, priority was given to the mother/child relationship. An important battle was directed at decreasing the amount of infant deaths from dehydration, a result of diarrhea. Some of the most dramatic accomplishments were the creation in 1980 of Oral Rehydration centers to deal with the serious problem of infant mortality due to diarrhea. By 1986 the creation of primary care units went from 189 to 606. The number of doctors increased by 58%, and nurses by 211%. Medical consultations increased 300% and infant mortality dropped from 120 per thousand to 69. The prevalence of infant deaths from diarrhea has decreased by a third (Scrimshaw and Hurtado 1988:97–104).

The accomplishments of the Nicaraguan health field are enormous for eleven years, as are the problems which still confront them (Ortega 1988). To transform an entire society from one like Nicaragua in which only an elite few had access to leadership and decision-making power, economic resources, and education to one in which everyone is given access to these things and are even granted the right to them is a complex task. "It creates rising expectations among the population and ever-expanding responsibilities for the state" (Envio 1988a:27).[3]

Health Care Activities in the Barrio

One of the permanent commissions of the barrio committee is that of health coordinator. The health coordinator is elected and works with a support group and the volunteer brigadistas. It is the responsibility of the coordinator to be in charge of general health issues of the barrio. The coordinator is supposed to maintain a census of health levels in the barrio, maintain contacts with the public health service, and mobilize the barrio around particular health issues or alerts (such as the dengue alert). A strong example of this is how vaccination campaigns are pursued.

The health coordinator of the barrio, in coordination with personnel from the nearest health center and numerous volunteer brigadistas carry out these vaccination campaigns for both dogs and children. In these campaigns, children are vaccinated for polio, measles, and D.P.T. These elected members, health officials, and volunteers also handle basic education, training, and treatment around diarrhea and the eradication of dengue. Dogs are vaccinated against rabies (Coen 1988).

In Barrio William Diaz Romero, the majority of volunteers are women. Due to the "double shift" (women are still the primary domestic laborers and caretakers of children), many women are unable to fully participate in the life of the grassroots organizations. However, for this reason, women participate more in their barrios than outside of them because they are close by and more accessible. These primarily women volunteers range in age from about 13–16 year old youth brigadistas (all female), to older women including several nuns who live in a convent in the barrio, a variety of other women volunteers from nurses to militant Sandinistas, current and ex-CDS board members, to an entire cadre of community members who frequently participate in barrio activities (females and males) (Coen 1988).[4]

Like the dengue campaign, the whole of these activities are planned at the National and Regional levels as well as at the local level. Interpersonally, these activities are primarily coordinated between several (generally between one and five individuals) from the zonal health center and the local barrio residents. Tania Perez, the director of the zonal health center is extremely energetic, accessible, and involved in all of these activities. She is visible and can be seen at many of the local barrio's organizational meetings exchanging ideas, listening to local participants, and just interacting in general (Coen 1988).

Given all of this, Barrio William Diaz Romero is reasonably healthy. This context is currently constrained by general and material scarcity and sky rocketing and rapid inflation and, by an inadequate supply of volunteers, community members, and health personnel to staff it. For the most part, the health of the barrio members and access to health services is adequate. There are definitely barrios in Managua which are worse off. Finally, the success of maintaining and improving the general health context of the barrio will be framed by the overall social/political context.

Current Conditions: 1990-1992

The last few sentences were written before the election of February 25, 1990. The structure and quality of the national health system was one of the main campaign issues. The Sandinistas wanted to continue the program as was, but with more grassroots support. This was beginning before the election. As was described in the previous chapter, the barrio had been able to attain a pre-natal clinic. UNO's health platform was to restructure the health services into a three-tiered system. They wanted to eliminate the requirement of social service for physicians. The current system requires the majority of physicians to work within some part of the public health system in addition to whatever private work they wanted to do. UNO also wanted to reintroduce a social security health program that would only cover certain types of job classification with workers paying for this system through wage deductions. The third part is to be a general public health service for those who could not afford private care or were not covered by social security.

The barrio committee has completed its community house and has moved its pre-natal clinic into it. This clinic has been staffed by a doctor and nurse and was open in the mornings Monday through Saturday. The barrio had to provide the space and food for the staff and public health paid the wages of the staff.[5]

Urban Renewal and Housing

Like their health accomplishments, the residents of the barrio consider the success in getting their housing project moving as a major accomplishment. The general dynamics of the project have been described in previous chapters; here we will focus on how this project was articulated to regional housing and urban policy in Managua.[6] Until 1989 housing and urban issues were handled by MINVA, which was the national and regional housing agency. This was a massive assignment. The Somoza dictatorship, the earthquake of 1972, the final years of the insurrection, the period of reconstruction, and the Contra war taxed the limited housing material needs for the whole country. The Sandinistas had made housing and land a priority for people. The land reform programs were particularly rural, with housing concerns focused on urban areas. We do not know that much about the agrarian reform, since it did not directly affect residents of the barrio.[7] In terms of urban and housing issues, the barrio was directly affected. In Managua, regional plans and projects went through three phases. First was the attempt to evaluate housing needs and develop strategies that could meet such needs. Besides the pressing need of houses was the problem of land status. Land status had two factors: ownership and geological quality. Ownership questions involved vacant land and unoccupied houses. Vacant land often becomes the areas for the construction of squatter settlements or as they were called in Managua "spontaneous communities" (Morales, Ardaya, and Espinoza 1987). The barrio of William Diaz Romero did not have any squatters of this type. What could be perhaps seen as squatters were the number of people who pay little or no rent. The vast majority of low income urban residents in Managua lived previously during the Somoza era in very minimal living conditions and paid very high rents. In the first years of the revolution, MINVA was able to freeze rents for the majority of renters. One factor that allowed many of the households in the barrio to survive was that they often paid no rent or an amount that was next to nothing. Households like Rosa's, Mabel's, Maria Felix's and Ephraine's paid almost no rent. There was an interesting twist to this law. Renters could not be evicted for any reason unless they had alternate housing available, which could include land to build a house on. Several persons who had received land in the housing project, found themselves being evicted from their rented houses before they could build their new houses.

The question of the geological quality of the land refers to the massive number of fault lines that occur across the region of Managua. The majority of land is on some kind of fault line. MINVA attempted to remove settlements from the most dangerous areas and relocate people to safer areas. With the large growth of the city, it proved nearly impossible to carry out such programs.

The next phase of urban planning was the attempt to develop organized housing projects. A large project was built with the aid of the Soviets near the old center of the city. These are two and three story buildings, with four to six units per building. However, since they were in areas with little or no services, they were not very popular. Also, most of the projects were conceived with the "honda" of the planners. That is, the planners felt that they knew what kind of housing the people needed better than the people, a general fault of urban planners wherever they are found. This possible conflict was avoided because of the war and the economy. Such "planned urban" communities were not economically possible. No such projects were attempted in the barrio. A second, more moderate urban planning style was developed that was referred to as the site service project. The government would provide land, and access to materials to build homes that would all be alike. The housing style that emerged from this plan is referred to as mini-falda (mini-skirt) for the base was built of cement blocks and top half was built of wood. This approach reflected better centralized planning, but was also severely limited by the war.

The third phase of the urban plan was to aid communities with the legal process to land and services. From this point communities themselves planned how they wished to develop their own projects. This is what took place in Barrio William Diaz Romero, and the dynamics we have presented in the other chapters.

In this third phase, an interesting political dynamic developed. In the latter part of 1988/89 the program of "compactacion" had eliminated MINVA. Questions of housing and urban development now were part of the city and regional government of Managua. Thus, to attain land titles and access to social services (lights, water, sewage, etc.) communities and their organizations would have to lobby the city urban agency now. There emerged a process where supporters of the revolution—such as committee and CDS regional advisors—were attempting to create grassroots strategies to push and protest the bureaucratic inertia of government structures that they were in support of. In the summer of 1989, those residents who had finished their homes, found that the water service that MINVA had promised was not there and that they would have to pay a lot more than they had planned in order to get water services. The residents again had to develop cooperative buying plans and strategies for obtaining water from the city government. It always interested and baffled us that the Sandinistas never seemed to have the political means to fully control the bureaucracy of the systems they were thought to be so in control of. This not only baffled us, but also baffled the community. However, it did reinforce for community members the fact that it was grassroots actions, not government agencies, that would solve their problems.

Housing needs will remain a critical problem for this community. Of the 42 lots allocated out in the project, about half of the people have finished and are living in the houses. Houses are in various stages of completion and have various stages of municipal services. As is common in the third world, those who have electricity and water share or sell it to their neighbors. For various reasons there has been little attempt by the current urban authorities to stop this. It remains to be seen what the new government agency will do. People in the barrio have been given other areas of land to build on and more families are attempting to build homes. From the summer of 1989 through the election of February 25, 1990, the current government has been ceding deeds to land directly to people. The

TABLE 5.1 Schools in the Barrio (school data, 1988)

Escuela Casa Nasaret	San Pancho
preschool--72	1st -- 182
1st --77	2nd -- 106
2nd --73	3rd -- 82
3rd --46	4th -- 123
4th --37	5th -- 81
5th --62	6th -- 69
6th --62	TOTAL 643
TOTAL 429	
Number of teachers: 13	Number of teachers: 26
With titles - 4	With titles - 6
Those in process of completing degrees - 2	

Totals are combined from the double session they offer.

original plan was that land was to be paid for over a twenty-year period at a low cost. The status of that plan is unclear with the ceding of land deeds. The biggest problem for everyone was the cost of building materials and access to them. With the new government, access to materials might be better (there had been a priority on sending materials to war areas over Managua) but we doubt that prices or earning power of the residents will be much different. Whether the new government will continue these types of urban programs or develop new ones remains to be seen. What they could do differently is hard to imagine. That they could do more would be appreciated by lower income groups, but such hopes are limited at best.[8]

Education

One of the major achievements of the Sandinista revolution was the opening up of education for the whole population of the country.[9] Educational development and access before the revolution was only for the middle class and above. Making the population literate was one of the main goals of the revolution. This was carried out through mass literacy campaigns, the development of adult education programs, and providing a context that would encourage people to value education. By the mid-1980's, there were over 1,000,000 people involved in some kind of formal education in Nicaragua. Like all other forms of social services, education in the latter part of the 80's began to suffer the effects of the war and economy. All schools faced the combined problems of limited basic school supplies, lack of space and development of educational facilities, and very low wages for educational workers. This can be shown by looking at the two primary schools in the barrio (Table 5.1).

Barrio Schools

Casa Nasaret has nicer physical conditions than San Francisco (commonly referred to as San Pancho). Both have very limited materials for use in the class room. A good job was attempted by all in very limited conditions.

Both schools in the barrio were affiliated with the Catholic church. San Pancho was located on the ground of the San Francisco Church. Casa Nasaret was located in a convent and orphans school. San Pancho ran three sessions; two during the day for children and one session at night for adults. San Pancho is a row of classrooms along a long corridor. There is an open play area for the students that is all dirt. The classrooms are very basic. They are open on one side with big windows looking out towards the play grounds. There are wooden chairs for the students, chalk boards in the front, and some space for bulletin boards. Roofs are of corrugated metal and the windows are louvered with slots. The classrooms and grounds are not very pretty or rustic. All of the materials and equipment are old and worn down. Both students and faculty have limited supplies. However, the "honda" (general ambiance) in the classroom was quite dynamic. Teachers worked quite hard to teach and students responded in kind. Classrooms were crowded and active. Students tend to gender segregate themselves, but were quite kinetic in the classroom. That is to say they did not remain in their seats very long. Teaching methods were somewhat traditional in terms of lectures, reactions, working problems on the chalk board, and writing assignments. The curriculum had been developed in cooperation between teachers, the ministry of education and local committees. However, in Barrio William Diaz Romero, there was not a great deal of interaction between the school, its projects, and those of the barrio. This was more of a factor of overload of needs and concerns for both groups and the dilemma of time needed to work together on common projects.

Current Conditions, 1990-1992

In the ten years of the revolution, Nicaraguans in general and people in the barrio in particular have become committed to the assumption that education is important and that all people should have access to education. Numerous families in the barrio have had members attain levels of professional education unattainable before the revolution. However, the concurrent problems of the war and the economy have left the material conditions of schools in very sad condition. Both of the schools in the barrio are underfunded and understaffed. Most of the more middle class families in the barrio, in fact, send their children by bus to private schools outside the barrio.

The school structure in Nicaragua involves six years of primary school, three of secondary, and then entrance into professions. All these levels of education have been free and have had open enrollment. There are special school programs for young students who have to work during the day. There are a limited number of day care facilities. There are none in the barrio. For those students who enter the university, there have been numerous opportunities for them to study overseas, especially in the existing socialist countries. The primary limitation in all these areas of education has been economic, that is, the lack of funds.[10]

Police and Legal System

During the Somoza dictatorship there was no police force in Nicaragua only the National Guard. After the victory, the Sandinista government had to set up a police force for domestic concerns such as traffic control, control of crime, and all those other things that police do. The police force was named the Sandinista Police force. It was localized to each large community. The government attempted to put together a police force that was responsive to local concerns, that was courteous and polite and, when possible, unarmed. Contrary to outside press accounts, they were very successful. Throughout Managua the police were affectionately referred to as "los dulces": the sweet ones. The Ministry of Interior was in charge of the development of this police force. Within the Ministry of Interior was also a police force that dealt with national security issues. This was the force that dealt with the problems of the "contras." The legal system involved an independent judicial branch. The overall system was a mixture of structures influenced by United Statesian and European models. The state acts as the prosecutor, and all defendants had rights of fair trial and representation by a lawyer. A high court system could overrule lower court decisions. In the war areas, ad hoc legal structures were put in place to deal with the immediate problems of contra activity. This is no longer in existence.

In the barrio people also saw the police as "los dulces." For people in the barrio the biggest concern was crime in the street. When we first visited Nicaragua (1984), Managua was one of the safest cities that we had experienced. However by 1987, urban crime had become a major problem. The bus lines were infested with pickpockets, robberies on the streets were common, and burglary seemed to be one of the major jobs in the informal sector. The barrio was particularly affected by this rise in crime because many of its commercial enterprises served the international community which was a primary target for the robbers. We have noted before, the barrio was the location for numerous boarding houses and cafeterias that served the internationalists. Boarding houses were often robbed on a monthly basis. One heard weekly accounts of people robbed on the street. In 1988, after a national baseball game (the stadium is near the barrio), a young woman from Denmark was killed on the street during a robbery. In the barrio, everyone maintained various complex systems of security to prevent robberies. The most common form of security was making sure that someone was always at home.

The cause for the increase in crime, again, was the war and the war's effect on the economy. It was easier and more profitable to attempt to steal one's earnings than to work. This was a problem that local residents and police worked closely on to seek solutions. Success had been minimal. Thus, unfortunately in this area, Managua is like many other capitol cities of the Third World and the developed world. However, crimes of propriety were more than crimes of violence.[11]

Military

Under the Sandinistas there were three levels to the military. There were local volunteer brigades which were the first line of defense against contra attacks. There had been such units in Managua in the early 1980's, but they had not been operational during our time in Managua. The second level were regional militia that were staffed by volunteers and reservists. The third level was the national army, the Popular Sandinista Army. This was the level of the professional army in which all males over sixteen years of age were subject to the draft. Women were all volunteers. It was the professional army that confronted and fought the Contras.

Military Relations in the Barrio

In the barrio everyone had some kind of relation with the military. This ranged from those who had fought in the insurrection, to reservists, to lifers, and young males who had been drafted. Though the barrio had a high number of young people who volunteered before they were drafted, people did not particularly like the idea of young children having to deal with the army because of the war. However, many people in the barrio had made the military their career. As in the U.S. the military offered many people a means to various forms of job training, whether it be in skilled jobs (welding) or using the military to stay abroad at a university level. Also, the military was a steady job with good benefits. Because of the age distribution in the barrio during the time we were there, not many of the young males were drafted. (They were too young or they had done their time in the early 80's.) More fortunately, few deaths were recorded in the barrio from having to fight the contras. However, everyone knew someone or had some "primo" or "tio" that had been affected by the war.

Also, some of the better-off families would get their children out of the country to avoid the draft.

For barrio residents the biggest problem with the military was the activities of off-duty military personnel. Mainly this involved circumstances relating to a law against serving liquor to any military personnel in uniform. However, since the barrio had many commercial activities that served liquor, military personnel sometimes could be found in these bars. People would often register complaints with the barrio committee over people who would illegally sell liquor to military personnel in uniform. Outside of this, we did not encounter any anti-military feelings. Like attitudes toward the police, military personal were seen as important and cooperative members of the community. People also respected the difficult and dangerous job they were doing in the war against the Contras. Though many worried about the draft of their children, they perceived those who attempted to avoid the draft very negative. Though there was no chapter of "Mothers of Heros and Martyrs" of the War, mothers of fallen soldiers were given a great deal of respect in the barrio.

Current Conditions, 1990-1992

The issues over the organization and future of the military are very sensitive and complex. Humberto Ortega has been retained by the new government as the provisional head of the military. Dona Chamorro has made herself minister of the Department of Defense. Also, for obvious reasons, the new government has been able to end the draft for now. Further, both the Sandinistas and the UNO have signed various agreements with the Contras over their demobilization. However, it still is not clear when and if they will demobilize themselves. Dona Chamorro says that metal from the guns must be melted down for machines and plows to rebuild the economy. This was what the people and the Sandinistas had always hoped for (Envio 1990b:3-18).[12]

Cultural Relations

In this section, we present various impressions of what we refer to as cultural activities. We are referring to those macro expressions of activities—beliefs, rituals, events, etc.—that have national character to them. These activities are not "indigenous" to the barrio, though these residents have their own constructions and interpretations of them. Thus, using the residents' views we separate these cultural relations into two categories: cosmopolitan and popular.

Cosmopolitan Cultural Activities

Don Orlando, during a barrio discussion group suggested that the barrio population was very cosmopolitan because it was surrounded by many cultural institutions, such as the radio station, research institutions, cultural centers, and recreational areas. This comment was met with skepticism, especially by Maritza—a professor of sociology—who thought that such a comment was some kind of crude determinism. However, Orlando did have a point of sorts. If there are cosmopolitan features to Managua, then many are in fact located near the barrio. On the borders of the barrio are located several research centers, the cultural workers' center of Managua, a couple of radio stations, and the national baseball park. The rate of interaction between most barrio residents and these institutions is quite limited; however, there are some forms of interaction. We would like to briefly present examples, but stress that this is an area that is marginal to the activities of the majority of the residents of the barrio.

Barrio Seminars. During the latter part of the summer of 1988, the barrio committee organized two seminars. The first was on the definition of socialism in Nicaragua and the other was on the history of the barrio itself. These took place on two Saturday afternoons in the meeting room of the committee. The seminars were attended by about ten to twelve people each time. The first meeting, dealing with socialism in Nicaragua was a discussion led by Hugo. He gave a long talk on the overall Frente position on socialism, which stresses that socialism was part of a general strategy for national sovereignty and self determination. This was followed by vigorous discussions between those attending on how socialism could be built into such a program in a country as poor as Nicaragua and what was socialist about Nicaragua currently with all the existing wealth differences present.

From this discussion came the idea to use the seminar approach to look at the history of the barrio itself. The following Saturday this session was held. About twenty plus people showed up for this session. This was quite a lively session with different residents having different views on the barrio's history. Maritza presented a lengthy discussion on the barrio's history particularly focusing on the period of Somoza and the insurrection. She had stated that the barrio had not been very progressive during the Somoza period, with little or no union activities going on. Manuel and Orlando both challenged that assumption, stating that they had both been active in union work during that time. Manuel stressed how he had been a union organizer in the barrio. In fact, most of the afternoon discussions got taken up by everyone contesting everyone else's particular micro views of barrio history. It was quite lively and was an enjoyable interchange for those involved. The national CDS had been encouraging barrio CDSs to form such discussion groups to get communities interested in doing their own analysis and research on both national and local issues. Though these sessions in the barrio were limited in terms of attendance, they did illustrate a level of skill and interest that was impressive. Especially in terms of the barrio's history, people seemed to really enjoy this arena of action.

Center for Cultural Workers. On the west end of the barrio's boundaries is located the Center for Cultural Workers. This elegant complex, lush with tropical foliage and contemporary brick buildings, houses a public art gallery, the national dance school, artisan shops, and a restaurant and coffee house. During the week various cultural events are presented at the center. Most often these are musical concerts. On Wednesday nights a reggae concert was presented. On the weekends it would be jazz or folk music. The admission to get into these concerts was high—several thousand cordobas depending on the current exchange rate. The primary clientele of these concerts were the young bohemian intellectual crowd of Managua, internationalists, and a few folks just looking for live music. Very few barrio residents attended. We took Consuelo several times to hear reggae concerts at the center. Though she seemed to enjoy the music, she was not too impressed with the "honda" of the place. For her, it was too middle class.

Sometimes residents would visit an art show there or attend special events sponsored by the center, such as a corn fiesta where all the different types of typical food dishes from corn were served. More frequently, barrio residents would use the park in front of the center or visit the grounds of the center. However, though the center was literally in the barrio's backyard, it is not part of the overall social space that the residents of the barrio use.

Research Centers. On the east end of the barrio, near the Hotel Intercontinental, are located several research centers of Managua. Because this is an upper class residential area, several of the larger houses or buildings were appropriated to house different types of agencies. Thus, near the barrio you can find the Institute of Economic and Social Research (INIES), the Center for Political Sciences Research (CRIES), the Center for the Study of Sandinismo (CES), and several other centers of this type. Though many of these centers conduct or sponsor research on topics of direct relevance to residents of the barrio, there is almost no interaction between the barrio and these agencies. This is an area that we have attempted to promote, but with little success so far. In the spring of 1988 we attended two workshops at INIES on housing, squatter settlements, and political action. INIES had just finished the first part of their investigation on squatter settlements in Managua. They found what many had found out about squatter settlements in other parts of Latin America. Squatter communities were not disorganized communities, but the exact opposite (Higgins 1974). However, what was most interesting about these workshops was who attended them. Those in attendance were researchers from INIES, other visiting social scientists, members of the city housing authorities and residents from the squatter settlements around Managua. This made for very lively and animated discussions. Further, it allowed for direct interaction between all these sectors and for the conveying of each other's points of view. This kind of encounter would have been useful for residents in the barrio. Often the barrio committee would have agency representatives come to the barrio to explain and give advise on barrio projects. However, these always had time and space constraints upon them. It would have been interesting to see such an exchange in a more relaxed atmosphere. However, though quite politically sophisticated, some barrio residents often felt a certain class bias in such interactions, that is a class bias directed toward them.

Women's International Solidarity Night with Nicaragua. In the spring of 1988, the International Women in solidarity with the Revolution sponsored a night with AMNLAE, the women's organization of Nicaragua. This was to be a social night and a chance for international women to exchange ideas with AMNLAE and for AMNLAE to explain its current projects. The international women were women who had been working in Nicaragua for several years in various solidarity projects. This was an event open to the general public. However, those in attendance were very similar to crowds at the cultural center. We invited Consuelo to go with us to this event. She was excited. She hoped this would bring women of various class backgrounds together. However, she did not like the event. She perceived most of the people there—both internationalists and Nicaraguans—as middle class and having no real interests in the working class people. Though in fact she had no way of knowing if her perceptions were accurate, she felt uncomfortable and we left halfway through the program.

Popular Cultural Relations

By popular cultural relations we are illustrating those activities that many people in the barrio perceive and act upon as part of their normal lives in one fashion or another. These range from going to baseball games, to sponsoring fiestas, to collecting funds for funerals.

The National Baseball Stadium. On the northern boundary of the barrio is located the national baseball stadium. This is a very attractive stadium and holds about 15,000 people. National baseball championship tournaments are held there and also international baseball competitions. Baseball is the national passion of Nicaragua, a true cultural phenomenon. Thus, this is clearly a cultural resource center that the residents of the barrio often use. Though they cheered their home teams on, there were not many die-hard supporters. We went with the Curtis family to a baseball tournament involving several Central American and Caribbean teams. Cuba had sent on its "B" teams to this tournament. We went to see the Cubans play against the Nicaraguan "A" team. By the third inning, the Cubans were leading by about 10 runs. Without remorse Nicaraguans started evacuating the stadium. We left along with the Curtises.

Popular Media. The only national cultural event that can compete with baseball would be the nightly "telenovelas" (soap operas) on television. At least in Managua, it seems that everyone is at home between 7:00 P.M. to 8:00 P.M. to watch the current soap opera. These are imports, with the ones from Brazil being the most popular. The rest of Nicaraguan television consists of some new programs, endless reruns of U.S. shows (*Dukes of Hazard, Moonlighting,* etc.), sporting events, and some educational programs. Also popular are local variety programs where people dance and lip-sync to their favorite songs and groups.

There are numerous radio stations. Most play contemporary pop music from Latin America and the United States. You do not hear a lot of contemporary Nicaraguan music on the radio.

There are three national newspapers: *Barricada, Nuevo Diaro,* and *La Prensa*. Since the election of February 25, 1990, the statuses of these newspapers have switched. Now *La Prensa* expresses the views of the current government, and the *Barricada* and the *Nuevo Diario* are the papers of the Sandinista opposition. With the exception of the screaming headlines and opposing editorial positions, the papers are very similar. They all have limited international news, intensive coverage of events in Managua, attempts at regional news, and very large sports sections with detailed coverage of all forms of baseball. There are some national magazines and some comic books. People in the barrio read all three newspapers on a regular basis. The pro-Sandinista papers come out in the morning whereas *La Prensa* is an afternoon paper.

Many people in the barrio like to read and have their own personal libraries. Peoples' interests run from contemporary writers like Galeano to historical, technical, and recreational material. This is also an expression of the mixed-class composition of the barrio. People like Hugo and Mabel are avid readers of anything they can get. Poorer or more marginal people, because of limits to their literacy, obviously do not use reading as a form of recreation.

Belief Systems About Health and Curing

Among the residents of the barrio there are not richly developed expressions of Meso-American cultural beliefs in the domain of health and curing. This is partially due to the urban quality of the residents, many of whom have gone through some kind of formal education that discourages such beliefs and to the fact that, throughout Nicaragua, such belief systems are not as richly developed as one would find in Mexico or Guatemala. This comes from the destruction of the Native American population during the colonial period. We had a hard time getting people to talk about such beliefs. People would say that only older people still believed in those kinds of ideas. There is limited organized discourse around such concepts as illness, curing, witches, and spirits as you would find in Mexico; nor is it very common for there to be any social roles like "curanderos" or "brujas" assigned to people in the barrio. We will summarize what limited information we did attain.[13]

Mal de Ojo (Evil Eye)

This is an illness that adults can indirectly give to children. It causes fever and nausea in the child. It is cured through wrapping the child in the clothing of the person(s) who gave the child the "eye."

Ojo Rosa (Pink Eye)

This is pink eye, the same aliment that we refer to by that name. They suggest that there are several herbs that can be used to cure this in a child.

Puje (Colic)

This seems to be some kind of intestinal ailment that small babies get, and it is very common. It sounds to us a lot like what North Americans refer to as colic in babies. Puje can be caused by strong winds hitting the child or the wrong kinds of foods being given to the child. Puje is also cured with various herb treatments.

Assorted Ailments

There are an assortment of ailments that people in the barrio say thàt they have heard of but are not too familiar with. For example, fallen fontanel, mal aire (bad air), or susto (fright). They know of these but have no specific cure for them or suggest that they do not exist anymore. There is a weakly developed hot/cold discourse on foods and activities; it is suggested that mixing hot foods (pork) with cold activities (bathing) can cause illness. There are some views on things that women should not do during menstruation (no bathing) and some ideas on the restriction of women after birthing, but again these are not well developed. We found that most of the references to witchcraft were in terms of the stereotypes barrio residents had about people from the Atlantic Coast (who are Indian or Black) or about people from Masaya, a Pacific coast town near Managua. These references were generally in terms of potions that could be used to make people fall in love with each other. Also, no one expressed beliefs in animal spirit companions (Higgins 1974).[14]

Calendar of Events

In terms of public rituals and celebrations in the barrio, the residents follow general national patterns. Below we will present a list of the major public celebrations and then a short description of the kinds of fiestas that people celebrate.[15]

Jan. 1	New Year's celebrations and the procession of Christ the King
Feb. 14	Day of the Lovers (Valentine's Day)
March 8	International Day of Women
March and April (varies yearly)	Semana Santa. This is Easter week. In Managua this is celebrated through processions and special masses in the churches. Though in fact this is the time when, if possible, everyone heads for some body of water, because this is also national vacation time.
May 1	International Day of the Workers
May 30	Mother's Day
June	Fiestas of San Luis, San Juan, and San Pedro (regional saints)
July 19	For the Sandinistas, the celebration of the revolution
Aug 1–5	Fiesta of Santo Domingo
Sept. 15	Central America Independence Day
Oct. 4	Fiesta of Santo Francisco (Saint of the barrio, though there is no organized celebration in the barrio)
Nov. 2–3	Days of the Dead
Nov. 28 through Dec. 24	Christmas celebrations, with Dec. 8, the day of the feast of the immaculate conception of Mary (la Purisima), the most popular event in Managua during these celebrations.

Household Fiestas

The most common fiestas occurring in the barrio were for birthday parties for small children. For us, these were kind of interesting. First, they would sing happy birthday in English. They would have pinatas, but when the children would get their turn to try to hit the pinata, they had to dance along to a salsa tune that would be playing. Also, guests were usually given gifts to take home.

We went to one celebration of a "quinceanera" a fifteenth birthday party for a young woman. Mabel and Noel threw a "quinceanera" for their oldest daughter, Noelia. This was quite an affair. Noelia wore a fancy dress. They had a mass, and put on a very large party at Mabel's friends house outside of the barrio. These are generally quite elaborate and expensive affairs for families to sponsor, and thus are not very common.

Funerals are also a form of a fiesta in the barrio. Caskets are placed at the home of the family. It is put in the front room where the immediate family sits by the coffin accepting the greetings from visitors. The barrio committee for the one we attended collected funds to help the family with the cost of the wake. People sat with the coffin throughout the night. The next day was the burial. Those not of the immediate family sit outside of the house, talking, drinking, and playing cards.

The other most common forms of fiestas in the barrio were different types of fund raisers. The committee or the school would have a party, where people would bring food and the group would sell beer to attempt to raise funds.

Also near the barrio was a public recreational facility where large popular dances were held and various sporting events. Depending on the cost of the admittance, young people from the barrio would attend.

In terms of representing activities that would express forms of cultural activities that are more richly textured, we present in some detail a description of popular religious events both in Managua and the barrio.

Popular Religion in Nicaragua

Among the urban popular classes in Managua, popular religion involves the blending of theological and popular concerns. This can be illustrated by looking at the fiesta of Santo Domingo and the celebration of the Martyr of the Barrio William Diaz Romero.

The Fiesta of Santo Domingo

The fiesta of Santo Domingo begins on August 1st and lasts throughout the week. The history of this fiesta goes back to the turn of the century and its organization is associated with a famed homeopathic curer of that time (Lancaster 1988). The fiesta of Santo Domingo begins with the arrival of the image of the Saint in the city from its village residence. The image of the Santo Domingo appears in Managua on August 1st and, at the end of the week, the Saint is returned to its village location. During the week that the Saint is in the city, there are numerous folkloric events taking place in the church courtyard.

What makes these fiestas of Santo Domingo interesting is the large following they have and the style and structure of the procession that brings the Saint into the city. This is a major summer event for the residents of Managua. It is a constant source of conversation for weeks before the event.

Mabel Curtis and her family attended the procession of Santo Domingo this year. They walked several blocks to the bus stop and, with the luck of the day, caught a bus that was not full. They went toward the main avenue (near the city market) where the Saint was to pass. Noel, Mabel, and the children began to search for the best place to sit and watch the procession. Several blocks down the street, they selected a small bluff where they joined numerous others who had already selected their seating. There were several thousand people in and on the street. The procession was still several hours away and many people were walking towards the procession to join it. From a village some 20 kilometers outside of Managua, more than 20,000 have been marching since late the night before. This procession brings the Saint into the city, places him on a large float in the shape of a boat, and then proceeds to the church.

The street scene is quite similar to religious fiestas in Mexico. There seem to be just as many vendors as spectators. People were there for the carnival quality of the event rather than the religious experience. Most of the people in the street and those watching seemed to be working class or rural peoples. Noel and Mabel's children were running about buying candy and playing various children's games. They were joined by several members of Noel's family who lived nearby.

Similar to other religious processions involving Saints or Virgins in Mexico and Central America, many people participated in order to repay favors granted by the Saint or Virgin. In Managua, those who have to show their faithfulness to the Saint do this with two types of costumes, either as a black native American or as what looks like a Plains Native American costume, except for the nose plugs.

The black native American costume is the following: whether adult or child, the person is dressed in a small skirt and wears numerous necklaces; the entire body is blackened with something referred to as burnt oil. This custom creates a second novel item, the attempt to spread oil on those watching the procession. Young children and adolescents will cover their hands with this burnt oil and then attempt to spread it on the faces of those watching the procession or those walking toward it. Most of these attempts are treated humorously and are seen as part of the event. The costumes of those dressed like Plains Native Americans involve the following; large headdress of feathers, leggings, nose plugs, numerous necklaces, vests of feathers, and carrying of bows and arrows.

At about 2:00 in the afternoon, the procession passed by where the Curtises were sitting. There seemed to be some 40,000 people in the streets. At least a third of the people in the procession seemed to be in the costumes described above. Many people were carrying "calindas." These "calindas" are large paper mache heads of cows, pigs, and other domestic animals which are carried in the procession. There are also paper mache "calindas" of very large women and the devil, in the form of "torros." There were also numerous people lighting sky rockets. In the middle of the procession, came the Saint himself. He is carried on a large platform with many flowers and candles by some ten or twelve people. The Saint sits inside a glass vessel. Its overall size cannot be more than ten inches in height.

Santo Domingo has "palanca" (personal power) similar to that of the people. He has the power to concretely help people with their material concerns. He encourages his faithful to express their devotion in outlandish costumes (like the painting of the body with burnt oil) or through rituals which reverse the common social order (the domination of the devil and large women "calindas" in the procession). Santo Domingo's "palanca" involves reminding the popular classes that the hegemony of the accepted social order is contestable (Lancaster 1988).[16]

The Barrio's Celebration

Ruth Arena was a member of this year's planning commission for the barrio's celebration of the martyrdom of William Diaz Romero. This position also involves being part of the general committee of the barrio (CDS). From this committee, Ruth and several others were chosen to plan this year's celebration. The martyrdom of William Diaz Romero is a very concrete reality for Ruth. All of her children participated in the insurrection and, from her view, by the grace of God they all survived. Others were not so lucky as Ruth's children. Over 40,000 "fell" during the insurrection (Massey 1988). Throughout Nicaragua, one finds schools, parks, factories, streets, and communities that are named after the thousands that died to build the new Nicaragua. William Diaz Romero was not the only martyr in the barrio. Many other families lost loved ones. The horror of his death and his resistance to the national guard so moved the people of the barrio that they chose him as their symbol of hope and struggle for the future.

Afuera del Barrio

Ruth and her commission had to plan the full day of events for the celebration. That involved inviting the priest who would offer the mass to begin the celebration. The commission was also responsible for inviting the guests of honor for the celebration. This always included the mother of William Diaz Romero and Sra. Saavedra, the mother of the president of Nicaragua, Daniel Ortega. Sra. Saavedra lives near the barrio and has many friends that live there. The commission also planned the speeches (which included Ruth's report on the health programs she had organized during the year), entertainment, and refreshments for those who attended.

Early on the morning of the 27th, Ruth's committee began cleaning the area around the house of William Diaz Romero for several blocks in each direction. This involves sweeping the sidewalks and streets, putting up banners, and whitewashing the curbs. While these activities are going on, other committees are preparing the refreshments, putting up chairs, and completing other chores.

The celebration begins about 1:00 P.M. in front of the house of William Diaz Romero where an altar had been erected. The altar contains various floral arrangements. Located above the altar are images of Jesus Christ and a photo of William Diaz Romero. The event begins with a mass. The priest gives a mass on the virtues of social change and commitment to salvation for all. The mass was followed by a short talk by the mother of William Diaz Romero on the importance of her son's death as an example of the type of strength that had built the popular revolution and that is now needed to defend it. This was followed by speeches by different members of the barrio on the importance of the day. Next there was some modern dancing by groups of young males and females. This was followed by an El Salvadoran singing group. Afterwards, awards of merit were presented to people who have worked hard on health or education projects in the barrio. During this time, refreshments were served to those in attendance (about 200). This was followed by a surprise: a teenage drum and bugle corps came marching down the street and played for more than half an hour.

In this celebration, elements of the community's symbols of cooperation, formal and popular religious symbols, and the revolution are blended together. There is no sense of being morbid or morose. Sorrow is felt for the family of Diaz Romero as well as for others in the barrio who lost loved ones in the struggle against the dictatorship. However there is also much joy in the community involvement. The martyred youth of the barrio, like William Diaz Romero, did not die to build some abstract new society. They died to begin that process in their own community. This also creates a form of "personalismo," not the "personalismo" of social and economic networks, but a network of involvement in the history of one's own community. This is a "personalismo" that emotionally and politically connects the spirits of this struggle (those who have fallen) to those who continue the struggle. The martyrs of the barrio become the daughters and sons of the whole community.

The activities of such events as the procession of Santo Domingo and the celebration of the martyrdom of William Diaz Romero are expressions of a general politicalization of popular religious action through the discourse of the theology of liberation (Lancaster 1988). The theology of liberation involves the mixture of popular religious concepts into strategies of political action. The fiesta of Santo Domingo can be seen as the construction by the masses of their own theological statement about society (Lancaster 1988). The martyrdom of William Diaz Romero is the politicalization of this process into people's everyday lives (R. Dalton 1987). People use their popular religious concepts and beliefs as cultural means to understand and act upon the hegemonic terrain of their everyday lives (Verese 1988:57–77).

Current Conditions, 1990–1992

During the period of the Sandinista political control, there never was a problem of religious freedom. As can be seen in the description of the fiesta of Santo Domingo and the barrio's celebrations of martyrdom of William Diaz Romero, the conflict in terms of religion has been over who has the authority to appropriate the symbols. That is, it is the people of the barrio who have placed the photo of William Diaz Romero next to that of Jesus Christ, not the church. There never has been any form of prohibiting people from practicing their particular spiritual concerns.

People in the barrio have not seen any contradiction between political action and religious beliefs. Representing many views held by people in the barrio, Orlando (the barrio coordinator) defines the popular revolution as a Christian movement. Given the constant interweaving of political and religious symbolism within the social discourses of Nicaragua, it would be safe to assume that will continue within the new hegemonic terrain. The theology of liberation is not limited to Nicaragua or its popular revolution, but is a worldwide movement that will continue. The people of Nicaragua will continue to celebrate the fiesta of Santo Domingo in the fashion described here, and barrio residents will continue their reverence for their fallen martyrs as expressed in the history of William Diaz Romero.

Political Structures

Here we wish to briefly discuss the political dynamics in the barrio that are not framed in terms of the barrio committee structure. That is national and international political relations that are articulated into the barrio in some fashion. The most active political group in the barrio is the Sandinistas. The Sandinista party is structured into cell groups that are based within communities. This involves those formal party members who organized into local base groups. They are supposed to develop their local issues or work on national and party issues at the local level. The cell groups are articulated to various other larger units that go up through the general party structure. There is a great deal of overlap between many of the most active members of the local barrio committees and cell members. In fact, Sandinista party members are strongly encouraged to work as helpers to the various commissions that are developed by the barrio committee.

In the barrio itself, the only other political party represented in the barrio is the office of the New Central America Party. This was one of the various parties that participated in the election this year. While we were there, there was no formal office or expression of UNO. Clearly, as in other parts of Nicaragua, many people in the barrio, without publicly expressing support for UNO, voted for them. Many people in the barrio related that during the Somoza era they were in opposition parties like the socialist or conservative parties. (Remember that Somoza controlled the liberal party.) In our various interviews and investigations, we found no one who had a history of participation in the Communist party. This is interesting in that in Cuba, Lewis found that many of the urban supporters of Castro's July 26 movement had long political histories involving either participation or membership in the Cuban communist party (Lewis 1977a, 1977b and 1978).

Numerous people in the barrio were quite open and vocal in their dislike for the Sandinistas and their policy. This is not surprising given that many residents of the barrio worked in commercial areas in both formal and informal sectors of the economy and felt that the economic policy of the government was directly detrimental to them.

International Community Relations in the Barrio

As we have stated several times in other chapters, the barrio is an area where numerous inexpensive boarding houses and eating places are located. Because of this, there is always a kind of floating international population in the barrio. For outsiders, the barrio is often referred to as the gringo barrio (in Nicaragua a gringo is any non-Nicaraguan). This presence of international visitors in the barrio has had both positive and negative factors. Positive factors have been the income and resources that have been gained by those whose businesses or trades serve this international clientele. However this did not generate a lot of work for residents in the barrio. Most of the businesses serving this international clientele are small businesses that are run by particular households. There is only one somewhat fancy hotel in the barrio that has a large working staff (8 people). What has been negative is that the barrio, because of the larger number of international visitors, is perceived as a place where either nothing much happens in terms of the local population or perceptions that the local barrio residents do not need much because it must be such a rich barrio reaping the benefits of so many of the international visitors.

The other important international component in the barrio is the sister barrio project between this community and the North Side of Greeley, Colorado. This sister barrio project is one that we as authors are actively involved in and is a significant factor in the development of what we refer to as ethnographic praxis.[17]

Notes

1. Under the current city government of UNO the barrio falls in the jurisdiction of district two. The local barrio CDS continues to lobby the mayors office in terms of health, housing and community development projects. Examples of these activities are the attainment of their sports center, basketball court and legalization of housing and land titles.

2. Between 1942 and 1959, various sectors of the work force became organized to provide these services as a result of the expansion of commercial agriculture, industry, and the state bureaucracy. Not until 1957, 70 years after Germany passed health care legislation, was the Social Security foundation in Nicaragua founded. It was elitist and primarily symbolic as it served a small population in only Managua, the capitol, and Leon, the second largest city in Nicaragua. Even in 1978, only a year before the overthrow of Somoza, only 16% of the economically active population was covered and only 8.4% of the total population. Only 30.7% of these worked in the productive sector, the majority of these being bureaucrats of Somoza. In 1974, the Ministry of Health budget accounted for only 16% of health care expenditures. Of this, 81% was allocated for operating expenses. 75% of the budget was spent in Managua, which accounted for only 25% of the Nicaraguan population. These policies obviously excluded the vast majority of the population, especially in the rural areas where it was necessary to scrape up the leftovers which were so "charitably" available in the private or traditionally health sectors. This extreme misallocation of health resources obviously reflected on the morbidity and mortality rates (Donahue 1986 and Envio 1988a:24–30).

3. Diarrhea among children and the war among adults have been the biggest killers. A total of 43,176 people to date have been killed, wounded or kidnapped (1.35% of the population were direct war victims, while .7% were actually killed) and some 11,000 war orphans and more than 250,000 displaced, signifies that there is a new illness that needs treatment and represents a high human and social cost. The war and relocation of those in war zones have indirectly caused malnutrition by the interrupting of planting and harvesting and have made the distribution of foodstuffs to new locations difficult. Population relocations and

Afuera del Barrio

troop mobility in the mountains are associated with new outbreaks of diarrhea, measles, malaria, and dengue. Numerous programs and health campaigns carried out by volunteer health brigadistas have seriously been affected due to fighting and the continued harassment directed at health workers by the counter-revolutionaries. The actual health structure has suffered also. Reagan's freedom fighters have "burned or otherwise destroyed 60 primary health units since the start of the war in 1981" (Envio 1988a:29); they have destroyed 29 health centers and left another 99 virtually uninhabitable (Donahue 1986 and Ortega 1988).

4. "Double shift" refers to the fact that many women work outside the home and are still responsible for domestic chores and child care within the house.

5. The general health system is extremely underfunded both in terms of material and staff. In the barrio, the public health service still sends a doctor to the clinic, but all material costs including medicine are the barrios responsibility. To meet this need the barrio committee has decided to charge a small consulting fee of c2. each visit.

6. For more information on the issues of housing and urban renewal in Managua see Morales, Aradaya and Espinoza "Asentamientos Espontaneos No Son Causas de la Crisis Urbana"(*Boletin Socio-Economic*, INIES, April, Managua, Nicaragua, 1987) and Vance "More Than Bricks and Mortar: Women's Participation."(In Moser and Peaker (eds.)*Women, Human Settlement and Housing*. London: Tavistock, pp. 139–165, 1987).

7. For information on agrarian reform see Gary Ruchwarger's book *Struggling For Survival: Workers, Women, and Class on a Nicaraguan State Farm*. (Boulder: Westview Press, 1989.)

8. In terms of attaining legal title to house sites in the barrio residents must go through the following procedures with the current city housing authorities. First, they must file plans of their house and lot. Second, a full listing of residents within the household. Third, affidavits from their neighbors are required confirming that they behave in a civil manner. Of the two housing projects in barrio William Diaz Romero, people in Camilo Ortega have successfully completed the construction of their houses. In the other housing project Carlos Calero about two-thirds of the residents have completed the construction of their houses. It is in the barrio Martha Quezada (one of the three newly aligned barrios) that the comité del barrio anticipates the most difficulty in attaining legal titles to house sites.

9. For a general analysis of education and the revolution see Vilas' *The Sandinista Revolution* (New York: Monthly Review Press, 1986). The specific information in this section is from our field notes (1986–90).

10. Current fees for primary school are c5. per student per month. For secondary students fees are c10. per student per month. University fees are in the process of being reevaluated. Although the Ministry of Education stresses that the fees for primary and secondary are voluntary, people in the barrio feel that if they fail to pay the fees that they will encounter delays in their children's graduations.

11. This information is from our field notes (1986–1992).

12. UNO is in the process of reducing the overall size of the military. This is having a negative impact on the economy since there is no employment for the returning military personnel. Also, as of January 1992 there were reports of armed

conflicts taking place in the north between recontras and recompas. Recontras are former contras who do not feel the promises of the new government are being fulfilled. Recompas are those rural residents who are defending their gains from the Sandinista period.

13. For more general information on such beliefs systems in Nicaragua see Hernandez' *Folklore de Nicaragua* (Guatemala: Editorial Predira Santa, 1986) and Valle's "El Folklore en la Literatura de Centro America," *The Journal of American Folklore*, Vol. 36, April-June, No. 140, pp. 43–67, 1923.

14. This information is from informal interviews with mostly older women in the barrio.

15. This information was written by Cony Blanco, a resident in the barrio.

16. This section is taken from Higgins's "Virgins and Martyrs," in Dow and Stephen (eds.) *Popular Religion in Mexico and Central America* (Washington, D.C.: AAA Manuscript Series, 1990).

17. Part of the praxis we are seeking in our study is the recognition of the various alternately abled members of this community and their organizations. We strongly encourage others in the future to ethnographically present the "culture" of this group. We are sorry that we were not able to focus much attention on this population.

6

Vamos a Seguir

Well, I picked this barrio because I liked it. I came from Masaya. I came here because of a tragedy. I lost one child in the war. My oldest son. So I came to Managua. I lived in San Judas. I did not like it there and we kept looking for a small lot so we could stay. We found one here in this barrio. I liked it here and we stayed.

We rented a house. After a while the owner kicked us out. So that is when I went to the comité del barrio, and told them my problem. By telling them my problem they gave me support and helped me solve my problem. The committee sent me to MINVA (the housing authority) to fill out a request to get land. I put in all the family's names and they gave me a little lot. With the help of all my children we built the home here. We moved into the new house on February 27, 1989, so I have been living here for four months. I like living here. I feel much better because now I know this is my land until the lord takes me. That's when I will leave it.

The way I analyze this crisis is in terms of the war. When the war against Somoza ended, the country was left very poor. Somoza took everything. He took things; he destroyed things. The war against Somoza caused a lot of suffering and all of these actions left us poor. Now things are very expensive and we have to fight and fight. But we think that in another ten years we will have a different situation in the country. We have to see that it is not only Nicaragua in crisis. If you go to Costa Rica you will see that everything is expensive, like here.

(Like I said), prices are very high. If we go to the supermarket for a pound of tomatoes, the small kind cost 2,200 cordobas. But if we go to the local store here in the barrio—sometimes our pockets don't have enough money to go the supermarket so we go around here (in the barrio)—the little tomato is cheaper, only 500 cordobas for each little tomato. In the barrio store a dozen eggs cost 10,000 cordobas, a pound of sugar right now is 5,000 or 6,000; a pound of rice is 7,000. The prices are variable. The cheapest you can find the rice for is 6,000 here in the barrio.

The achievements that we have made here in the barrio during these ten years? Well, right here is the housing project. That is a big achievement for us. This was a priority for the poor people here. We are building the community house which will give us a place to use for our activities. The other improvement has been the health of children. Soon we are going to have a doctor, who will attend our children and

---

Translated from the Spanish, the chapter title means "We Will Continue."

adults. It has been the "comité del barrio" that worked for these things. The committee also organizes campaigns to keep the barrio clean, we all get together to clean our streets. This is a very healthy barrio. I have my neighbors, who are healthy, honest, and friendly.

Well, I never imagined this . . . what we are living through now (the war). I never imagined this. Before the victory of the Sandinistas, many people hoped we would live better than we did with the National Guard in power. They really did torture and massacre people. We the people, have done a lot of things and I call it better living than before.

I do not think of the future without wishing that this war ends for good. I wish that my grandchildren can grow up in peace. I wish that your government or president could understand how hard this war is for us. I have cried too much. This war has hit my family very hard, it has been a tragedy. I want the president of the USA to understand our wishes and let us live in peace. What I ask for is for my grandchildren to grow up in Nicaragua with peace. Is this too much too ask?

—Elisa Torres–Age 53
Ten-year resident of the barrio

Introduction

In the first part of this conclusion we summarized what we think we have presented about the everyday lives of the residents of the Barrio William Diaz Romero. This involves expressing what we find to be the social linkages between levels of existential actions, community involvement and national identities. In the second part of the conclusion we describe what we feel can be stated as demonstrations of what we have been searching for in terms of an ethnographic praxis. In the last section of this chapter we present what the future of this community may look like in the context of "Government from Below."

Everyday Life in the Barrio

The reality that framed other realities for the residents of the barrio was that of their socio-economic struggles. It seemed that almost everyone worried about how they were going to maintain themselves, their families, and the mode of living in what seemed to be an a neverending economic crisis. This was also a social crisis for it was how one fared in the economic terrain that influenced how one could socially construct particular actions. We have provided detailed coverage of these struggles in Chapter 3, and also discussed how this economic crisis had affected the outcome of the election. The weariness that many of the residents expressed about their economic struggles, though generated by the dynamics we have discussed, are part of the everyday realities of the majority of the peoples of the

Third World. At the most macro level, the struggles of the people of this barrio are representative of the chasm between the affluent world and the developing world. It also illustrates that political and economic models based upon modernist assumptions have little or no relevance in terms of how the world is operating currently. The leftist Sandinistas followed monetarist policies to fight this economic crisis, whereas the rightist Chamorro government has kept state control over the banking system in order to restore the "market economy" (Envio 1990a:105–106). How to cover the cost of a fair and just society is a process dearly in need of new visions (Heller 1988). At the local level, such as in Barrio William Diaz Romero, many things can be accomplished through community action. There is at this point no form of community action that can alter how international currencies are valued.

This leads to the other profound reality that is expressed in the everyday lives of these residents: their own experimentation with local political empowerment. For all the rhetoric, proclamations, factions, frustrations, and hard work, this quixotic phenomenon referred to as empowerment was a reality for these people of the barrio. In the chapter titled "Quiero Decir Esto" we provide detailed information on how this worked in the barrio. One of the things we learned about revolutionary action—that creates the social space for empowerment—is how ordinary it is. The issues to which these residents directed their new power were not about changing the whole world, but about getting a polluting battery shop closed or attempting to get the prices of cheese lowered. It involved long hours of work to organize and carry out a vaccination campaign or to disinfect the barrios water system of dengue larva. For these residents, empowerment does mean a process for local control and development. It means that they are the designers of their community within the boundaries of the power to which they have access. What continues to be both ironic and sad is that such a simple exploration of community action seems so threatening to the outside world. This leads to the other important reality that framed these people's everyday lives: the world outside the barrio.

In the processes of confronting their immediate economic and political problems, the residents of this community were aware of the forces outside the barrio that placed real limits on their experiment in self governance. They constantly attempted to organize programs that would provide some kind of economic aid directly to the community—such as the rice buying cooperative—which were just as often thwarted by economic dynamics beyond their control and access. They were also aware that their exploration of self governance placed them in conflict with other class interests in Nicaragua and in opposition to various international forces, primarily that of the U.S. government. The recognition of these constraining hegemonic boundaries also made some members of the community sensitive to internal contradictions of class, gender, and sexuality in the barrio itself. This is to say that, in terms of these people's everyday lives, they were quite aware that their local actions were taking place in a much broader social arena of meanings and actions.

Now, more than ever, they are aware that they have to rethink their experiment with self governance with the change in the hegemonic terrain produced by the election of February 25, 1990. How much social space they will have to continue with such forms of local empowerment remains to be seen.

Social Linkages

In this section we explore the types of social linkages that have been constructed in terms of the revolutionary experiences of the last ten years. We frame this analysis in terms of three categories: existential, community, and national identity.

Existential

During our times of residency in this community, we have come to know many of the people in this barrio as close and personal friends. Within that group of friends most have been strong supporters of the revolution, while many have been quite open critics (either from the left or the right). All of these people have been through a long-term period of armed struggle, ending in a general insurrection against the Somoza dictatorship, the victory of the popular forces, ten years of the Sandinistas political power, the U.S.-sponsored Contra war, and now a new period of political drama with the Sandinistas being the opposition political forces. These powerful realities have made people aware that their self concepts are social constructions. Their perceptions of their existential selves are driven from the experiences of these revolutionary changes. For many, like Consuelo, Luis, Dona Hydee, or Dona Olga, they see the process as one of being reborn through the political dynamics of this revolution. They see their lives and the concepts they have of themselves as immediately linked to their involvement and support of the popular revolution and their affiliation with the Sandinistas. Others, like Don Pedro, Mabel, Don Carlos or Rosa Esmeralda, see their self concepts as a mixture between their affiliations with the revolution and its affects on their lives and their families. They talk about how the totality of all these experiences have changed the way they look at their experiences and those in their family, especially their children. They recognize the contradictory contexts within which they have had to construct their own self concepts and within which their families and friends have also constructed their identities. Thus, some may see themselves as being militant supporters of the revolution while some of their family members are equally militant in their opposition to the revolution. There are also others, like Don Ephraine, Julia, Maria Felix, and others who worked in the informal sector who are quite negative in their perceptions of the revolution but seem to be able to construct a strong self concept through such opposition. That is they see little positive about this revolutionary experience. Ephraine states that there has not been a clear day since the revolution, and he sees himself and his ability to stand outside this revolution as a positive accomplishment.

Thus, we would suggest that these people have become aware of the social processes involved in defining themselves and their own immediate context. This does not mean that they support or do not support the revolution. Instead, the revolutionary experience has opened up to them the reality that concepts such as the self are socially constructed. Hence people in the barrio do not experience their realities as abstract concepts, but as daily activities in a context that affirms such understandings.

Community

The residents of this barrio do consider themselves as part of a community. People talk about and accept that they have a responsibility to their community. This acceptance of community responsibility both predates the revolution and has been redefined by that process. The Barrio William Diaz Romero has a residential history of over a hundred years. Many of the households that we worked with have family histories of three to four generations that have lived in this community. People have known each other in this barrio. Gossip networks are strong and active. This produces minor problems of conflicts and disagreements, but also produces networks of cooperation when households face a particular crisis—such as a death or sickness. People enjoy talking about the history of the barrio and who has the best recollections of past events and where things used to be before the earthquake of 1972.

What the experience of the revolution has added to this social history is the opening of space for political action at the community level. Prior to the revolution, this community had no real political space for locally developed action. Those who had some kind of "palanca" with the Somoza regime would have been able to lobby for particular benefits, but there was no community-wide structure for such actions. The revolution added formal politics to the community's reality. We have described this in the chapter on the politics of the barrio. With the development of the CDS in the barrio, community responsibility took on a concrete form: Will you support the vaccination campaign? Will you help with the clean-up campaign? Will you work on the committee to organize the children's day party or help organize a committee to seek funds to build the community center? How residents decided to respond or not respond to such questions reshaped concepts of what it meant to work for the community. For some, all such requests were legitimate and required positive responses because some such requests were responded to on the assumption that it would help the particular concerns that they were negotiating with the CDS, whereas others would reject any request coming from the CDS, reflecting feelings that the organization did not act in the best interests of the community. However residents reacted, they all recognized a political level to their community, and that being part of that community required some kind of interaction (even if it was avoidance) within the political space.

This recognition of a political space within the community also reinforced the communities awareness that political issues generated by the revolution were not issues outside their community, but were dynamics within their own everyday lives. The popular revolution was a process that was both constructed and contested within the social space of the barrio itself, but not outside. This is not to say that the larger social and political networks of power and authority did not frame the overall space for such action, but to stress that at the community level people felt themselves to be in support of or in opposition to that revolution not as an abstract principle but as part of their everyday lives.

National Identity

How do these local or community realities link to a phenomenon that we could refer to as national identity? We would suggest, for all the reasons we have been exploring, with those factors being in some case good/bad/positive/negative, that people in this community have a sense of themselves as historical subjects. Because of the Sandinista revolution and the terrorist response of the U.S. government to that revolution, people like the residents of the Barrio William Diaz Romero found themselves as active players in a world drama. For centuries most of the world cared little about Nicaragua and what was happening there (even though little had changed). Though Nicaragua has had the unfortunate history of being contained within the hegemonic boundaries of U.S. government geo-political concerns, this never translated into any kind of concern about what any particular Nicaraguan thought about the world one way or the other. For the residents of this barrio particularly (because of the boarding houses and the international visitors) it now seemed that everybody was interested in what they thought about almost anything. The majority of the residents of the barrio seemed to enjoy the experience. Vendors, taxi cab drivers, tortilla makers, merchants, drunks, university professors, and lawyers would loudly and proudly tell you what they thought about Nicaragua, the United States and the current world problems. Whether they supported the Sandinistas or not, people seemed to understand that it was the revolution that the Sandinistas had organized that had brought the "gaze" of the outside world into their everyday lives. Now for the first time in modern Nicaraguan history, the outside world seemed to be interested in what Nicaraguans thought about their own experiences. We are examples of this. We could not say that Nicaragua was a lifetime interest and that we always wanted to spend months in Managua. Clearly the drama of this popular revolution brought us to Nicaragua and to this community. Thus, there has been a new national identity that has emerged from this revolutionary context—Nicaraguans, especially many people in the Barrio William Diaz Romero, feel that they are now historical subjects in a world drama. They may not be able to direct this drama, but now at least they feel they have more than a walk-on part. For a while at least, the world seems to be concerned with what happens in Nicaragua. Thus, good or bad, Nicaraguans are enjoying that aspect of the attention.

Ethnographic Praxis

This project of doing a study of the Barrio William Diaz Romero has been grounded by our search for what we have referred to as ethnographic praxis.[1] We have defined this as involving the combination of ethnographic analysis, applied anthropology, and critical advocacy or solidarity with the groups with which one is working. For us, ethnographic praxis does involve the anthropologist(s) identifying with the aspirations of personal self-determination of those with whom one is working with. For us, the obligation central to ethnographic praxis is to construct a relationship between the anthropologist(s) and the community that is concrete, not abstract.

Thus, in terms of how we have defined ethnographic praxis, what have we accomplished in this pursuit?

We have helped to place two communities together. There is a social linkage between the communities of the North Side of Greeley, Colorado and that of the Barrio William Diaz Romero. In terms of the linkage with the North Side of Greeley, Colorado, this extends beyond the North Side. We are members of a community group that is based in the North Side. This group is called Al Frente de la Lucha. It began in the late sixties as a civil rights action group which has developed into a community-based action group. However its membership is composed of people from throughout the city. Over the years, this group has been involved with the rights of undocumented workers, the struggle for fair treatment of the

North Side residents in terms of relations with police, city and county government, and schools. The Frente owns a small house in the North Side that is decorated with murals depicting the history of the Chicano and working class struggles in Northern Colorado. Currently this house is used as a day center for homeless people in Greeley. The North Side is predominately Latino, with the majority of the Latino population being Mexican or Chicano. However, as we have stated, the membership of the Frente is multi-ethnic and multi-class. The majority of the non-Latino members of the Frente tend to be associated with the academic or community action segments of the city's population. Thus, not only has there been the development of social linkages between the North Side and the Barrio William Diaz Romero through this sister barrio project, it has also encouraged ethnic and class interaction within the city of Greeley. All of the solidarity activities that we have organized over the four-year period of this sister barrio project have been held in the North Side, thus bringing people into this community. Sometimes it is the first real visit for some Greeley residents.

What does this social linkage between these two communities mean in concrete terms? Well, each has become part of the narrative realities of the other. What does that mean? There have been three visits of Greeley residents to the barrio of William Diaz Romero.[2] These visits have been covered by the media in Greeley, the Denver media, and the media in Managua. The various visitors from Greeley have written about their visit to the Barrio William Diaz Romero, and have had these accounts published in local media sources, including radio interviews. This has also taken place in Managua. The two groups that have negotiated this sister barrio project have also exchanged numerous written documents that define and redefine the scope of this exchange project. The local barrio committee has copious notes in its minutes that address the idea and scope of this exchange and so does the Frente in Greeley. There have been written exchanges between medical and educational groups in Greeley and those associated with the barrio in Managua. The Greeley local newspaper (The Greeley Tribune) has given fair and extensive coverage of this exchange project, including editorials supporting the concept of the exchange. Ironically in one editorial interpreting the February election results, the writer was commenting on the importance of the events taking place in Nicaragua after the election because of Greeley's sister city project with the Barrio William Diaz Romero. However, we have a sister barrio project, not official sister city support. We as anthropologists have given numerous talks in Greeley and in Managua about what we are doing in terms of this exchange project and our research associated with it. We have also given formal presentations at academic meetings and published papers on what we have been doing between these two communities. We are writing

Vamos a Seguir

this ethnography now and have completed a video documentary on the Barrio William Diaz Romero.

Why do we suggest that the placement of these social linkages between these communities into various narrative discursive fields is a concrete accomplishment that illustrates something about this pursuit of ethnographic praxis? From Michel Foucault to Donna Haraway we are learning that narrative discursive fields are materially real hegemonic terrains (Foucault 1977). How particular realities are narratively framed and presented involves various levels of representation about power and authority over the issues of class, colonization, gender, and sex (Haraway 1989). Narratives are part of contested conflicts over who gets to explain and who gets explained to about such hegemonic processes. These various narratives in which the concerns and hopes of the various actors who make up this exchange between two communities are expressed, add to the heteroglosia of these debates and confrontations. At the local level, for many people in Greeley, Colorado, the people of Nicaragua or at least the people of Barrio William Diaz Romero are not empty rhetorical categories (of either the right or the left) but real people involved in struggles of everyday life. Concurrently, many people of Nicaragua, or at least the people of the Barrio William Diaz Romero, can relate to people of the United States or Greeley, Colorado also as real people. We are not suggesting excessive profundity of this or that narratives by themselves will transform the world or win the revolution. However, it is important to understand that construction of collective praxis for progressive social changes is one that is contested on many fronts that include narrative confrontations.

What other forms of concrete accomplishments have been achieved through this project? Through the combined efforts of both communities of this exchange, the following has been accomplished in the Barrio William Diaz Romero:

1. The completion of a community center for the barrio;
2. The development and maintenance of a pre/post natal clinic for the barrio;
3. The equipping of two baseball teams for the barrio;
4. Various donations of clothing, medicine, money, and building equipment for the barrio;
5. Exchanges of information between the two communities in terms of health programs, education, and community development.[3]

The first four we have talked about in other sections of this monograph. Here we explain the fifth one a little more. In these areas of international solidarity work, especially in the case of Nicaragua, there tends to be a one way form of communication. That is, it is the North American (including Canadian) or European groups that visit and bring things to Nicaragua more so than Nicaraguans visiting and bringing things to North American or European compatriots. This is often because of limited resources for Nicaraguans to make such visits. In the case of the United States, during the Sandinista political period, it was quite hard to get a visa for Nicaraguans to enter the United States. This has been true for our project. We want to bring people from the Barrio William Diaz Romero to visit Greeley and give us advice on what we could be doing locally to develop more forms of community political empowerment. Those who have gone to the barrio in Managua—especially those from the North Side—who return with such feelings of how much they need to learn from the experience of the people of Barrio William Diaz Romero. The health and education professionals from Greeley that have visited the barrio also return tremendously impressed with how well their compatriots work within such limited conditions, and that there is much to learn from such experiences. The future of this exchange has to involve getting the people from Barrio William Diaz Romero to the community of Greeley and the North Side.

So What Makes Any of This Ethnographic Praxis?

This involves our personal positions on the search for an ethnographic praxis. What this search does for us is to provide a means to explore how to link our personal/political concerns to our ethnographic and anthropological pursuits. This is not a recipe that all other social anthropologists should follow if they are to do good anthropology. We are not attempting to define a mode or method for doing politically correct anthropology. We are attempting to illustrate that good anthropology or ethnography can be political and seek solidarity with the groups that one is working with. We are attempting to present, in an open and honest fashion, how we have combined these various interests for ourselves. For us that contains a search for the praxis of doing ethnography. We are aware that as a narrative form, ethnography does not require linkage to a position of praxis. However, we are equally aware that such an assumption is a modernist one and does not always address the full range of issues of power and authority that are also contained within narrative forms. Nor are we suggesting that a post-modern position is to be associated with progressive actions. There are numerous contradictory and reactionary possibilities contained within the post-modern discourse. We wish to use the hegemonic space generated by post-modern argumentation to situate ourselves, these communities, and this work into the contested realities of metropolitan intellectual production and Third World struggles of self-determination. We are well aware of the overdetermined hegemonic terrain within which these contestations take place. If we were so naive as not to understand that, then the election of February 25, 1990, has been the call to wake up and smell the coffee. We are also aware that these actions that we are part of are minimal, and can make one feel as if he/she is pissing in the ocean to bring up the tide.[4] But then if a whole lot more people were pissed off, perhaps the tides could rise faster. Again, the stress is on "can" or "could be," not "ought to be." We do not know what "ought to be" is. We only have various fragments of different-colored threads that at different times are woven into dramatic patterns that can and do come undone.

If we desire that our work be seen as a search for an ethnographic praxis, then how are others to judge the various levels of objectivity and subjectivity in our accounts? We have stated in the introduction that such judgments, in fact, have to come from the readership not us. We honestly feel that readers should have no such trouble making use of the various forms of objective and subjective information contained in this narrative. There is no hidden text to this narrative. Certain critical readers should be able to enlighten us about certain presuppositions to our search for ethnographic praxis or see contradictory forms of presentation. We welcome such readings. We also assume that some people will find elements of this narrative as lacking in value and as not a useful contribution to the field of ethnography. To those we stress that this may, in fact, be true, for our primary goal is to not only make a useful contribution to the field of ethnography, but make ethnography a useful contribution to the somewhat larger social field of realities and interests. We are not concerned with attempting to determine the outcome of the events we have narratively described, but with being co-participants in the construction of a social process seeking a fairer world. We hope that such narrative accounts of social action (including ethnography) can contribute to the general praxis of such a quest. Is that enough? To that question we always respond with a paraphrasing of Fidel Castro's defense speech to his tribunal: history will be the judge of that.

The Struggle Continues

In this concluding section we report on our impressions of the barrio and Managua during our visit at the end of July this year (1990). This was almost six months after the elections of February and three months into the governing of UNO at the national and local levels. We found numerous fragmented images of changes taking place. Thus we have divided this section into four parts. First we discuss what is a renewed spirit of action on the part of many people in the barrio, then the new factors of polarization, followed by a discussion of the development of forms of political distrust, and we conclude with our observations on how the action of "Gobierno de Abajo" is in fact operating.

Renewed Spirit and Sense of Action

In the barrio and around Managua people still speak of the shock and surprise at the Frente's defeat. They speak with sadness that the victory of UNO carries with it no vision or view of what society should be, only a vague and unfocused protest against the errors of the Frente. People recognized that the election was lost due to errors of the Frente and its leadership. People stress the role of the war, USA manipulation of the election process, and the economy as the larger processes that affected the election. But the factors that people stressed the most were the errors of the Frente. Many suggested that the Frente should have ended the draft. Others stressed that the Frente did more talking than listening, that they solicited suggestions for programs that never seemed to develop, or that too many of the Frente officials were taking more than their fair share of privileges. People seem to feel that it is important to stress the awareness of such errors as part of the rebuilding of the political and social movement that could recapture political power in six years or sooner. Clearly these are the views of people still involved with the Frente or still supportive of the goals of the popular revolution. They feel that by analyzing these errors they can be sure not to repeat them. Further, by providing the context of their own political errors, they can better illustrate their dissatisfaction with the direction that UNO is taking as it attempts to govern. For example, in admitting that Frente officials were receiving more than their fair share of privileges, it is also stressed that this is in no way similar to the new government officials receiving thousands of dollars to head agencies or ministries of the government. Also in confronting their errors they feel able to redefine and remobilize themselves for the current struggle.

What evidences do people in the barrio offer to illustrate this new spirit? First and foremost was their experience with the second general strike that had ended the week before we had arrived. Though not well reported outside of Nicaragua, this general strike had shut down the entire country, not just Managua. It was a clear drawing of the line between the popular classes of the country and the new government. It was an illustration that though the majority of the country had voted for UNO, that did not mean that the majority of the country wished to undo the accomplishments of the revolution. They recognized that the election of UNO did bring an end to the contra war and of the economic blockade, but from that they wanted to see new forms of cooperation, not a return to class dictatorship of the rich over the poor. People built barricades and armed themselves to illustrate these feelings. The country was at the crossroads of civil war. In the barrio, there were five armed barricades maintained during the strike. Some of those who had maintained the barricades had ironically been voters for UNO. For many in the barrio, the strike was an affirmation that the power of the popular classes was real and would still be part of how politics were to be enacted in Nicaragua. For them this was further illustrated by this year's celebration of the revolution.

Manuel, Consuelo, Elisia, Orlando, Hugo, and many others reported to us how wonderful this year's celebration of the revolution (the first since the Sandinista loss) was—bigger and more exciting than last year's. Everyone told us how the UNO government had attempted to discourage people from attending the celebration. They ran t.v. announcements encouraging people not to go, they gave people the day off, and stopped bus service for the day. All to no avail. Thousands attended the celebration from all over the country. The plaza of the revolution was full and people stayed through a hard rain storm. Again this indicated to us and the people from the barrio the continued strength of the Frente and the people's commitment to struggle for their popular revolution.

This commitment to popular struggle was expressed in people's willingness to continue to work on the various programs of health, education, and community development. Those who were still strong Frente members talked of how they had to replant the roots of their revolution to make for stronger branches to support new programs. In the barrio this was evidenced by their new community center. Through the help of our sister barrio project they had finished their center. It was a large, very well made one-room structure. They had the inauguration of the house in June on the anniversary of the martyrdom of William Diaz Romero. The people said it was the largest attendance in the history of the celebration. They had moved their clinic into the center, and it was operating on a six-day-a-week basis. Through the clinic, the barrio committee now represented not only the Barrio William Diaz Romero, but the neighboring barrio of Martha Quezada and several other smaller colonias in the area surrounding the barrio. The barrio had several new commissions to work on new problems, and what was most impressive were the number of new people now attending and participating in the community actions. The political support for the barrio committee has increased since the election in February. Viewed from this fragmented image, events and opportunities were hopeful and optimistic. However this was not the only image present.[5]

Polarization

More so than we had seen in our previous visits, were strong feelings of doubt, confusion, and tension. These were expressed at the local level, with neighbors being angry and suspicious with each other. People were concerned about what they said and who they would say it too. Everyone suggested that it had been someone else who had voted for UNO and that they were now "repenting" their vote.

The factor that was generating the most tension, however, was the economic crisis. In the three months that UNO has been in power, the state of the economy had gotten worse. When UNO entered the government, the cordoba was valued at about 40,000 cordobas to the dollar; when we left on the second of August, the cordoba was valued at 620,000 to the dollar. People were angered that with the war over and the blockade ended, there had been no improvement in the economy. Thus, those who favored the Frente saw this as evidence of UNO's lack of governing skill. Those who still sided with UNO, blamed the Frente unions and the two general strikes the unions had called.

Three processes were fueling the economic crisis—people's earning power was getting lower, the government had ended subsidies on basic municipal services (transportation, gas, and utilities), and the government planned to introduce the Cordoba de Oro (the gold cordoba). The gold cordoba was to be valued at one cordoba for one dollar. Though this was clearly a form of voodoo economics on the part of UNO, it was the general population that was feeling the pain of pins being stuck into their everyday lives. As of yet, the Cordoba de Oro had not been introduced, but the government and certain businesses were already charging at this rate. One had to pay one's taxes and utility bills at the rate of the gold cordoba. Thus, Manuel Ruiz had to pay monthly taxes on his metal business. These were at about 15 to 20 dollars a month. So what he had to do was pay in the old or current cordobas the value of 15 or twenty dollars. His 15 dollar tax bill required that he pay somewhere around 9,300.00 cordobas. Some people in the barrio were reporting that their water and electricity bills were running at about 10 to 15 dollars also. No one knew where or how they were going to get money to pay these kinds of bills. Foods prices were incredibly high. We visited a supermarket near the barrio and prices were higher than in the United States. In fact, prices in Greeley, Colorado were cheaper than in this supermarket in Managua.

The economic crisis also involved increased unemployment. The UNO government is continuing the Sandinista attempt to reduce the public work sector. However, their approach has been less than successful in terms of the two general strikes and the current needs of the country's population. There also seems to be a purge in process. People who have public sector jobs—such as teachers—fear that they will be losing their jobs because of their support for the Frente. Also, because of the recession, the private sector is laying people off. Numerous households in the barrio reported family members being out of work for months. Many people voted for UNO in the hope that they would somehow work economic miracles. This has not happened.

Another factor in terms of the tensions of Managua, is the presence of urban political violence. While we were in Managua there were several accounts of barrios strongly affiliated with the Frente being attacked by UNO supporters. There have been several killings associated with political differences. At the end of the inauguration of the barrio community center, there was a stabbing blamed on a UNO supporter attacking one of the youths of the barrio. The vice-president of Nicaragua—Victor Godoy—is openly organizing an armed militia that he refers to as National Salvation Brigades. Many people feel that this private militia is fomenting much of this urban violence. What is different here is the perception that these forms of urban violence are political. Over the last three years urban crime has been on the increase in Managua. We often heard warnings about using the bus or being out too late at night because of the problems of youth gangs in the area or throughout Managua. However, this was not seen as politically motivated but as a fault in the conditions of urban life. Now people are seeing these activities as political in nature. If you support UNO, these actions are seen as encouraged by the Frente; if you are supportive of Frente, the actions are seen as organized by UNO. The evidence is limited and much of it is hearsay, but it is clear that certain factions in UNO, such as the vice president, are openly calling for forms of direct violence against Sandinista supporters. In fact, the police are attempting to reorganize volunteer police groups in barrios to fight against these forms of violence.

What we encountered in the barrio that we had not seen in any of our previous visits were residents fearful of each other because of the political climate. Many are fearful of this kind of violence; others worried about what others are saying about them in terms of how they voted. Before the election, people in the barrio felt that their community allegiance transcended their political positions. Now it is one's political position which seems to be defining one's community allegiance. People speak in more political terms than before. Many people who had been moderate Frente supporters now speak with very strong political metaphors. They refer to people who voted for UNO as traitors and reactionaries. They speak of their own situations as forms of class warfare, and they see that the new government is attempting to strangle the working class and poor. Those who actually voted for UNO in the barrio are not vocal about their support. Many asked not be quoted about their support. This is odd. Like the rest of the country, the barrio went about 60% for UNO and 40% for the Frente. We had never encountered people in the past concerned about expressing their views on political subjects openly; now some are afraid to do so.[6]

Distrust of the Political Process

Concurrent with this polarization of political positions within the barrio is the emergence of more people who now are disinterested or distrust the political process in general. Those who voted for UNO had hoped for some kinds of rapid and positive changes that would affect their daily lives. Instead, they got more negative changes, especially in term of the economy. A few open UNO supporters felt that things might still get better, but were very worried about the economy. The comment we heard over and over again immediately following the Sandinista loss was how people everywhere are now repenting their votes for UNO. They do not understand or accept that things should have gotten worse, things were supposed to get better within 100 days as UNO had so boldly promised. No one saw anything as better. The war was over, but they now had to fear dying of hunger. The original blockade was over, but there was a new kind of blockade; no one had any money to buy anything.

These feelings are producing new reactions from people in the barrio. Socorro and her family are thinking about leaving. Their plans involve a move to El Salvador and working with revolutionary groups there. Mabel Curtis wants to leave. She recently lost her job as a director at a school and she fears that Noel's job at the Pepsi plant is not secure either. She is tired of the hassle of marriage, household maintenance, and the political realities of Nicaragua. She does not want to wait six years for the return to power of the Frente. She wants to go to the States to find work. She wants to go alone. Others, like Pedro or Julia, feel that the current realities of Nicaragua reinforce what they have always known—the rich are getting richer, while the poor get poorer. Julia feels that both Dona Violeta and Daniel Ortega are doing fine while she and her family only get poorer. Bolivar Espinoza, an urban researcher at INIES, finds this sentiment actually hopeful. He hopes that in the next six years a new leftist political base can grow that will go beyond the programs of the Frente. He feels that neither UNO nor the Frente will be able to develop programs and a vision that will fit the actual reality of how dependent capitalism controls Nicaragua's export economy. He clearly thinks that the popular classes will suffer the most during this time. It will be deteriorating living conditions that will be the basis of new and stronger leftist politics. This view is an odd mixture of classic Marxist hopes for revolution and insights into the popular classes of Nicaragua.[7]

Gobierno de Abajo

After the electoral defeat, the Sandinistas took the position that they would continue their popular struggle through governing from below. This seemed to mean the maintenance of the mass organization as a foundation from which to defend the gains of the revolution and to continue struggling for such groups' various hopes and plans. No one knew exactly what this was to mean or what form it would take. The two general strikes illustrate the overall political power of what this meant but not what government from below meant in terms of daily activities, such as those in the barrio. We were lucky that during our stay this July we were able to attend a meeting between representatives of the new city government controlled by UNO and the barrio's committee.

The barrio housing project is in legal trouble. The new government wishes to review all land and housing projects developed during the Sandinista period. As we have reported, the barrio was quite successful in getting these lands for people and the people were successful in getting their houses built. Now they are not sure how legal their titles to these lands are. Since the election, the barrio residents have been attempting to meet with the new city government to clear these issues up. On July 26, they had their first meeting with the new government on this issue. The city of Managua is divided into various districts, with each district having an Alcalde (Sub-Mayor) in charge of the particular district. The Barrio William Diaz Romero is in district two. The Alcalde of district two sent two representatives of his office to this meeting. They were members of UNO. The meeting was held around six in the evening in what is now the new community center. In attendance that evening were over a hundred people. There were people from the barrio and people from the neighboring barrio that were using the committee to represent their issues. People were anxious to hear from these representatives. What was interesting was that of those in attendance, the majority had most likely been people who had voted for UNO, never envisioning that their votes would put them in jeopardy of losing their newly acquired lots and homes. The UNO representatives showed up about a half hour after the starting time for the meeting. They stayed in front of the room with Don Orlando who was chairing the meeting. They walked in with a defensive manner and seemed to act as if those in attendance were hostile to them. We think this was their first political error of the evening. The committee is clearly still composed of militant Sandinistas. Orlando, Hugo, Maritza, Luis, and Olga all still have commissions on the committee and they have in no way lessened their commitment to the Sandinista revolution. But this was not true of the those in attendance. The UNO representatives were in fact confronting people who had, for various reasons, voted for them. However, they assumed the audience shared the militancy of the committee. By the end of the evening, they did. Orlando explained that the community wished to discuss three issues with them. First was the status of the title of the land in the housing project; second, the status of particular lots in the barrio that people had built houses on; and third, the problems of people who were renting their houses. The UNO representatives stated that they were open to discussing these concerns, but from practical not political points of view. On the issues of the housing project, they stated that since the land had been confiscated by a previous city government, the current government wanted to review each case separately. This met with a total refusal by those in attendance. Various speakers stated that there were no separate cases, all of them had the same problem and wanted the issues to be dealt with collectively. The residents had their own commission to represent them and wanted these representatives to negotiate this problem directly with the commission. The UNO representatives attempted to counter this position with the claim that, for particular households, it would be better to solve their problem separately. No one accepted this offer. They finally agreed to work with the commission. Then the question was, "When?" After further discussion, a meeting the following Thursday was accepted. Residents then asked if a decision on the issues of land entitlement at the upcoming meeting would be made. The UNO representatives were confused over this request. They were not sure about their authority to act or whether the problem could be solved so fast. This was met with cynical comments from the audience, such as "Why not? UNO had promised to solve all problems within a 100 days."

On the issues of individual lots and renters, it was accepted that those would have to be dealt with on a case-by-case basis, but the UNO representatives stated that no one would be evicted until all the factors in each case were investigated. At this point in the meeting, the people began airing more general grievances. They wanted to know when their streets would be cleaned and the pot holes filled, what was going to be done about public safety, and most dramatically, what was going to happen to lots that the handicapped and mothers of soldiers killed in contra attacks had received. The UNO representatives felt that these were political issues which they did not have to address. This was not accepted by the audience, especially since there were numerous handicapped persons there. These issues had previously been crucial. One of the UNO representatives and a gentlemen in a wheelchair got into a heated argument over these issues. The other UNO representative charged the person in the wheelchair with only being concerned about his own problems and wanting to make everything political; that his plight was his own problem, not the government's. This brought a hiss from the crowd. Hugo stood up, stated that regardless of anyone's politics, the reality of the handi-

Vamos a Seguir

capped and martyred mothers was one they had to accept and one that deserved everyone's respect. There was immediate, loud applause for Hugo's comments. The meeting then addressed a few more issues and was drawn to the normal vague ending that meetings have in the barrio and throughout Nicaragua. As the meeting was breaking up, Orlando thanked the representatives for attending, requested another meeting with them soon, and asked that people show their thanks for the meeting with a round of applause for the city representatives. There was only a momentary silence as people began leaving the building. While they were exiting people were commenting on the lack of political skills on the part of the UNO representatives and on how rude and defensive they had been to everyone. The committee members of the barrio felt that they had gained some leverage because on the most important issue—that of the housing projects—the UNO representatives agreed to deal with the problem collectively. No one trusted what they had been told by the UNO representatives. People felt that they had not been honest or truthful. In a matter of some two hours, the barrio committee had strengthened its position as the spokepersons for the barrio independent of political position, whereas the UNO representatives seemed to have alienated the whole audience which, on paper at least, was composed of those who had supported them in the election.

The barrio residents and the committee strongly feel that they will continue with their own community programs. This will involve getting the titles to the land in the barrio housing projects legalized, including the community house; keeping the clinic going and staffed; developing more youth programs; sponsoring dances on the weekends to make money; developing programs for the elderly in the barrio; and seeking out new alliances with the other barrios near them. Orlando envisions Barrio William Diaz Romero as being the best-organized barrio in all of Managua. There are still factions in the barrio. There are some who still do not trust Orlando and feel that there should be a more representative leadership, one more sensitive to the non-sectarian approach required for the fight of a government from below. There are still many people who are hoping that UNO will be able to deliver on some of its promises. What the politically active people see as needed now is to reach out to all the residents of the barrio in order to rebuild the spirit of the popular revolution.

We were also able to witness these new approaches in action. As part of our sister barrio project, we brought down with us five duffle bags of used clothing for the barrio. When we brought the clothing to the community house, they had a meeting where they vigorously debated how to make sure that this donation went to the most needy in the barrio, independent of their politics. Criticism was offered that suggested that in the past committee members too often took the best of the offerings and that the neediest were not always served. A plan was constructed where representatives from the different sections of the barrio and the new sections of other barrios would do a mini-census (we tried not to smile at the census idea) of the poorest members of their section. Based on that census, the packages of clothes would be given to those poor households. On the night before we left, they gave us a going away party at which they had us hand out the clothing packages. More than fifty packages were given out. Without any doubt, they went to the poorest members of this community. Further, we knew from personal knowledge, that many that received these packages where those who had not been active in barrio affairs and had, also without a doubt, been those who had voted for UNO. At least in this barrio, "Gobierno de Abajo" was a process in action. How this process was operating in other barrios in Managua or throughout Nicaragua we do not know. Clearly it is too early in the process to make any kind of judgement or prediction. What everyone says is "vamos a seguir"—we will continue.[8]

For us, as anthropologists searching for forms of ethnographic praxis, we too share the sentiment of "vamos a seguir." We too will continue our involvement with this community, with our commitments of solidarity to their struggle for self and collective determination. In terms of our professional lives as anthropologists (one closing in on three decades; the other finishing a half decade of work), it was an impressive and moving feeling to return to this community and to see the community house finished. People are still able to envision positive actions to be planned and carried out, and people still have the hope of a better life for themselves and others. These feelings are tempered by all the current events in Nicaragua and the world. Also, as we have stated, there are many other fragmented views present in this community that express equally real concerns of fear, confusion, and suspicion. For us, we truly feel that we have a place in this community. As much as possible, given the differences of history, culture, and social classes, we feel a part of this community. What started in 1986 as a vague plan to write an ethnography of this community while helping them with their own projects has come to certain levels of concrete affirmation. At our going away party, over one hundred residents showed up. The committee had bought a new sound system to be used in the community house for parties and dances like this. The currently popular worldwide party song of the "lambada" was blasting from the new sound system. People of all ages were on the dance floor attempting to dance to this "hot" dance. People were drinking, talking, dancing, and having a very good time. Their futures are uncertain. Two weeks before, the country had been ready for civil war. That night, they were ready to dance. Numerous friends thanked us for the things we and the group from

Greeley had done for the barrio. Ausmundo stated, as he was drinking his beer and watching people dancing, that this was what they were struggling for, the space to have fun and enjoy themselves. We agree. Vamos a seguir.

Notes

1. As part of this overall project we are starting a field project in Greeley, Colorado. This involves an ethnographic investigation of the North Side of Greeley, and working with community-based groups within this community. One of these groups is Al Frente, the community that sponsored the sister barrio program. Currently we are working on getting people from the Barrio William Diaz Romero to visit Greeley, and we are developing a newsletter for the North Side. We are also working with a Christian based community group through one of the local Catholic churches.

2. Some time in the near future we are planning to have Consuelo, Lesbia, and Hugo visit us in Greeley. We are planning to have them organize workshops with local groups in Greeley on what they have learned in terms of grassroots organizing in Nicaragua.

3. We have produced a video documentary on this community also. The documentary is also entitled ¡Óigame! ¡Óigame! (Camp, Coen, Higgins, Payne; EMS: Univ. of Northern Colorado, 1991). This video is available through the EMS division of the University of Northern Colorado. We have also produced two video documentaries on Mexico: *When Will Our Turn Come? The Urban Poor of the City of Oaxaca* (Camp, Higgins, and Payne; EMS: Univ. of Northern Colorado, 1982) and *La Vela: Tradition and Change in Juchitan, Mexico*, (Barco, Camp, Higgins and Payne; Greeley: EMS-University of Northern Colorado, 1986).

4. This was a common phrase of F.F. Higgins (my father) used to express goals that were beyond attainment.

5. During our visit in January of 1992 those still active in barrio affairs were maintaining a spirit of optimism and hopefulness. People such as Hugo, Consuelo, Orlando are still quite active. At the level of the comité del barrio (barrio council) numerous new people have become quite active. Currently the most active participants at assemblies are those having conflicts over the legalization of their house sites. This is because this is the most immediate need of these constituents.

We would like to emphasize the fluid quality of community participation at the barrio level. For example, the configuration of the comité del barrio and other active supporters is quite cyclical. Manuel has been quite active in the past years. Currently he is not involved. Consuelo's intensity of participation in the last 5 years has ranged from heading commissions to avoidance of local barrio affairs while maintaining stronger affiliation with the Sandinistas on National issues. This cyclical participation seems to be either motivated by personality conflicts (such as Francisco Perez' and Manuel Ruiz' conflicts with Orlando over leadership style) or differences over policy and direction of local actions (such as Maritza Palacio's feeling that the local comité should be more closely articulated with the direction of the national movimiento communal). This general fluidity, we feel is the ethnographic reality of grassroots political processes.

6. In comparison to these observations there seemed to be less noticeable social tension in our visit (January 1992) than before. This may have been simply that is was a year later and that it was the holiday season. Though it should be noted that in November 1991 there had been massive demonstrations in Managua over the attempted destruction of Fonseca's tomb. Also barrio members described various acts of vandalism against the community center and that crime on the street was worse than ever. People currently feel that the Markets such as the Oriental and Huembes are so dominated with street thieves that it is not even safe to wear your eye glasses while shopping. These fears of crime seem to be motivated by the unabated economic crisis.

7. More militant members of the Sandinistas in the barrio felt that the national political situation continues to be quite volatile. Though many people expressed optimism that the Sandinistas would return to power in 1996, these more militant members expressed doubt of this taking place unless the Frente is able to form new political alliances and restrengthen its grassroots support.

8. Ironically under UNO, the comité del barrio (barrio council) is attaining many of their goals that were initiated during the time of the Sandinistas. This comes from the particular organizational talent of members of the committee such as Hugo, Elisia, Orlando and others who have kept the barrio mobilized around various issues regardless of what may be occurring at the national level. Concurrently there has been the necessity of UNOs city government to demonstrate that it can actually do something at the local level. This ironic marriage of convenience more than anything else is grounded in the long term planning, organization, and commitment of barrio participants to see their projects to fruition. The combination of all these factors has placed the barrio in a unique lobbying position to attain its long term goals. Though we have no comparative information on the activities of other barrios in Managua it would seem that the residents of William Diaz Romero and their new allies from the surrounding barrios have quite successfully governed from below.

Bibliography

Arevalo, Juan Jose. *The Shark and the Sardines.* New York: Lyle Stuart, 1961.

Barco, Julia; Camp, Ron; Higgins, Michael J.; and Payne, John. *La Vela: Tradition and Change in Juchitan, Mexico.* Greeley, CO: EMS Video Production. University of Northern Colorado, 1986.

Bartolome, Miguel; and Barabas, Alicia, eds. *La Dinamica Etnica En Oaxaca.* Mexico, D.F.: INAH, 1986.

Bauman, Zygmunt. *Legislators and Interpreters.* New York: Cornell University Press, 1987.

_____ . *Culture as Praxis.* London: Routledge and K. Paul., 1973.

Bennholdt-Thomsen, Veronika. "Subsistence Production and Extended Reproduction." In Young, Wolkowitz, and McCullugh, eds. *Of Marriage and the Market.* London: Routledge, Kegan and Paul, 1984, pp. 41–44.

Bermann, Karl. *Under the Big Stick.* Boston: Southend Press, 1986.

Black, George. *Triumph of the People.* London: Zed Press, 1981.

Boas, Franz. "Methods of Ethnology," In Boas ed., *Race, Language, and Culture.* New York: Macmillan, 1940.

Borge, Tomas. "Tomas Borge on the Nicaraguan Revolution." *New Left Review* 164, 1987, pp. 53–65.

Cabezas, Omar. "No Se Debe Mandar Memos a Las Masas," Managua, Nicaragua: *Barricada,* June 22, 1988a. p. 5.

_____ . "Nueva Linea de los CDSs," Managua, Nicaragua: *Nuevo Diario,* July 8, 1988b, p. 7.

Camp, Higgins, and Payne. *When Will Our Turn Come: The Urban Poor of the City of Oaxaca.* Greeley, CO: EMS Production. University of Northern Colorado, 1982.

Camp, D., Coen, Higgins, Payne. *Oigame, Oigame: The Sights and Sounds of a Popular Revolution.* Greeley, CO: EMS Production. University of Northern Colorado, 1991.

Castells, Manuel. *The Urban Question.* Cambridge: MIT Press, 1977.

Chambers, Erve. *Applied Anthropology: A Practical Guide.* Engelwood Cliffs, New Jersey: Prentice Hall, 1985.

Chance, John. *Race and Class in Colonial Oaxaca.* Stanford, Calif: University Press, 1978.

Clifford, James. *The Predicament of Culture.* Cambridge, Mass.: Harvard University Press, 1988.

_____ . and Marcus, G., eds. *Writing Culture.* Berkeley: University of Calif. Press, 1984.

Close, David D. *Nicaragua*. London: Pinter Publication, 1988.

Coen, Tanya. "Images of Urban Household Organization in a Barrio in Managua, Nicaragua." Paper read at the Rocky Mountain Association of Latin American Studies. Fort Collins, Colorado, 1988.

Coraggio, Jose Luis. *Nicaragua: Revolution and Democracy*. London: Allen and Unwin, Inc., 1985.

_____. "Social Movements and Revolution: The Case of Nicaragua." In *New Social Movements and the State in Latin America*. Holland: CEDLA Publication, 1985, pp.23–37.

Crad, Joseph. *I Had Nine Lives. Fighting for Cash in Mexico and Nicaragua*. London: Sampson, Low, Marston & Co. Ltd., 1930.

Dalton, Roque. *Miguel Marmol*. New York: Curbstone Press, 1987.

D'Ciofalo, Giovanni. "Crisis Economica y Sector Informal." *Boletin Socio-Economico*, May 1988, INIES, Managua, Nicaragua, 1988, p. 12–17.

Dimen, Murial. *Surviving Sexual Contradictions*. New York: Macmillan, 1986.

Diskin, Martin. ed. *Trouble in Our Backyard*. New York: Pantheon Books, 1983.

Donahue, John. *The Nicaraguan Revolution in Health*. Bergin and Garvey Pub., 1986.

Doubleday, C. W. *Reminiscences of the "Filibuster" War in Nicaragua*. New York: Putnam's Sons, 1886.

Eitel, Jim. "Health Care Revisited: An Editors Journey." *Nicaraguan Perspectives* Berkeley: Nicaraguan Information Center. 12. 1986, pp. 30–34.

Evans-Pritchard, E.E. *The Nuer*. Oxford: Claredon Press. 1940.

Envio. "Revolutionizing Health: A Study of Complexity." *Instituto Historico Centroamericano* Vol. 7, No. 7: 80:24–30., 1988a.

_____. "The New Economic Package." *I.H.C.* Vol. 7, No. 86:14–42. 1988b.

_____. "Sandinistas Surviving in a Percentage Game." *I.H.C.* Vol. 7, No. 89:10–23. 1988c.

_____. "In the Hurricane's Wake." *I.H.C.* Vol. 7, No. 89:2–8. 1988d.

_____. "In Brief." *I.H.C.* Vol. 8, No. 91:5–16. 1989a.

_____. "There is No Where Else Quite Like Managua." *I.H.C.* Vol. 8 No. 91:17–33. 1989b.

_____. "Update." *I.H.C.* Vol. 8, No. 93:10–30. 1989c.

_____. "From a Mixed Up Economy: Toward a Socialist Mixed Economy." *I.H.C.* Vol. 8, No. 94:33–55. 1989d.

_____. "Economy." *I.H.C.* Vol. 8. No. 95:11. 1989e.

_____. "Making the Economy Our Own: Interviews with UNAG Leaders." *I.H.C.* Vol. 8. No. 15:35–44, Managua, Nicaragua, 1989f.

_____. "Economy." *I.H.C.* Vol. 8. No. 96:8, 1989g.

_____. "The Nicaraguan Environment: A Legacy of Destruction." *I.H.C.* Vol. 8, No. 100:38–42. 1989h.

_____. "Economy." *I.H.C.* Vol. 8. No. 101:9, 1989i.

_____. "Central America 1989." *I.H.C.* Vol. 9. May 1990a.

_____. "Playing With Fire." *I.H.C.* Vol. 19. No. 107:3–18, Nicaragua, 1990b.

_____. "UN's Balance of Power-On a Tight Rope." *I.H.C.* Vol 9. No. 107:26–32, 1990c.

_____. "Municipal Autonomy in Nicaragua." *I.H.C.* Vol. 9. No. 107:23–38, 1990d.
_____. "Tomas Borge on Revolution and Democracy." *I.H.C.* Vol. 9 No. 107:44, 1990e.
Evers, Tilman. "Identity: The Hidden Side of Latin America." In *New Social Movements and the State in Latin America*. Holland: CEDLA Publications, 1985, pp. 130–154.
Fagan, Brian. *People of the Earth*. Glenview, Illinois: Scott, Foresman and Co., 1989.
Foucault, Michel. *Discipline and Punish*. New York: Pantheon Press, 1977.
Frazier, Charles Edward. *The Dawn of Nationalism and Its Consequences in Nicaragua*. PhD. Thesis: University of Texas, 1958.
Galeano, Eduardo. *Memory of Fire*. Vol. 1–3. New York: Pantheon Books, 1985.
Gamio, Manuel. *La Poblacion del Valle de Teotihuacan*. Mexico: Secretaria de Agricultura y Fomento, 1922.
Gibson, Bill. "A Structural Overview of the Nicaraguan Economy." In Spalding, ed. *The Political Economy of Revolutionary Nicaragua*. Boston: Allen & Unwin, Inc., 1987, pp. 1–41.
Giroux, Henry A. *Teachers as Intellectuals*. Massachusetts: Bergin and Garvey, 1988.
Gonzalez Casanova, Pablo. *El Poder al Pueblo*. Mexico, D.F.: Oceano, 1986.
Haraway, Donna. *Primate Visions*. London: Routledge, 1989.
Harris, Marvin. *The Rise of Anthropological Theory*. New York: Cromwell, 1968.
Harris, R. and Vilas, Carlos. *La Revolucion en Nicaragua*. Mexico, D.F.: Ediciones Era, 1986.
Harvey, David. *The Condition of Postmodernity*. London: Blackwell, 1989.
Heller, Agnes. *General Ethics*. London: Blackwell, 1988.
Henry, E. "Urban Social Movements in Latin America: Towards a Critical Understanding." In *New Social Movements and the State in Latin America*. Holland: CEDLA Publication, 1985, pp. 155–176.
Hernandez, Enrique Pena. *Folklore de Nicaragua*. Guatemala: Editorial Piedara Santa, 1986.
Herring, Hurbert. *A History of Latin America*. New York: Knopf, 1968.
Higgins, Michael and Coen, Tanya. "Jodido Pero Contento." In *City and Society*, 1990, pp. 156–164.
Higgins, Michael James. "Martyrs and Saints." In *Popular Religion* in Mexico and Central America. Dow and Stephen: Washington, D.C.: SLAA Publication Series, Vol. 10 1990, pp. 107–206.
_____, "Quienes Son Los Migrantes Al Teatro Urbano del Valle de Oaxaca." In *La Dinamica Etnica en Oaxaca*. Bartolome and Barabas, eds. Mexico, D.F.: INAH, 1986.
_____. "Somos Tocayos." Lanham: University Press of America, 1983.
_____. "Somos Gente Humilde." Mexico, D.F.: INI., 1974.
Hodges, Donald C. *Intellectual Foundations of the Nicaraguan Revolution*. Austin: University of Texas Press, 1986.
Hooks, Bell. *Yearning: Race, Gender, and Cultural Politics*. Boston: South End Press, 1990.
Jackson, Michael. *Paths Toward a Clearing*. Bloomington: Indiana Press, 1989.

Karnes, Thomas L. *Tropical Enterprise: The Standard Fruit and Steamship Company in Latin America*. Baton Rouge: Louisiana State University Press, 1978.

———. *The Failure of Union: Central America, 1824–1960*. Chapel Hill: University of North Carolina Press, 1961.

Kroeber, A. L. *Handbook of the Indians of California*. Bureau of American Ethnology, Bulletin 78. Washington: Government Printing Office, 1925.

Laclau, Ernesto and Chantall Mouffe. *Hegemony and Socialist Strategy*. London: Verso, 1985.

Lancaster, Roger. *Thanks to God and Revolution*. New York: Columbia University Press, 1988.

Lange, Frederick W. and Doris Z. Stone, eds. *The Archaeology of Lower Central America*. Albuquerque: University of New Mexico Press, 1984.

Lanuza, A., J. Vazquez, A. Barahona, A. Chamorro. *Economica Y Sociedad en la Construccion del Estado en Nicaragua*. San Jose: ICAP, 1983.

Levi-Strauss, C. *Structural Anthropology*. New York: Basic Books, 1963.

Lewis, Oscar. *Four Men: Living the Revolution*. Urbana: University of Illinois Press, 1977a.

———. Four Women. *Living the Revolution*. Urbana: University of Illinois Press, 1977b.

———. *Neighbors*. Urbana: University of Illinois Press, 1978.

MacLeod, Murdo J. *Spanish Central America: A Socioeconomic History 1520–1720*. Berkeley: University of Calif. Press, 1973.

MaCulay, Neill. *The Sandino Affair*. Chicago: Quadrangle Books, 1967.

Maier, Elizabeth. *Nicaragua, La Mujer en la Revolucion*. Mexico D.F.: Ediciones de Cultura, 1985.

Malinowski, Bronislaw. *Argonauts of the Western Pacific*. New York: Dutton, 1922.

Marcus, George, E., and Fischer, Michael. *Anthropology as Cultural Critique*. Chicago: The University of Chicago Press, 1986.

Mascia-Lees, F., Sharp, P. and Cohen, C. "The Postmodernist Turn In Anthropology." In *Signs* Vol. 15. 1989, pp. 7–33.

Massey, Doreen, *Nicaragua*. Philadelphia: Open University Press, 1988.

May, Jacques M. and Donna L. McLellan. *The Ecology of Malnutrition in Mexico and Central America*. New York: Hafner Publishing Company, 1972.

McBirney, Alexander R. and Howell Williams. *Volcanic History of Nicaragua*. Berkeley: University of Calif. Press, 1965.

Mead, Margaret. *Coming of Age in Samoa*. New York: Morrow, 1928.

Melucci, Alberto. *Nomads of the Present*. Phil.: Temple University Press, 1989.

Molyneax, Maxine. "Mobilization without Emancipation? Women's Interests, State, and Revolution in Nicaragua." In *New Social Movements and the State in Latin America*. Holland: CEDLA Publication, 1985, pp. 123–154.

Morales, N. R. Ardaya and B. Espinoza. "Asentamientos Espontaneos No Son Causa de la Crisis Urbana." In *Boletin Socio Economic* INIES-April. Managua, Nicaragua, 1987.

Moser, Caroline O. N. "Introduction." In *Women, Human Settlements and Housing*. Moser and Peaker, eds: London: Tavistock Press, 1987, pp. 12–32.

Mosser, Don. *Central American Jungles*. New York: Time-Life Books, 1976.

Newson, Linda A. *Indian Survival in Colonial Nicaragua*. Norman: University of Oklahoma Press, 1987.
"Nicaragua-Diez Anos en Cifras." Instituto Nacional de Estadisticas Y Census. Managua, 1989.
Nicholson, Linda J. *Feminism and Postmodernism*. New York: Routledge, 1990.
Oliphant, Lawrence. *Patriots and Filibusters*. London: Blackwood and Sons, 1898.
Ortega, Daniel Saavadra. "Nadie Hizo Tanto por Los Ninos." *Barricada*. August 7, 1988.
Perez, Tania. "Interview with Tania Perez." Field Notes of T. Coen. Managua, Nicaragua, 1988.
Powdermaker, Hortense. *Stranger and Friends*. New York: W.W. Norton, 1966.
Radell, David R. *Historical Geography of Western Nicaragua: The Spheres of Influence of Leon, Granada, and Managua*. PhD Diss. University of Calif. Press, 1965.
Roberts, Bryan. "The Informal Sector in Comparative Perspective." Paper presented to the Society for Economic Anthropology. Knoxville, Tenn., 1987.
Rodriquez, Mario. *The Cadiz Experiment in Central America: 1808-1826*. Berkeley: University of Calif. Press, 1978.
Ruccio, David. "The State and Planning in Nicaragua." In *The Political Economy of Revolutionary Nicaragua*. Spalding, ed. Boston: Allen & Unwin, Inc., 1987, pp.127-148.
Ruchwarger, Gary. *People in Power*. South Hadley: Bergin and Garvey, 1987.
_____. *Struggling for Survival: Workers, Women, and Class on a Nicaraguan State Farm*. Boulder: Westview Press, 1989.
Ruis, Eduardo del Rio. *Nicaragua for Beginners*. New York: Writers and Readers. Publishing Cooperatives, Ltd., 1984.
Ryan, John Morris, (ed). *Area Handbook for Nicaragua*. American University Press, 1970.
Said, Edward. *Orientalism*. New York: Pantheon Books, 1979.
_____. "Post-Modern Anthropology." Talk given at AAA Meetings. Chicago, Ill., 1988.
Scherzer, Carl. *Travels in the Free States of Central America*. London: Longman, Brown, Green, and Roberts, 1857.
Scrimshaw, Susan and Elena Hurtado. "Anthropological Involvement in the Central American Diarrheal Disease Control Project." *Social Science and Medicine*. 27.1, 1988, pp. 97-104.
Selser, Gregorio. *Sandino*. New York: Monthly Review Press, 1979.
Service, E. R. *Primitive Social Organization. An Evolutionary Perspective*. New York: Random House, 1962.
Sherman, William L. *Forced Native Labor in Sixteenth Century Central America*. Lincoln: University of Nebraska Press, 1979.
Slater, David. "Social Movements and a Recasting of the Political." In *New Social Movements and the State in Latin America*. Holland: CEDLA Publication, 1985, pp. 57-84.
Spalding, Rose J. "Introduction." In *The Political Economy of Revolutionary Nicaragua*. Spalding, ed. Boston: Allen & Unwin, Inc., 1987, pp.1-11.
Squier, E. G. *Nicaragua: Its People, Scenery, Monuments*. New York: Harper and Brothers, 1860.

Stevens, Beth. "Women in Nicaragua." In *Monthly Review Press* Vol. 39. 1987, pp.1–18.

Stone, Doris. *Pre-Columbian Man Finds In Central America.* Cambridge: Peabody Museum Press, 1972.

Trinh, T. Minh-Ha. *Woman, Native, Other.* Bloomington: Indiana Univ. Press, 1989.

Utting, Peter. "Domestic Supply and Food Shortages." In *The Political Economy of Revolutionary Nicaragua.* Spalding, ed. Boston: Allen & Unwin, Inc., 1987, pp.127–148.

Valle, Rafael Heliodora. "El Folklore en la Literatura de Centro America." *The Journal of American Folklore* Vol. 36, No. 140, April–June, 1923.

Vance, Irene. "More Than Bricks and Mortar: Women's Participation in Self-Help Housing in Managua, Nicaragua." In *Women Human Settlements and Housing.* Moser and Peaker, eds. London: Tavistock Press, 1987, pp. 139–165.

VanWilligen, John. *Applied Anthropology: An Introduction.* Massachusetts: Bergin and Garvey Publishers Inc., 1986.

Varese, Stefano. "Multiethnicity and Hegemonic Construction." In *Ethnicities and Nations.* Guidilri, Pellizzi, and Tambiah, eds. Austin: University of Texas Press, 1988, pp. 57–77.

Vilas, Carlos. "Troubles Everywhere: An Economic Perspective on the Sandinista Revolution." In *The Political Economy of Revolutionary Nicaragua.* Spalding, ed. Boston: Allen & Unwin, Inc., 1987, pp. 233–246.

———. "The Sandinista Revolution: National Liberation and Social Transformation in Central America." New York: *Monthly Review Press*, 1986.

Voget, Fred. *A History of Ethnology.* New York: Holt, Rinehholt, Winston, 1975.

Walker, Thomas W. *The Land of Sandino.* Boulder: Westview Press, 1981.

———. *Nicaragua in Revolution.* New York. Praeger Publishers, 1982.

Weeks, John. "The Mixed Economy in Nicaragua: The Economic Battlefield." In *The Political Economy of Revolutionary Nicaragua.* Spalding, ed. Boston: Allen & Unwin, Inc., 1987, pp. 43–60.

West, Robert and John Augelli. *Middle America: Its Lands and Peoples.* Englewood: Prentice Hall, 1976.

Wolf, Eric. *Sons of Shaking Earth.* Chicago: University of Chicago Press, 1959.

———. *Europe and People Without History.* Berkeley: University of Calif. Press, 1982.